I08103900

IMAGES
of America

EARLY SANTA FE

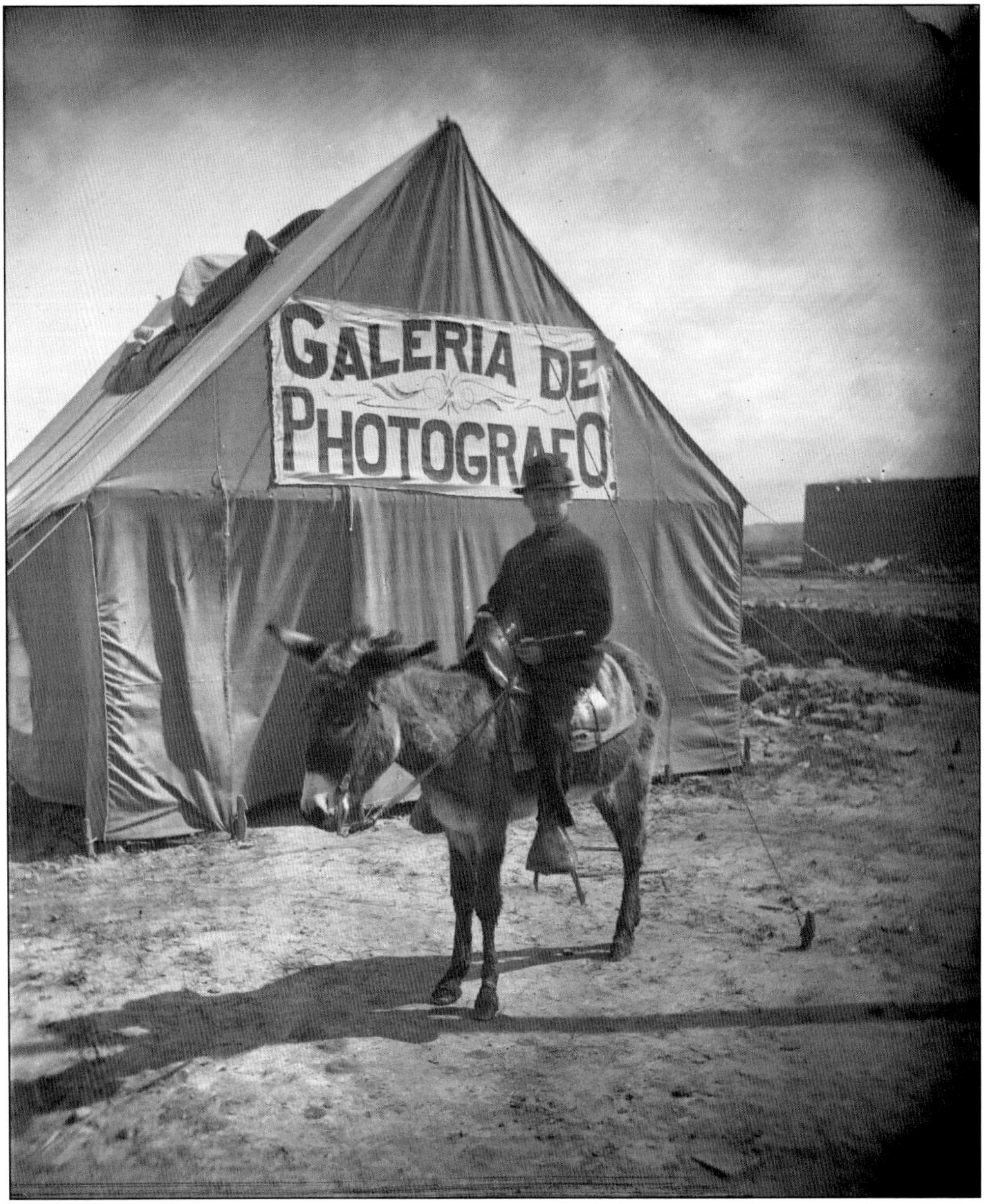

Since the mid-19th century, photographers have captured the essence of Santa Fe through the camera lens. Many of these visionary pioneers were just passing through while documenting the great expanse of the West. Others found the open space and the ever-changing sunlight of this ancient city captivating, decided to make it their calling in life, and, in the process, their home. (Photograph by Ben Wittick, courtesy Palace of the Governors [NMHM/DCA], No. 015864.)

On the Cover: Jesus Sito Candelario opened his curio shop on San Francisco Street in Santa Fe during the latter part of the 19th century. Working directly with members of the surrounding Indian pueblos, Candelario became one of the most successful curio merchants in New Mexico. (Courtesy Palace of the Governors [NMHM/DCA], No. 093714.)

IMAGES
of America

EARLY SANTA FE

Ana Pacheco

ARCADIA
PUBLISHING

ISBN 978-1-4671-2590-1

Published by Arcadia Publishing
Charleston, South Carolina

Printed in the United States of America

Library of Congress Control Number: 2016957461

For all general information, please contact Arcadia Publishing:
Telephone 843-853-2070
Fax 843-853-0044
E-mail sales@arcadiapublishing.com
For customer service and orders:
Toll-Free 1-888-313-2665

Visit us on the Internet at www.arcadiapublishing.com

To the early photographers whose vision speaks volumes of their love for Santa Fe.

Contents

Acknowledgments

I am deeply grateful for the expertise and help of the staff at the Palace of the Governors Photograph Archives. A special shout-out goes to Hannah Abelbeck, who worked diligently with me on my photograph choices for this book, and to Patricia Hewitt in the Fray Angélico Chávez History Library, who made it all the more enjoyable as the two of us pieced together historical facts for this narrative. I'd also like to give belated thanks to the late Richard Rudisill, who worked with me at the archives back in the 1990s. Even while working on this book, I came across correspondence by him that made my life easier. Also thanks to Art Olivas, Richard's counterpart back in the day. Their knowledge of the museum's photograph collection far surpassed any computer system I have ever come across!

Lastly, my gratitude goes to Emily Olson and the Amon Carter Museum of American Art in Dallas for diligently protecting the legacy of photographer Laura Gilpin.

Introduction

Historians are like deaf people who go on answering questions that no one has asked them.

—Leo Tolstoy

Imagery is a powerful medium in this era of social media. Fortunately, the early pictorial history of Santa Fe emerges like sand through an hourglass. For the past 25 years, I've been fortunate to have at my disposal the vast collection at the Palace of the Governors Photograph Archives. I've been doing research there since the mid-1990s, when I began publishing *La Herencia*, a quarterly magazine on New Mexico's Hispanic history and culture. This was in the pre-digital era, when I had to go through each file photograph by photograph. Like any good prospector, I was after the gold, but what I found while sifting away were unexpected nuggets of Santa Fe's rich history. These old photographs of people, places, and events came alive with each image I held. That's also when I fell in love with black-and-white photography. I began to appreciate the expertise that each of these different photographers possessed. It took a lot of skill and talent to take photographs back then, with no fancy computer software to clean up mistakes.

Back in the 1980s, I had taken some photography classes at the School for Visual Arts in New York. It was all very complicated for me—the shutter speeds, the angles of light, not to mention the process of developing film with all of those solvents and chemicals. In the mid-19th century and through the beginning of the next century, these photographers were working with daguerreotypes and glass-plate negatives when photography itself was in its infancy. How did these early photographers make it look so simple?

The idea for this book, documenting the early history of Santa Fe through images, came from the photographers themselves. While doing research on a gamut of subjects, I kept running across many of the same photographers over and over again. They had witnessed history, and I wanted to know more about them. The last chapter in this book is devoted to their lives, at least the ones where I could find information. Some of the early photographers were just passing through, leaving images but not a paper trail. In some instances I was able to connect the dots, discovering friendships and professional alliances that explained their portfolio of work. I was surprised that some left families and friends behind to pursue their calling as photographers. Some scraped by doing odd jobs to be able to do the work they loved. And I was fascinated to learn of some of the unusual ways they died.

The photographs represented in this book are but a small fraction of their work. Virtually all of these photographers have a huge collection of photographs documenting Native Americans from the surrounding pueblos and the region. Since I couldn't do justice in one book to all of their work, it is my hope to eventually write about the Native American life that they so richly documented.

To my dismay, there were no collections of women photographers to speak of at the photograph archives. The period I chose was an era when women were not represented in many fields. The only woman photographer featured in this book is Laura Gilpin. To my astonishment, none of the photographs that she took in a career that spanned more than 60 years were available at the archives. Although she lived in Santa Fe for more than 50 years and died here in 1979, her photograph collection is at the Amon Carter Museum in Dallas.

Some of Santa Fe's better-known people who made history won't be found in this book because I have already written about them in *Legendary Locals of Santa Fe*, which Arcadia published in 2013. Also, some aspects of Santa Fe history have been omitted, either because images were not available or they did not represent the work of the early photographers.

The book begins with photographs from 1851 and ends with World War II, roughly a century of history. I chose World War II as a cutoff because Santa Fe began to change drastically after the war. That's when the town experienced rapid growth, with many people moving in while others left. This period also coincides with the advent of wide access to color photography, but I wanted to keep the history of Santa Fe in black and white, just like the photographs represented. Finally, in writing this book, I came to believe that the camera not only preserves history, more importantly, it keeps it alive.

One

Plaza Environs

The Santa Fe Plaza has been at the heart of the city's growth since it was founded more than 400 years ago. The wheels of commerce, civic celebrations, and religious devotion have converged on this quadrangular parcel of land with the Sangre de Cristo Mountains as a backdrop since the early 1600s. Events of historic proportion have taken place on the plaza, including the re-conquest of 1692 for the Spanish Crown and the beginning of American occupation in 1846.

It was on the plaza that Don Diego de Vargas and his soldiers negotiated a peaceful re-entry to the capital city. It was on the plaza that Gen. Stephen Kearny and his soldiers rode into town claiming sovereignty for the United States.

Over its history, four flags have flown on the plaza: the main ones were Spain (1610–1821), Mexico (1821–1846), and the United States (1846–2016). The US flag was planted atop the Palace of the Governors on the morning of August 9, 1846, when Gen. Stephen Kearny declared it for the American government. And believe it or not, the Confederate flag flew over the plaza for three weeks in the spring of 1862, when the city was under Confederate rule during the American Civil War.

Four historic routes, like arteries extending from the heart, have connected to the plaza: the Camino Real from Mexico City to San Juan de los Caballeros in northern New Mexico; the Santa Fe Trail, which began in Independence, Missouri, and ended right on the plaza; the Spanish-American Trail from Santa Fe to Los Angeles; and Route 66, the Mother Road, from Chicago to Santa Monica, whose original route passed down the block from the plaza on Water Street.

Manifest Destiny and the 1846 American occupation opened the floodgates of humanity in Santa Fe. This rapid growth led to development beyond the plaza area. By the mid-1800s, businesses, schools, and government institutions were being built in areas outside of the plaza's perimeter. With the exception of a few photographs in this chapter, most of the buildings are long gone. Fortunately, the 17th-century concept of a community square brought by the Spanish settlers still looks the same.

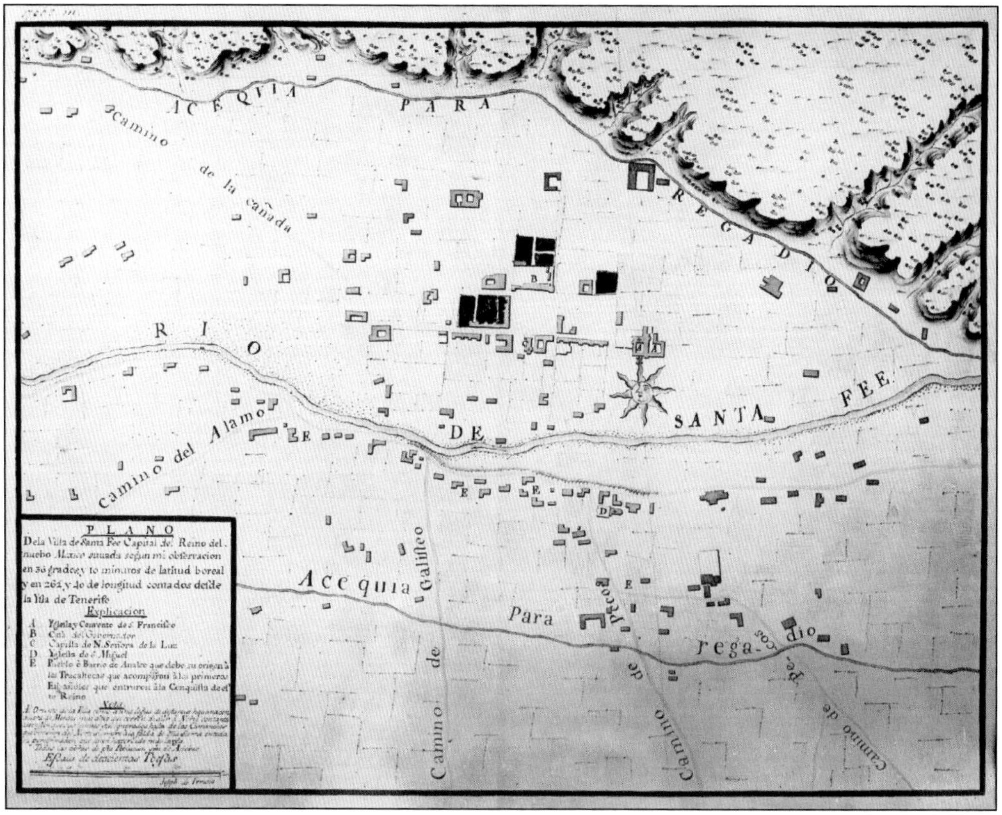

In 1930, while studying at Oxford University, an unknown Santa Fean came across an old 1776 map by José de Urruitia of La Villa Real de la Santa Fe. To this day, the ancient map is of historic value because it provides a blueprint of the 17th-century building laws of Spain brought to the New World. The document shows that as early as 1607, city planners put in place a quadrangular Plaza de Armas, with four main gates into Las Casas Reales, which are now the Palace of the Governors. (Photograph by Jesse Nusbaum, courtesy Palace of the Governors [NMHM/DCA], No. 015048.)

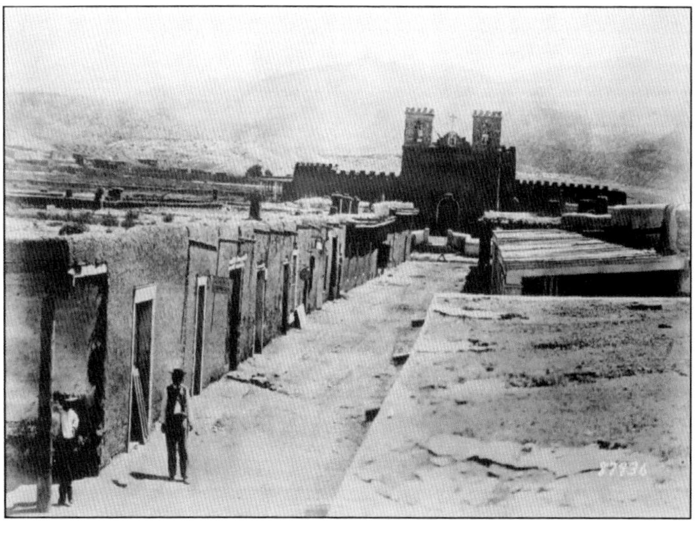

This 1885 photograph of the parish church shows La Parroquia, which was built between 1714 and 1717. The first church built at this location, in 1626, was destroyed by fire during the Pueblo Revolt of 1680. In 1869, construction of St. Francis Cathedral began. Today it is known as the Basilica Cathedral of St. Francis of Assisi. (Courtesy Palace of the Governors [NMHM/DCA], No. 011330.)

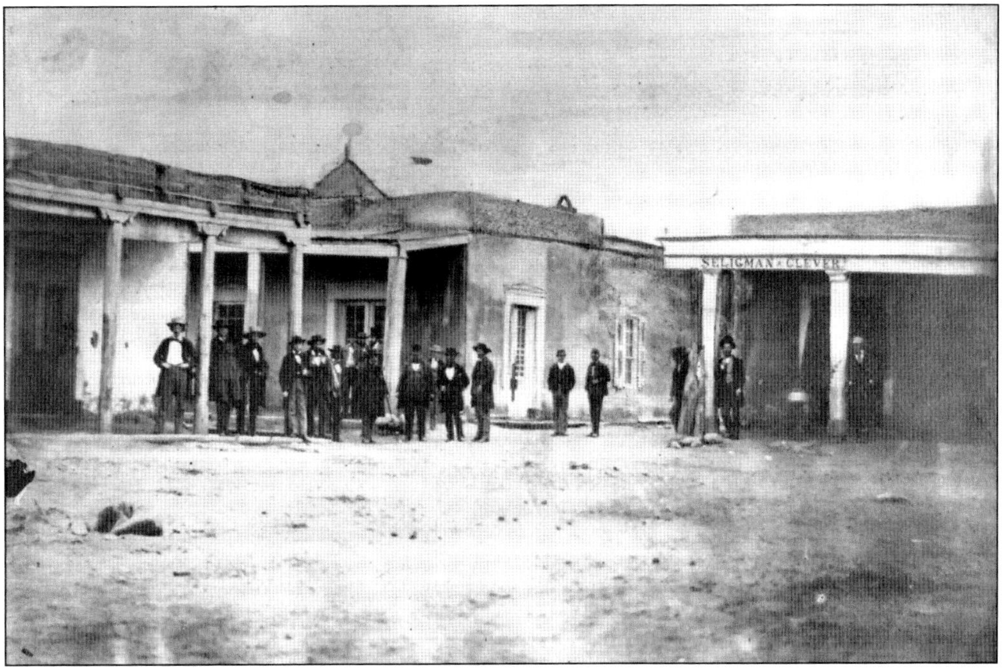

This 1855 photograph shows the southeast corner of the plaza with the Exchange Hotel and Seligman and Clever Store on the right. The Exchange Hotel, former called the US Hotel, was built in 1847. Since the early days of the Spanish settlement, the southeast corner has been some type of lodging. Currently on that site is La Fonda Hotel, which means "the inn" in Spanish. Two Jewish merchants, Sigmund Seligman and Charles P. Clever, opened their mercantile store on the plaza in 1852. Like many other entrepreneurs, they sought their fortune traveling the Santa Fe Trail, which began in Independence, Missouri, and ended at the plaza in Santa Fe. (Courtesy Palace of the Governors [NMHM/DCA], No. 010685.)

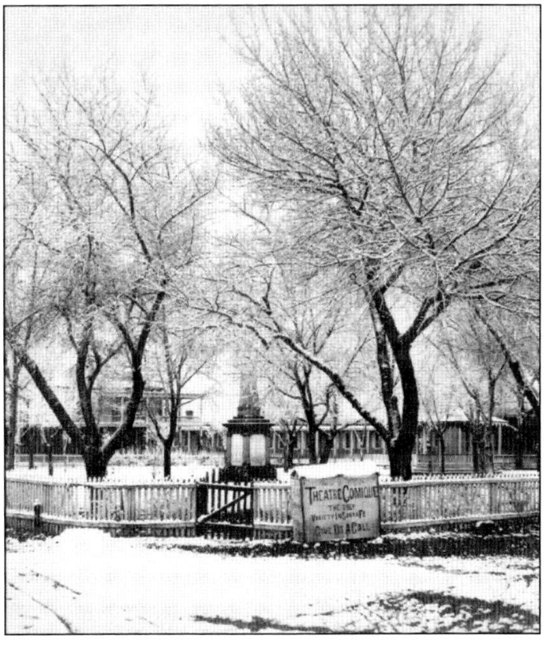

The Santa Fe Plaza was the stage for performances and all civic and public gatherings, which continues to be true in the 21st century. This 1880 winter image with the Soldiers Monument features an advertisement for the Theater Comique, a traveling theater visiting that year. (Photograph by Bennett and Brown, courtesy Palace of the Governors [NMHM/DCA], No. 011260.)

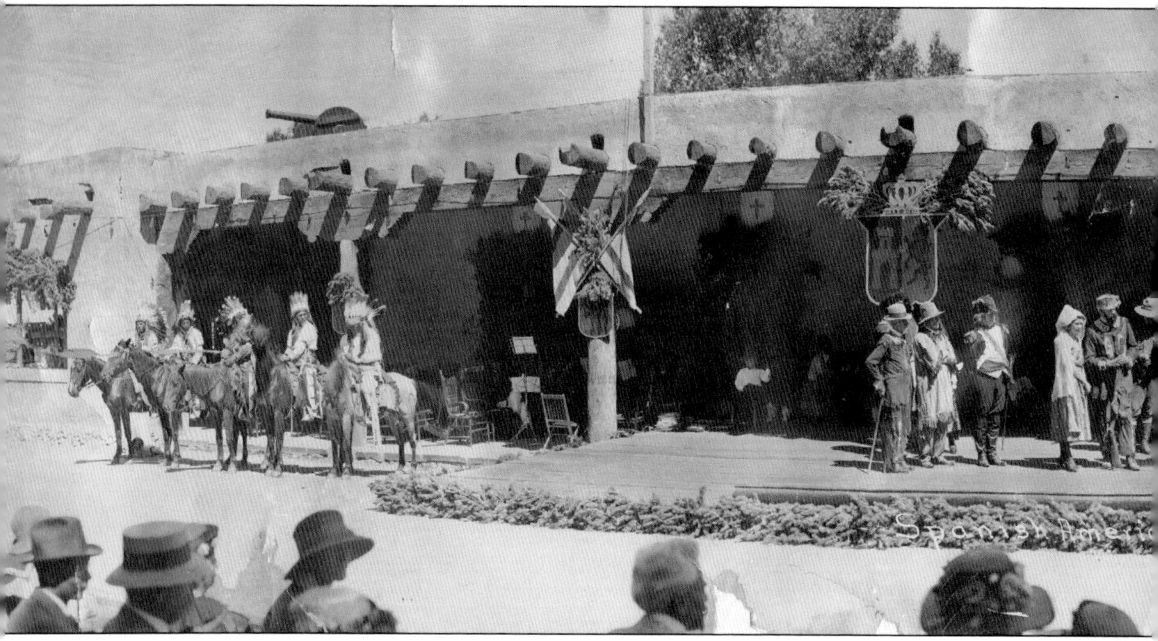

This panorama of the Palace of the Governors was taken in 1921. The construction of Las Casas Reales (the Royal Houses) was completed in 1610. The newly constructed building represented the Spanish crown and government of the capital city of New Mexico. The part of the structure that has stood the test of time and remains today is the Palace of the Governors. It is the oldest continuously occupied government building in the United States. Since its completion, it has served as the home of governors and their families through the Spanish, Mexican, and early American eras. During those years, it was the political hub where decisions made in Spain, Mexico, and

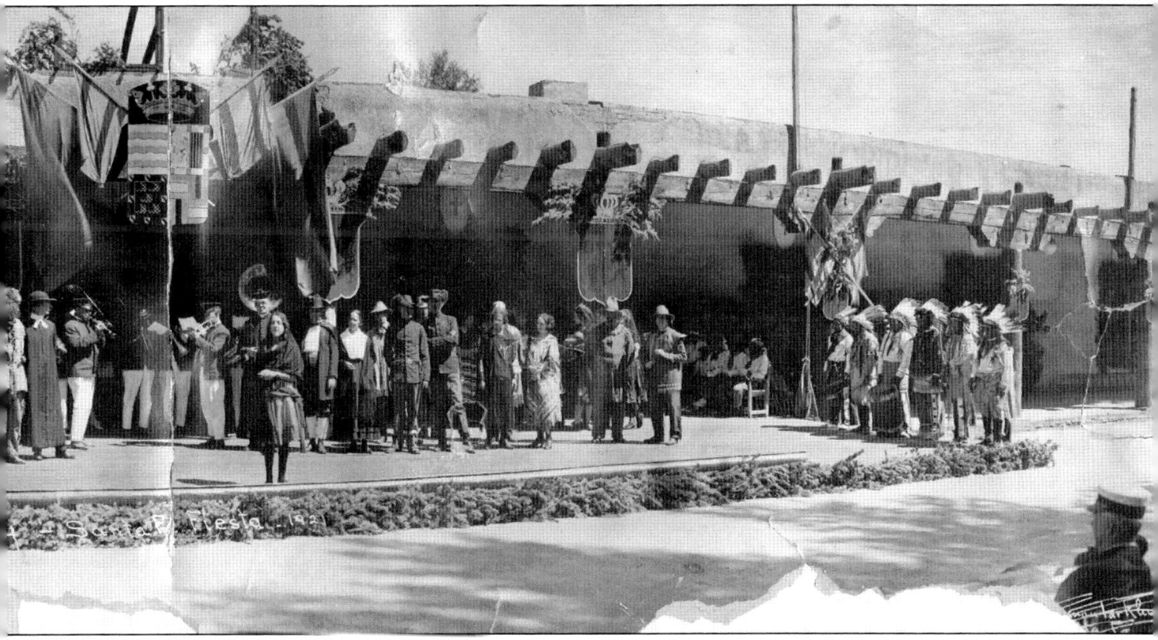

Washington became mandate in New Mexico. Since the latter part of the 19th century, tourists and locals have had the opportunity to purchase jewelry, pottery, basketry, kachina dolls, and other handcrafted work under the portal of the Palace of the Governors. This 1925 photograph of the daily commerce represents New Mexico's Pueblo Indians and other Native American tribes from the region. The Palace of the Governors became a registered historic landmark in 1960, and in 1990 it was declared an American treasure. (Photograph by Harmon T. Parkhurst, courtesy Palace of the Governors [NMHM/DCA], No. HP.2015.74.01.)

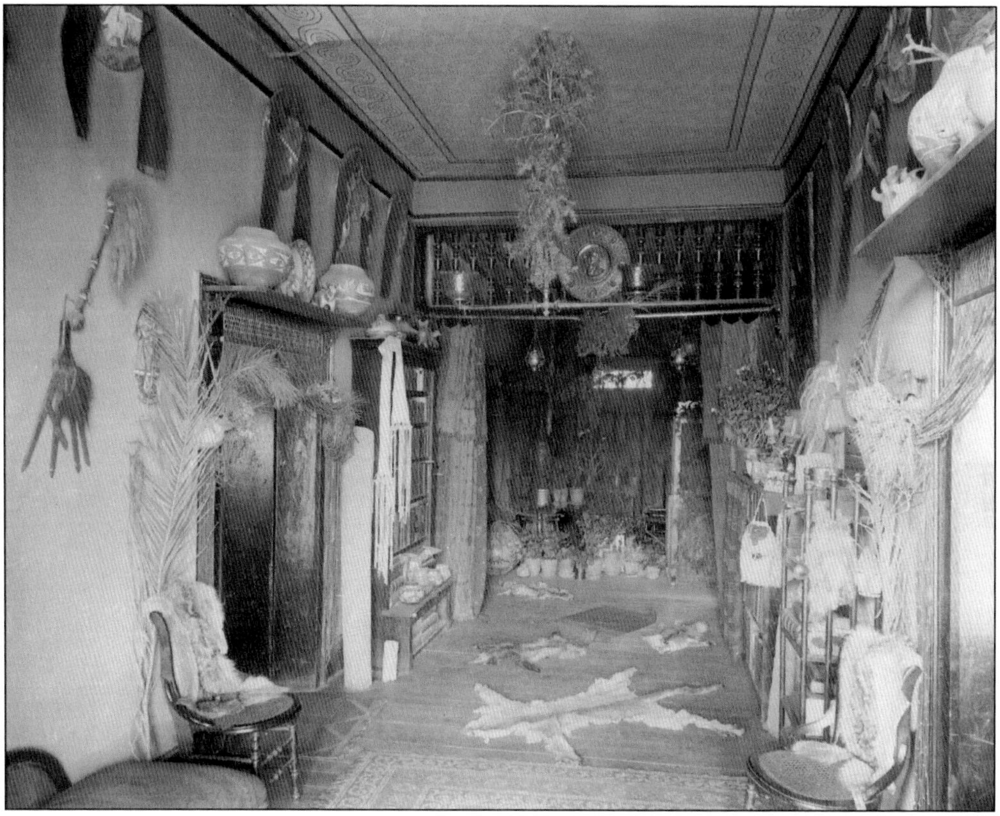

The Palace of the Governors' hallway is shown in 1893, while Gov. L. Bradford Prince was in office. When Prince became the governor of New Mexico in 1889, he held many church-related functions in the reception room at the Palace of the Governors for the Holy Faith Episcopal Church. (Photograph by Thomas J. Curran, courtesy Palace of the Governors [NMHM/DCA]. No. 046776.)

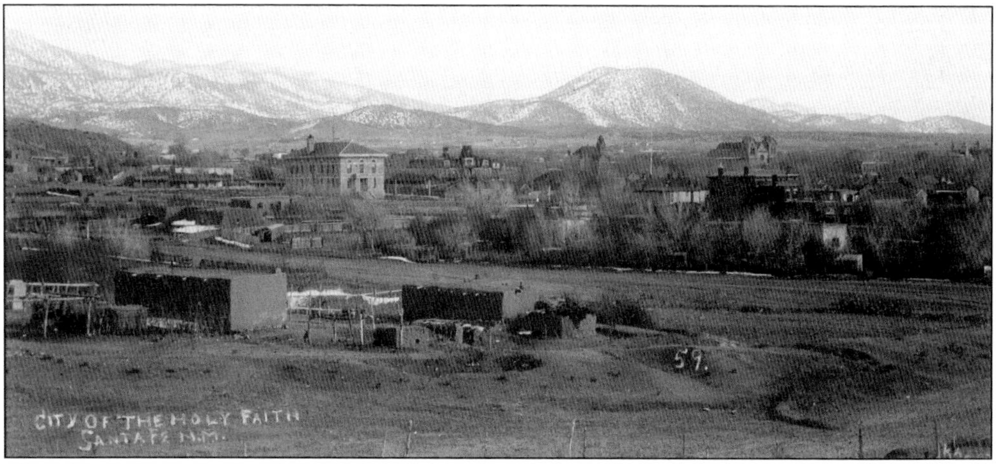

This 1895 bird's-eye view of Santa Fe, the City of Holy Faith, was taken looking southeast, with the Sangre de Cristo Mountains in the background. Business development was centered on the Santa Fe Plaza area through the early part of the 20th century. (Photograph by Christian G. Kaadt, courtesy Palace of the Governors [NMHM/DCA], No. 030768.)

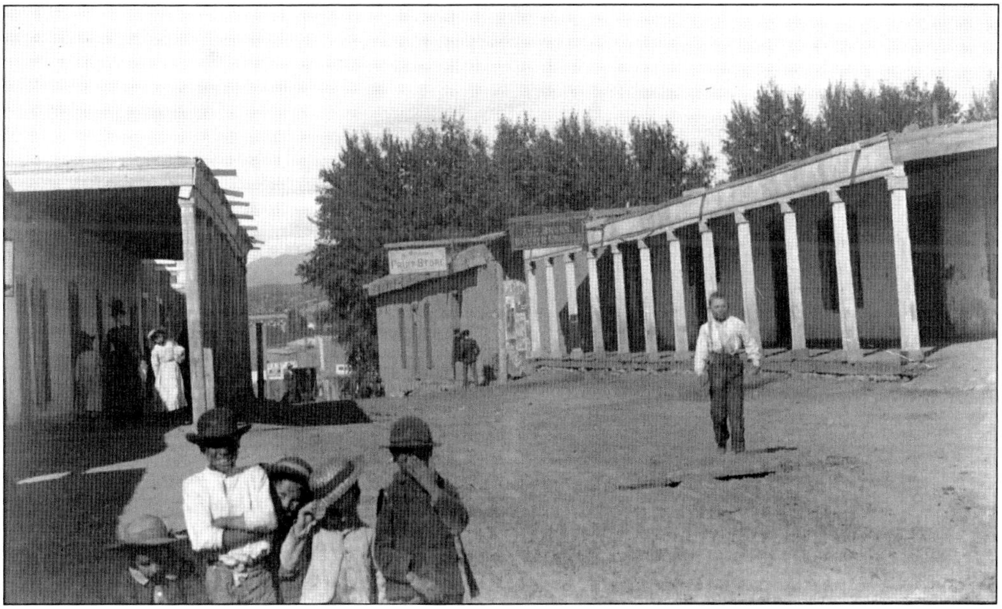

This 1884 photograph shows Bridge Street, which was later renamed College Street in recognition of St. Michael's College, whose building occupied most of the block. In the 1950s, the street name was changed to Old Santa Fe Trail by real estate developers trying to enhance the history of the neighborhood. (Photograph by Dana B. Chase, courtesy Palace of the Governors [NMHM/DCA], No. HP.2009.64.1.)

The La Sallian Christian Brothers came to Santa Fe in 1859 and opened St. Michael's College, an all-boys Catholic school. It remained in that location on College Street through the mid-20th century, when it moved to Siringo Road, where it is currently located. This photograph was taken around 1872. (Photograph by H. Gurnsey, courtesy Palace of the Governors [NMHM/DCA], No. 011118.)

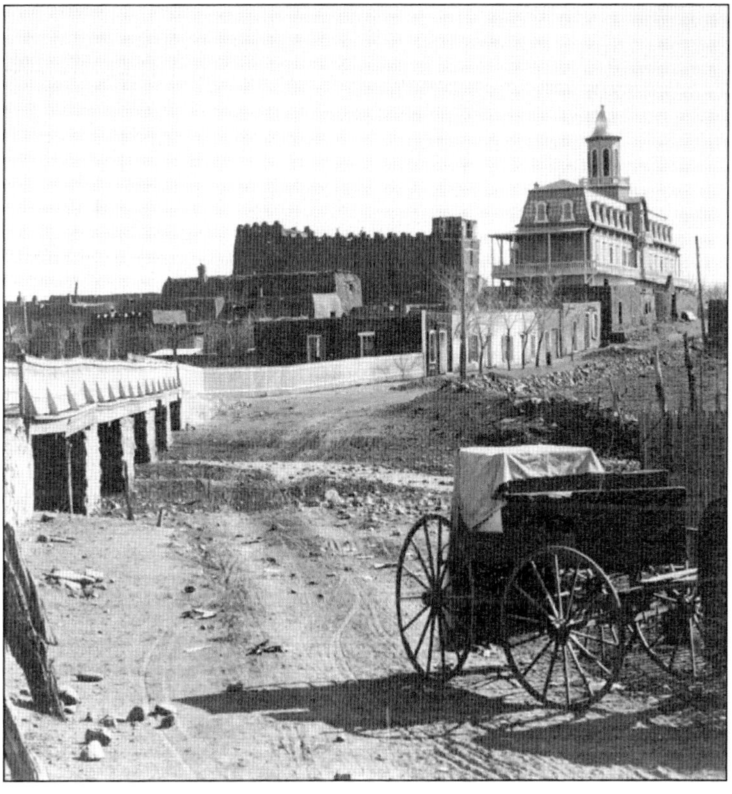

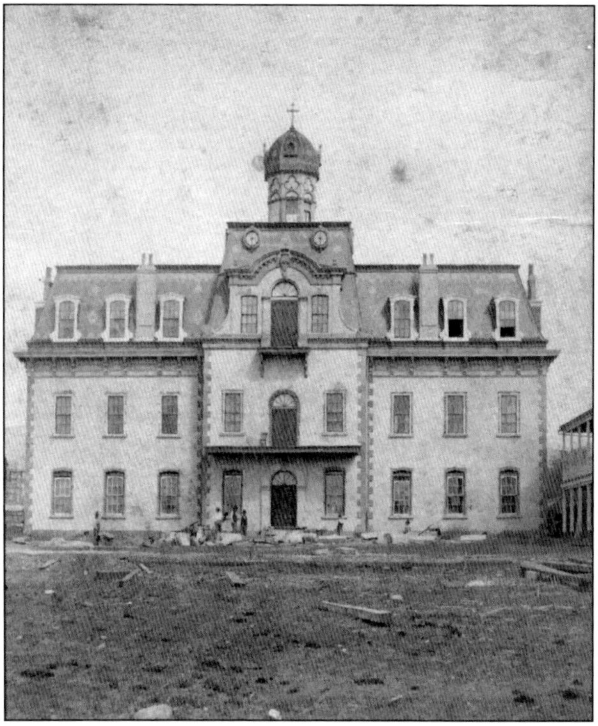

In 1865, four nuns of the Sisters of Charity arrived from Cincinnati at the behest of Archbishop Jean-Baptiste Lamy. They opened a hospital that later became St. Vincent Hospital and St. Vincent Orphan Asylum. Two of the sisters, who had been nurses during the Civil War, had to support themselves on their way to Santa Fe by begging at mining camps and railroad stations. St. Vincent Hospital was the first organized healthcare facility in territorial New Mexico. (Photograph by Bennet and Brown, courtesy Palace of the Governors [NMHM/DCA], No. 138221.)

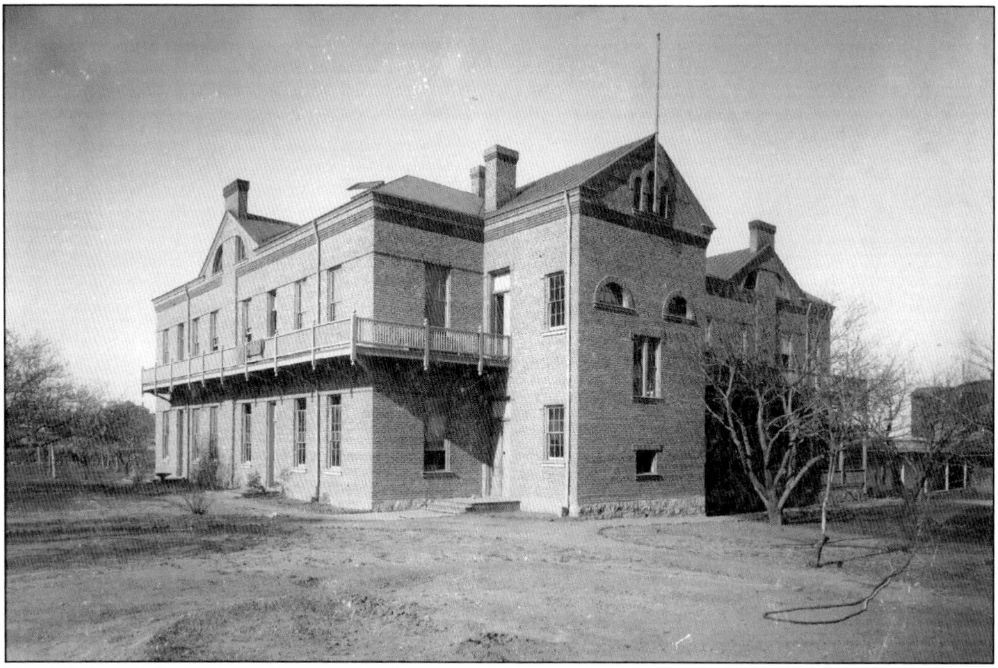

Founded in 1891, St. Vincent's Orphan Asylum was under the direction of Sr. Theodogin Farn and Sr. Catherine Mallon. Sr. Vincent O'Keefe and Sr. Pauline Keo founded St. Vincent Hospital. All four nuns lived in an L-shaped adobe home with a dirt floor that later became the hospital. (Photograph by Thomas J. Curran, courtesy Palace of the Governors [NMHM/DCA], No. 016517.)

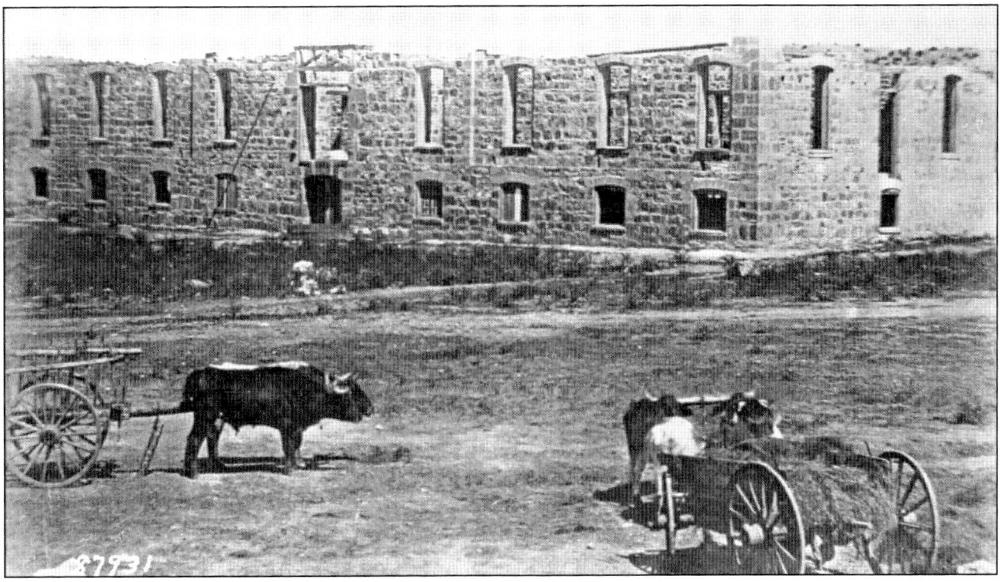

In anticipation of the 333rd anniversary of the 1550 Coronado expedition, construction of the federal building began in the early 1880s. During Santa Fe's Tertio-Millennial Celebration and Exposition of 1883, a racetrack was built at Federal Place to accommodate the celebration. In 1884, a monumental obelisk was erected in honor of Christopher "Kit" Carson for his bravery in the Mexican-American War and the American Civil War. In 2005, the building, formerly known as the US courthouse, was renamed for Justice Santiago E. Campos. (Photograph by Nicholas Brown, courtesy Palace of the Governors [NMHM/DCA], No. 010242.)

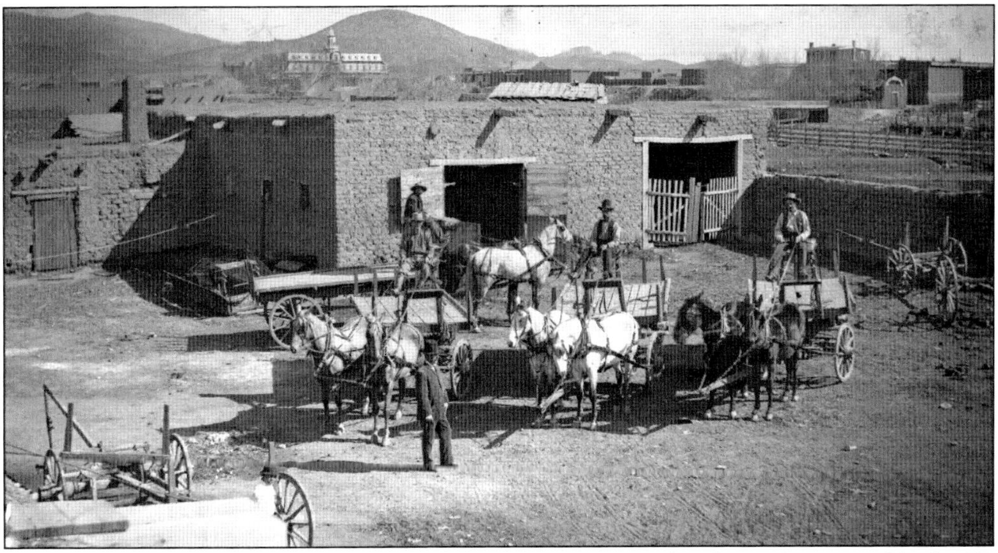

Dudrow & Bear's Transfer Corral, pictured here in 1881, was a family-run business. Charles W. Dudrow came to Santa Fe between 1869 and 1872. He had been a driver for the Barlow and Sanderson stage lines that ran from Pueblo, Colorado, to Santa Fe. When he arrived in Santa Fe, he married Cora Bear and became a business partner with her father, Samuel Bear. They opened Dudrow & Bear Ice, Transfer and Livery (also referred to as Dudrow & Bear's). The business was located near the train depot and Our Lady of Guadalupe Church. (Photograph by Ben Wittick, courtesy Palace of the Governors [NMHM/DCA], No.015826.)

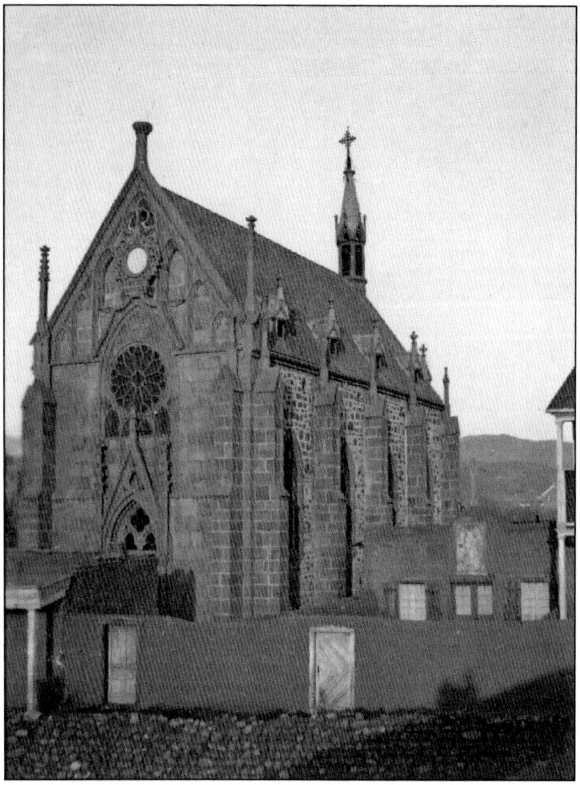

Loretto Chapel was built in 1878 by Archbishop Lamy to accompany the Sisters of Light Loretto Academy. The Gothic Revival chapel was inspired by Sainte-Chapelle in Paris and was designed by architect Antoine Mouly, who had worked on the restoration of King Louis IX's Parisian chapel. Legend has it that the Loretto Chapel's unique spiral staircase was miraculously built by St. Joseph the Carpenter between 1877 and 1881; it has no visible means of support. The chapel was closed in 1968 and deconsecrated by the Catholic Church. It is now run as a privately owned museum. (Photograph by Bennet and Brown, courtesy Palace of the Governors [NMHM/DCA], No. 052452.)

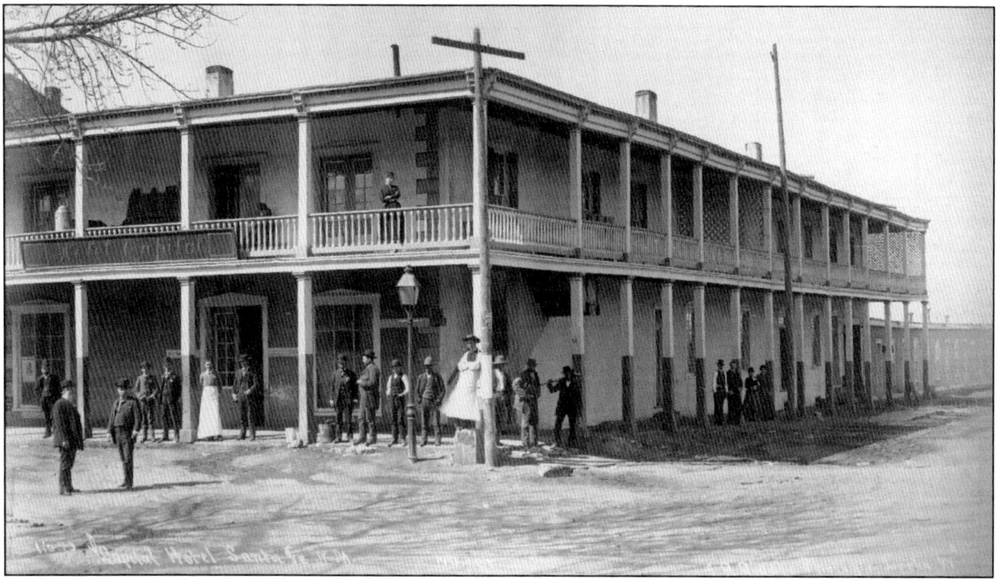

The Capital Hotel was built in 1863 by Gustave Elsberg and his cousin Jacob Amberg. Located at the corner of Lincoln and Palace Avenues, the first floor of the hotel was used for retail businesses. The *Santa Fe Mexican* was located there, and there was also a grocery store. Elsberg and Amberg also rented out meeting rooms to the Masons, Odd Fellows, and other fraternal organizations. The building, pictured around 1886, was destroyed in 1917 by a gas explosion. (Photograph by J.R. Riddle, courtesy Palace of the Governors [NMHM/DCA], No. 056237.)

The Palace Hotel was built in 1881 in anticipation of the railroad coming to Santa Fe. The hotel was built on property owned by the Spiegelberg brothers. It was built in the French Empire style, in complete contrast to the surrounding adobe structures. The hotel was later renamed the De Vargas Hotel and is now called the St. Francis Hotel. (Courtesy Palace of the Governors [NMHM/DCA], No. HP.2013.33.10.)

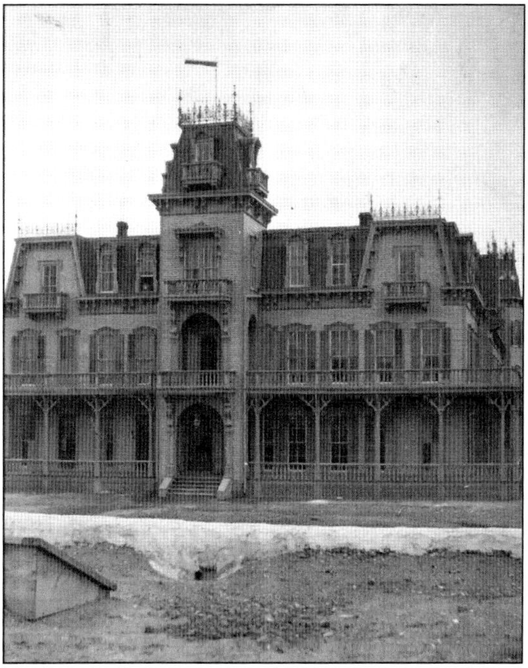

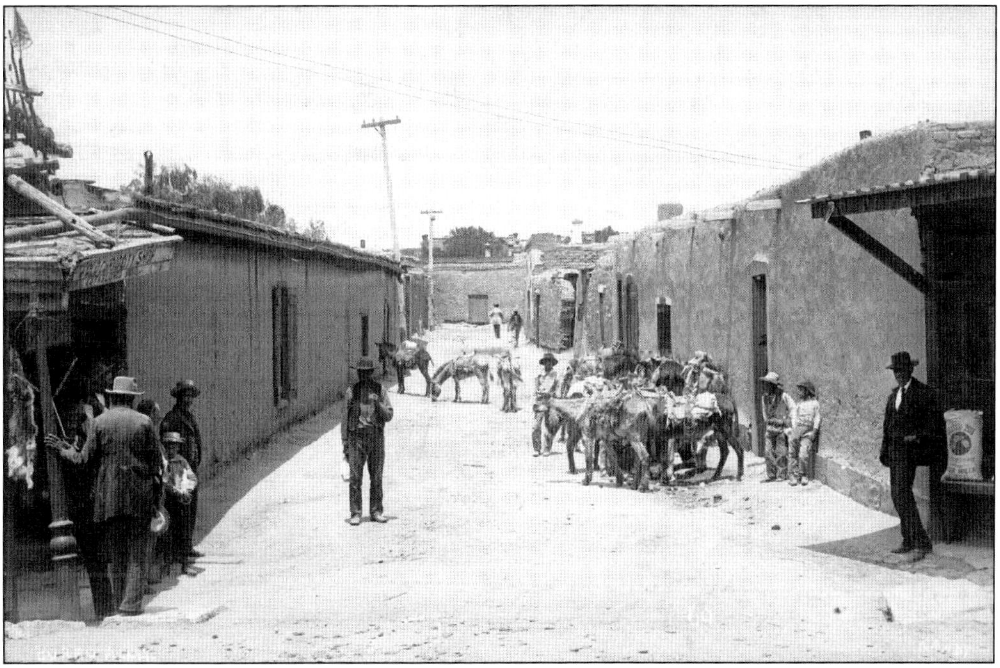

This photograph of Burro Alley was taken between 1889 and 1905. Burro Alley is a small street connecting Palace Avenue and San Francisco Street. During the 19th and early 20th centuries, vendors who sold salt from the Galisteo Salt Basin and firewood from the surrounding mountains would tie up their burros here to rest. While the animals recuperated, the vendors would frequent the local saloons and brothels. The gambling hall that was run by María Gertrudis Barceló, known as Doña Tules, was at the corner near Palace Avenue. (Photograph by Christian Kaadt, courtesy Palace of the Governors [NMHM/DCA], No.011071.)

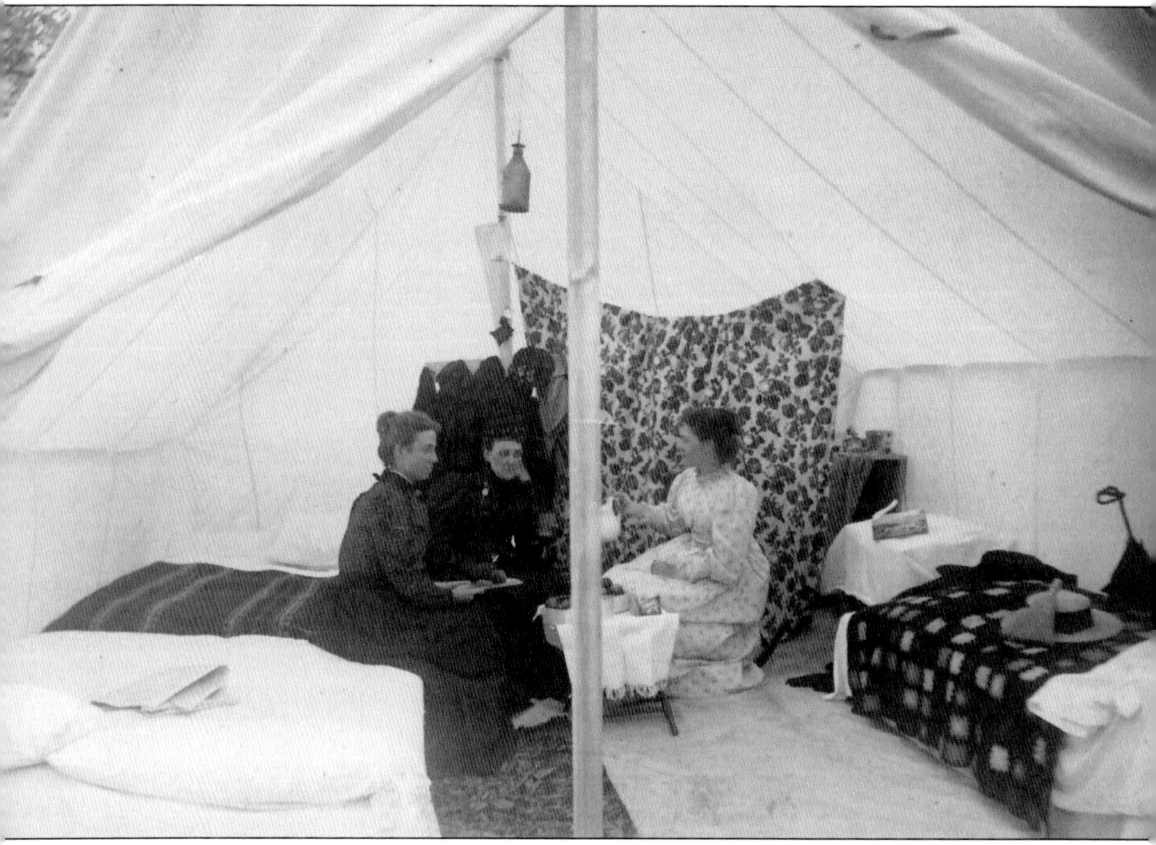

From the late 19th century until 1940, tuberculosis was the leading cause of death in the United States. Many people suffering from the disease came to the high-desert mountains of New Mexico in search of a cure. There were sanatoriums throughout the region that cared for the tuberculars. In the northeastern part of Santa Fe, Sunmount Sanitarium was nestled up against the Sangre de Cristo Mountains where the Immaculate Heart of Mary Retreat and Conference Center is located today. (Courtesy Palace of the Governors [NMHM/DCA], No. HP.2014.52.8.)

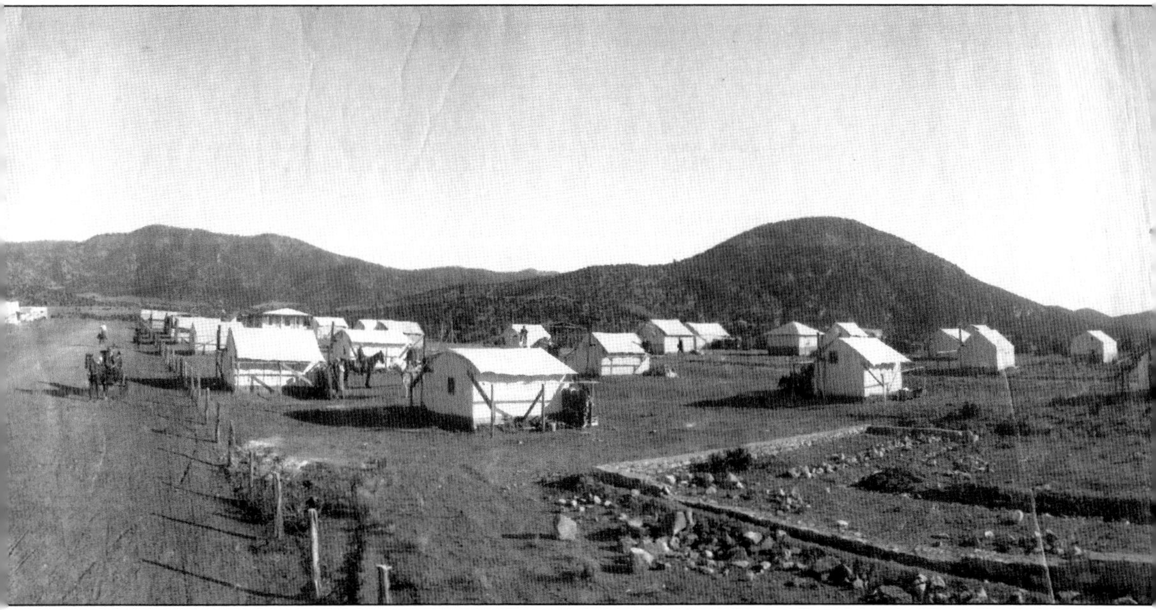

Sunmount Sanitarium began as a group of tent houses and small cottages in 1880. Dr. Frank Meara and his wife built a hospital where the Santa Maria building at the retreat center is located today to care for the "lungers," as they were called at the time. Prior to the advent of antibiotics, which destroyed the bacterial infection of the lungs, the primary treatment for the sick was pristine air, sunshine, and low humidity and pollution, all found in the high altitude of northern New Mexico. (Courtesy Palace of the Governors [NMHM/DCA], No. HP.2012.40.)

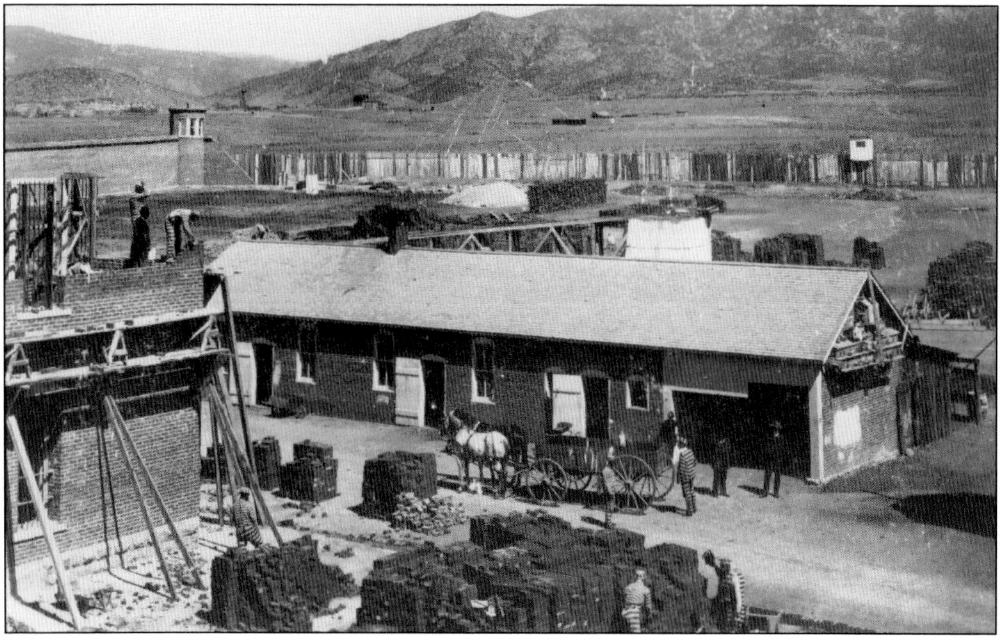

Construction of the Territorial New Mexico Prison, at the corner of Córdova Road and St. Francis Drive, began in the mid-1890s. The prison remained at that location until 1956, when it was moved to the southern part of town. Prior to 1884, for lack of facilities, New Mexico sent its prisoners to Nebraska and Kentucky. In 1884, the territorial legislature appropriated $150,000 for its first penitentiary. When the building was later demolished, the bricks were recycled to build fireplaces for the new residential neighborhood called Dale Bellamah. (Photograph by Thomas J. Curran, courtesy Palace of the Governors [NMHM/DCA], No. 15208.)

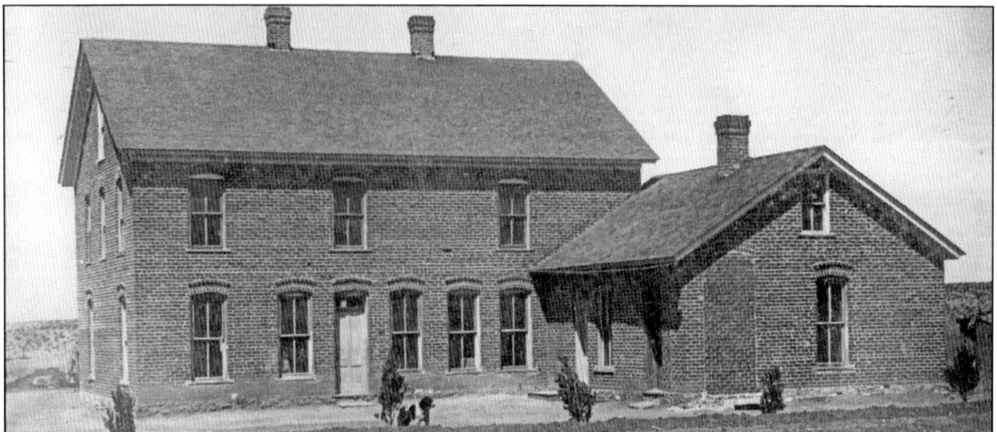

In 1885, Lars Larson and his wife, Belle, both of whom were deaf, began a school in their small adobe home. They taught the children with their own money. That was the same year that Congress passed the Education of the Deaf Act. The Larsons went on to petition for funding from the New Mexico territorial legislature. In 1887, the money was appropriated and the Territorial Asylum for the Deaf and Dumb was opened. During that era, the word "dumb" commonly referred to someone who was mute. The name was later changed to the New Mexico School for the Deaf. The school was the first mandated educational institution in New Mexico. (Photograph by Thomas J. Curran, courtesy Palace of the Governors [NMHM/DCA], No. 16540.)

Brown Moor School was as an all-girls school that opened in Santa Fe in 1931. At Brown Moor, students from well-to-do families from the East sent their daughters to experience a Western education. During the mornings, they were taught a standard curriculum. In the afternoons, they enjoyed horseback riding, archery, skiing, and other outdoor activities. The school closed in 1944, during World War II, because the trains were needed to transport soldiers. (Photograph by Laura Gilpin, courtesy Amon Carter Museum, P1979.235.347.)

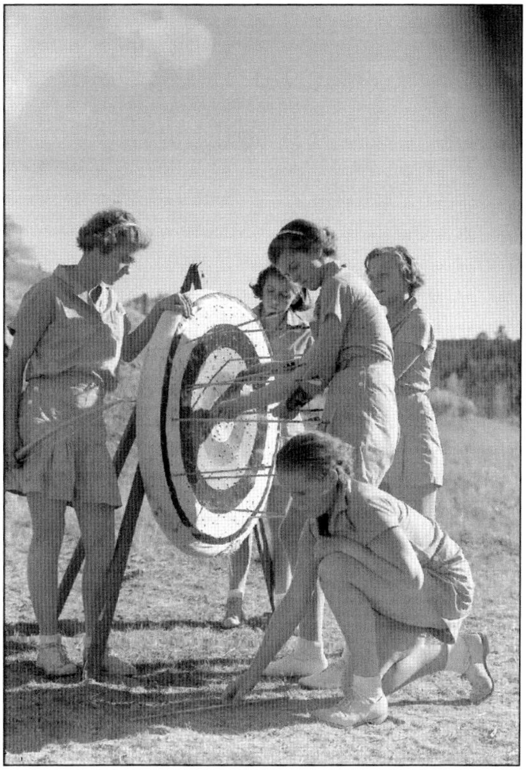

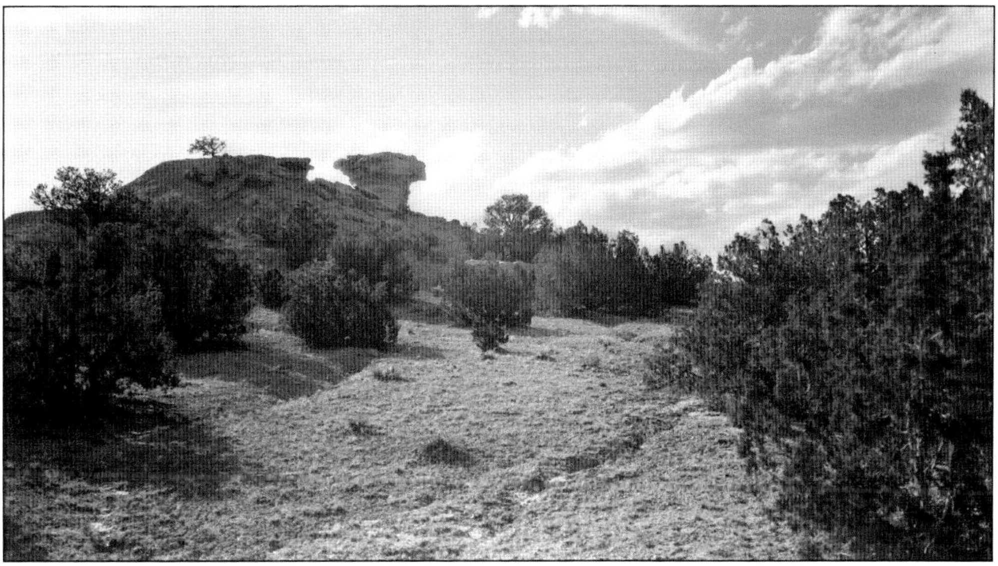

Wind and rain through the centuries have created the sandstone rock formation that looks like a camel, as seen in this 1925 photograph. Camel Rock is part of Tesuque Pueblo, the smallest of the eight pueblos in northern New Mexico. The name Tesuque derives from Te Tesugeh Oweengeh, "the village of the narrow place of the cottonwood trees." Located 10 miles north of Santa Fe on US Highway 84-285, Camel Rock is directly across from Camel Rock Casino. The rock monument is fenced off now, but through the 1970s, people used to climb on it and have picnics. (Photograph by Harmon T. Parkhurst, courtesy Palace of the Governors [NMHM/DCA], No. 067899.)

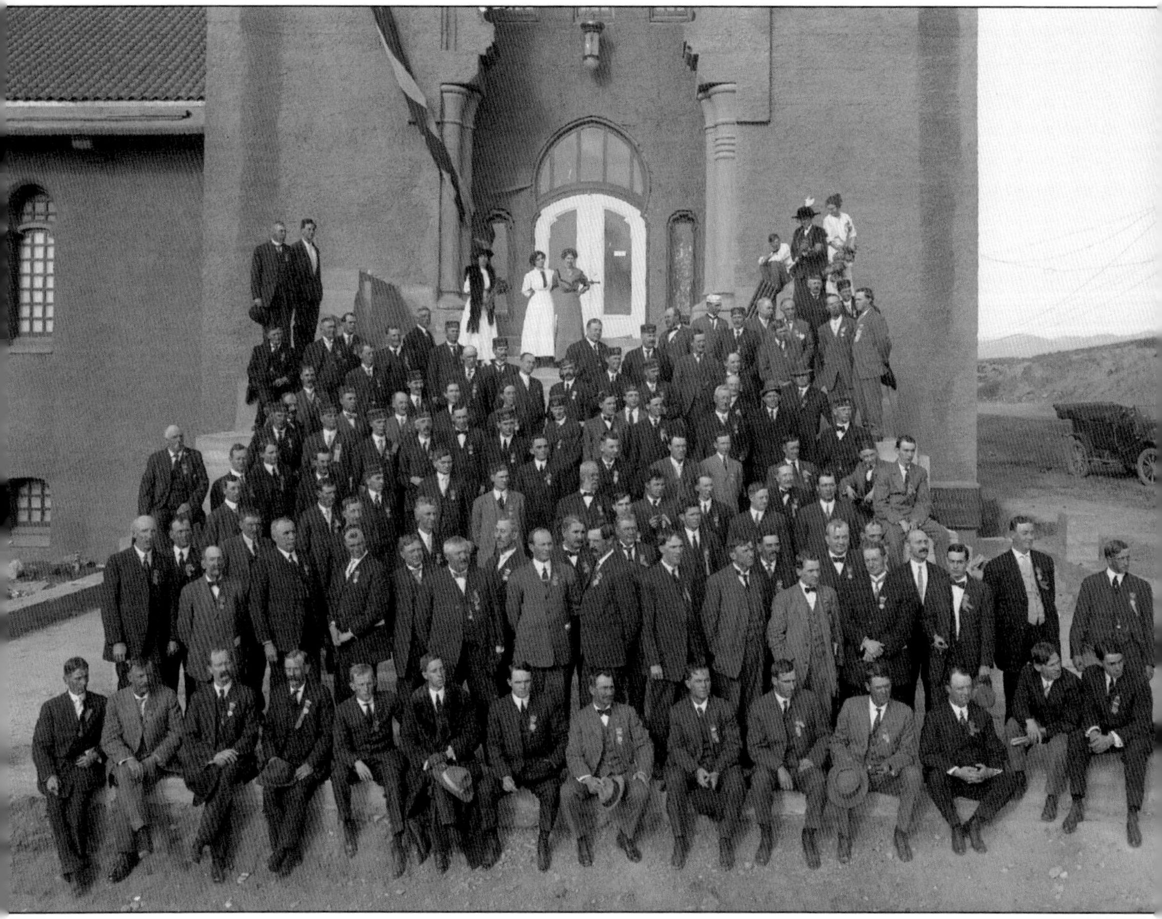

The Scottish Rite Temple was erected in 1912 at the corner of Paseo de Peralta and Washington Avenue. It was built to resemble the Alhambra in Spain. Its pink facade has always stood apart from the rest of Santa Fe's architecture, and it has been referred to by many as the Pepto-Bismol building. Many well-known New Mexicans were Masons, including merchant Abraham Spiegelberg (second row, second from left), archaeologist Sylvanus G. Morley (first row, sitting sixth from left), and Richard Henry Hanna of the Museum of New Mexico (fifth row, far right.) (Photograph by Jesse Nusbaum, courtesy Palace of the Governors [NMHM/DCA], No. 061384.)

Two

Business Moves

Under the Spanish flag, Santa Fe managed to eke out an existence via the traders, trappers, and farmers who came through town to sell their goods. But it was only after Mexico gained its independence from Spain in 1821 and trade opened with the United States that commerce established a foothold in the capital city. William Becknell, known as the father of the Santa Fe Trail, arrived in Santa Fe shortly after Mexican independence. Having established the trade route from Independence, Missouri, to Santa Fe, he received a warm welcome from its citizens. After years of isolation, Santa Fe was being introduced to people and merchandise it never knew existed. Initially only a few wagons made the journey, which took a month to complete, but by 1835, seventy-five wagons hauled an estimated $140,000 in goods. By 1843, the value of goods had risen to $250,000, and by 1855, the annual haul was about half a million dollars.

Santa Fe was not the only community in New Mexico to benefit from the new trade route. In 1826, the community of Las Vegas, 66 miles from Santa Fe, also established a thriving business community. Hispanic merchants like Miguel Romero and his sons brought merchandise west over the trail. They quickly opened stores, and Las Vegas also became a major trading hub in the Southwest.

The future of economic growth for Santa Fe was dependent on the coming of the railroad. In 1860, the Atchison, Topeka & Santa Fe Railway began with the intention of connecting those two cities in Kansas with Santa Fe. In 1873, the first train tracks reached the Kansas-Colorado border. Finding the terrain too difficult to lay tracks, the train never reached Santa Fe. Instead, a spur railway line was built in Lamy, 18 miles from Santa Fe. The economic stability that a railway in Santa Fe would have provided never came to fruition, but the name of the Atchison, Topeka & Santa Fe became synonymous with progress in the West.

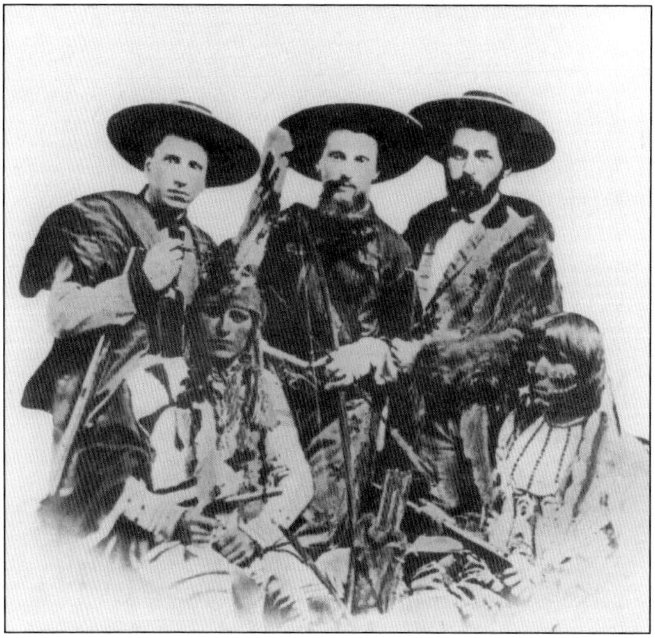

Sigmund Seligman arrived in Santa Fe in 1849 from Gau-Algesheim, Germany. His brother Bernard soon followed and helped establish Seligman & Clever, a dry goods store on the plaza. Some of the other early freighters to arrive via the Santa Fe Trail included Zadoc Stabb and Lehman Spiegelberg, who also established businesses. Standing from left to right are Bernard Seligman, Zadoc Staab, and Lehman Spiegelberg with Kiowa Indian scouts. (Courtesy Palace of the Governors [NMHM/DCA], No. 007890.)

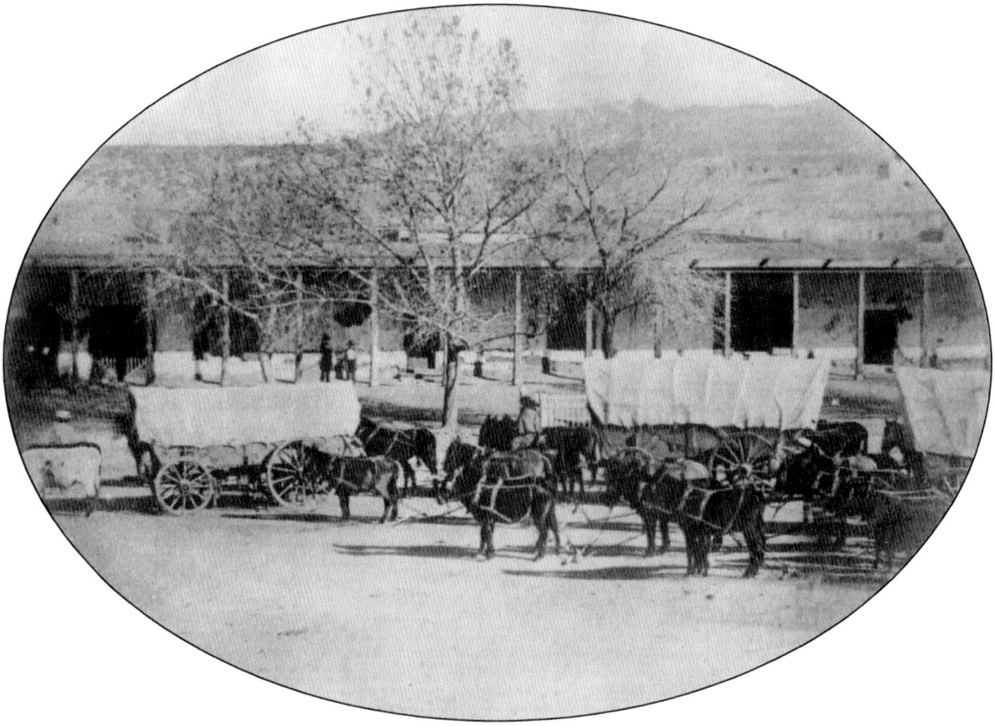

Jacob Amberg and Gustave Elsberg came to Santa Fe by wagon train in 1861. When Amberg emigrated from Germany, he began his trade as a merchant, going from farm to farm selling merchandise from a pack tied to his back. Eventually he received the help of investors, who financed a wagon train to the West. His cousin Gustave Elsberg joined him, and they opened a trading post in Santa Fe. Years later, Amberg settled in Chihuahua, Mexico, and started another trading post. (Courtesy Palace of the Governors [NMHM/DCA], No. 011254.)

This late 19th century photograph shows a Mexican woman selling chiles on the plaza. The chile plant arrived during the conquest of New Mexico by the Spanish-Mexican colonists, who arrived with their Tlaxcalan (Mexican Indian) servants in the 16th century. The Pueblo Indians adopted it immediately and incorporated it into their diet. From the first encounter between Europeans and Native Americans to the present, the chile has been an exemplary mediator between cultures and peoples. (Photograph by Christian G. Kaadt, courtesy Palace of the Governors [NMHM/DCA], No. 014225.)

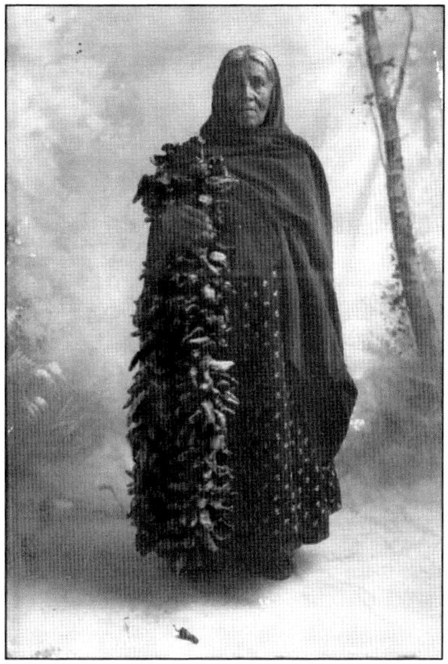

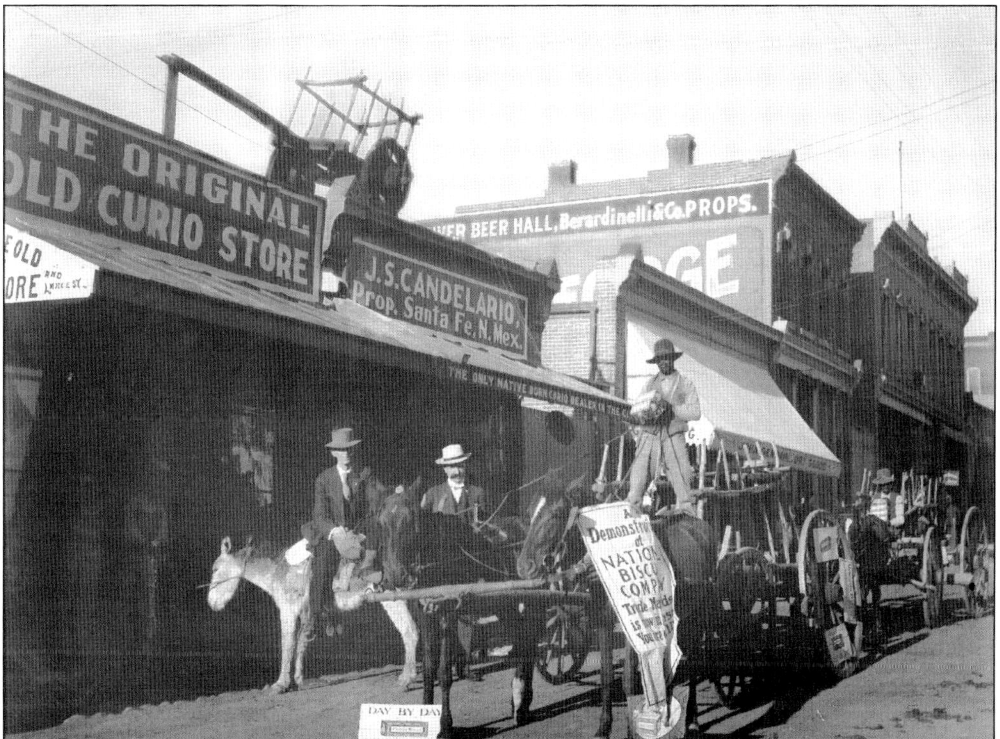

In 1890, the J.S. Candelario Old Curio Shop sold the largest selection of Native American craftwork in Santa Fe. When Jesus Sito Candelario opened his shop on San Francisco Street, he became one of the most successful curio merchants in New Mexico. He worked directly with members of the surrounding pueblos, who created weavings, baskets, jewelry, and pottery. His grandson, photographer John Candelario, eventually took over the business. (Courtesy Palace of the Governors [NMHM/DCA], No. 093714.)

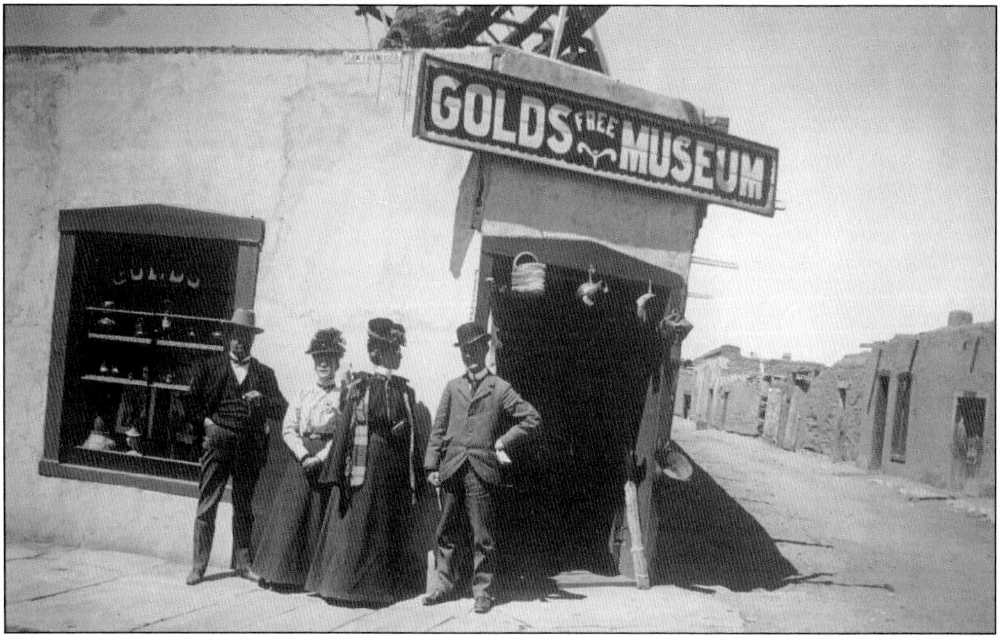

Luis Gold came to Santa Fe after the Civil War with three sons: Aaron, Abe, and Jack. Jack managed the J.S. Candelario Old Curio Shop prior to opening his own business. In 1890, he opened the Jack Gold Free Museum and Old Curiosity Shop on Burro Alley. The Gold family entered into partnerships with the Navajo and Pueblo Indians to supply native artifacts to a demanding public. (Courtesy Palace of the Governors [NMHM/DCA], No. 010731.)

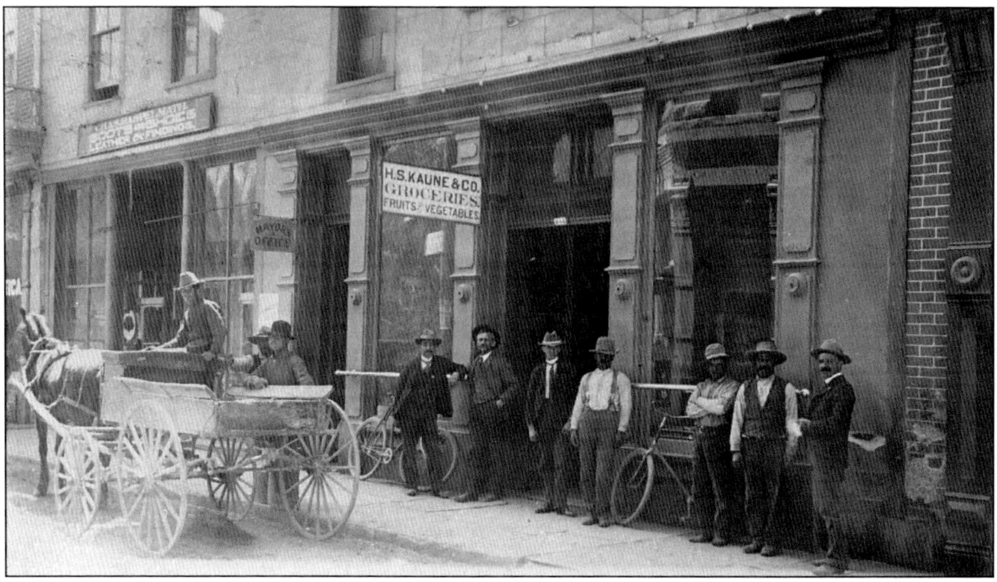

Henry Kaune and his sons stand for a photograph in 1900 in front of the H.S. Kaune and Company Grocery Store. Henry Kaune moved to Santa Fe in the late 1890s from St. Louis, where he operated a grocery store. His four sons—Alfred, Charles, Henry, and Gustave—followed in his footsteps. The family operated two stores, one on Old Santa Fe Trail and the other on Washington Avenue. Kaune Elementary School, which closed in 2014, is named for Alfred Kaune, who was on the school board for many years. (Courtesy Palace of the Governors [NMHM/DCA], No. HP.2014.14.1663.)

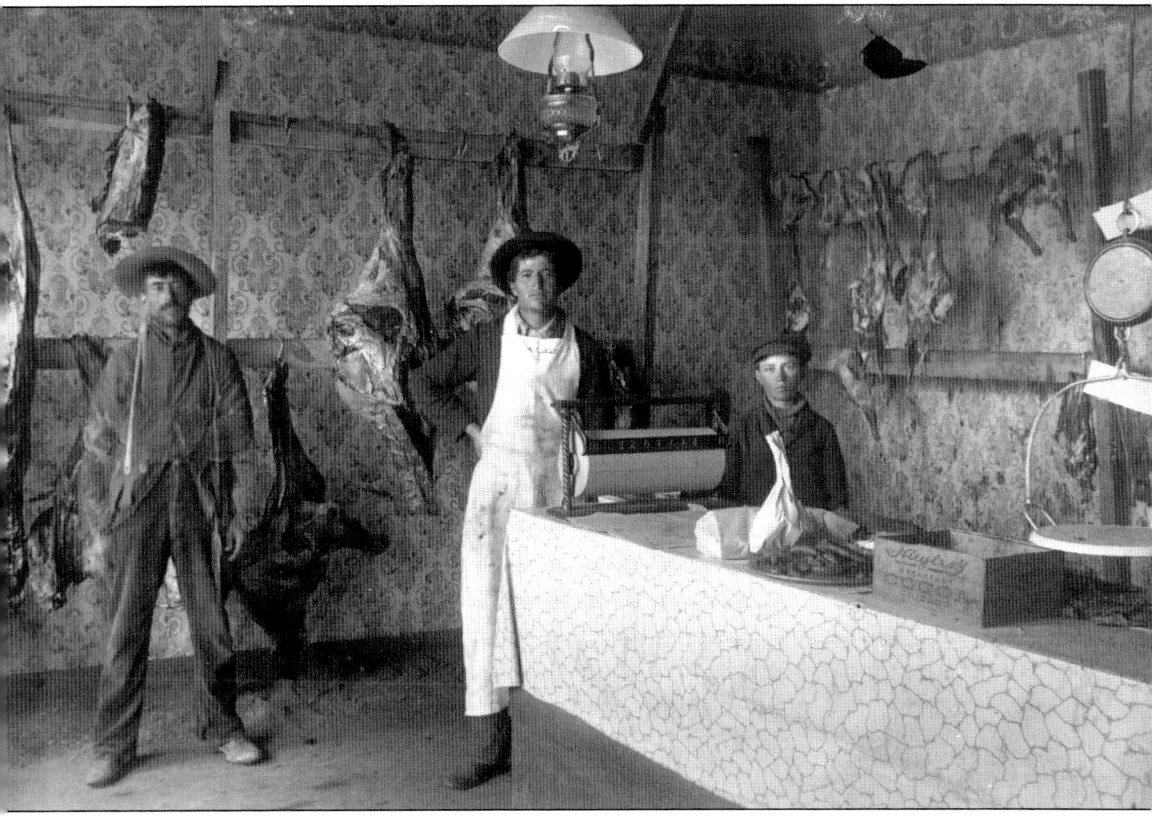

From left to right, Hilario, Hefinio, and Ramón Pacheco work in the family-run butcher shop on Water Street around 1918. Santa Fe was home to multigenerational tradesmen and their families. José de la Cruz Pacheco, for whom Pacheco Street is named, came to Santa Fe in the late 19th century from Santa Cruz in northern New Mexico. He and his family brought the trade of meat cutting and were known as *carniceros* (butchers). They also operated a slaughterhouse at Penn Road. Through the 1970s, virtually every male with the surname Pacheco was involved in the meat trade. (Courtesy Palace of the Governors [NMHM/DCA], No. 010663.)

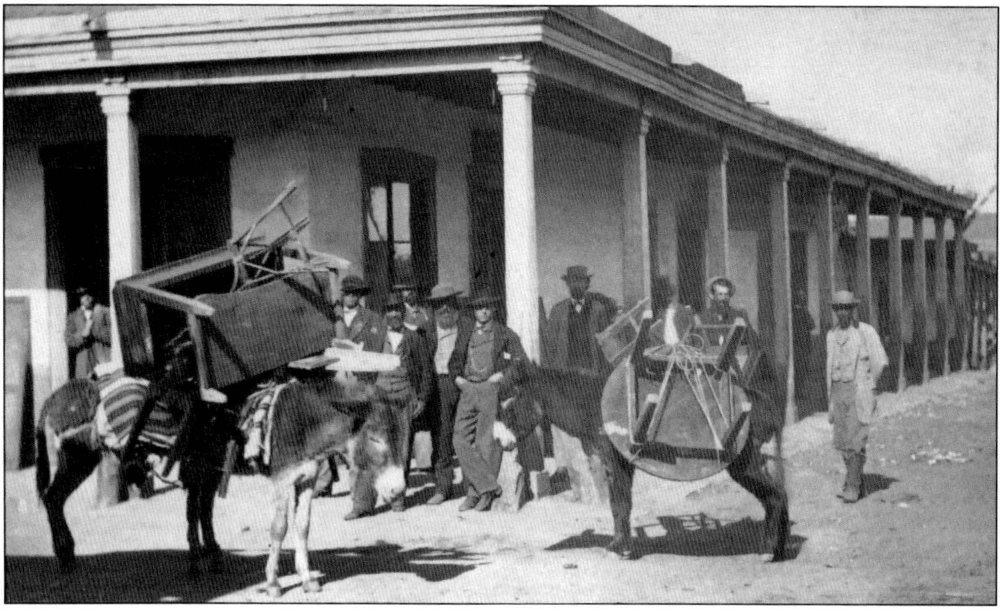

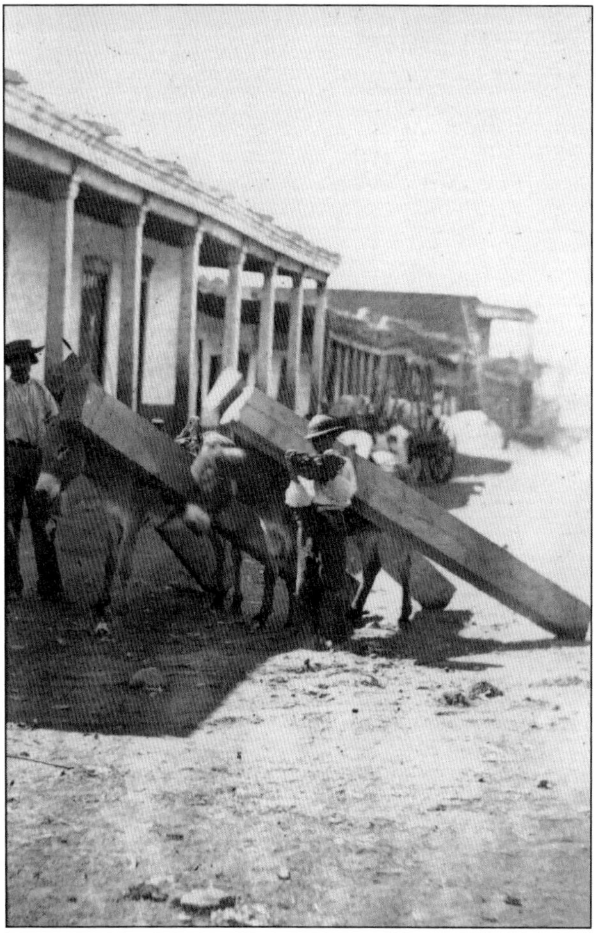

The burro is credited with the development of Santa Fe. These sure-footed animals were used for all types of transportation, including furniture, as pictured here around 1867. (Photograph by Nicolas Brown, courtesy Palace of the Governors [NMHM/DCA], No. 050311.)

Burros were the preferred animals for work in Santa Fe's surrounding mountains. They regularly transported processed timber into town tied to their backs. (Photograph by Nicolas Brown, courtesy Palace of the Governors [NMHM/DCA], No. 011760.)

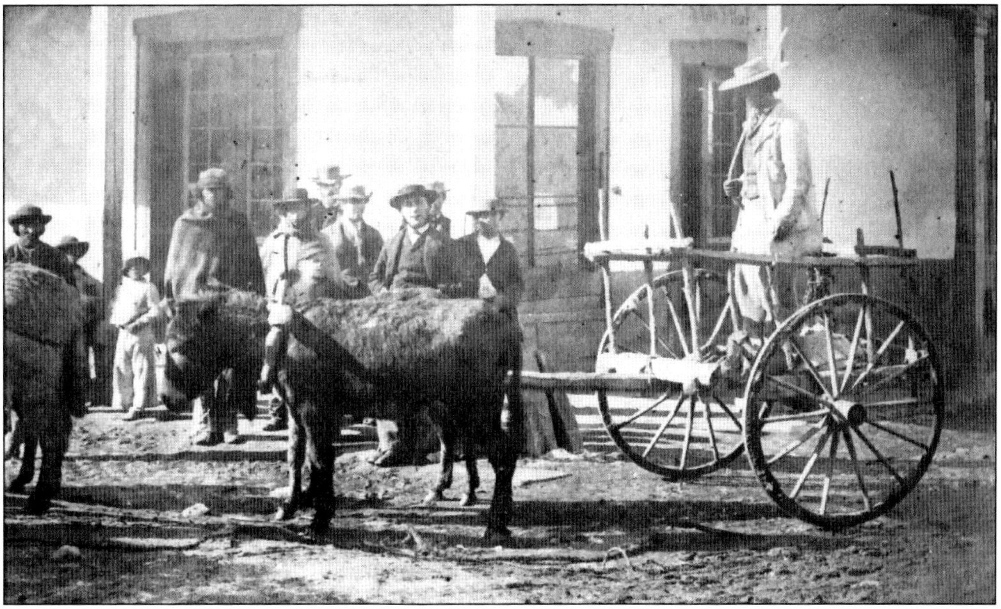

The burro was one of the most common domesticated animals found in Santa Fe during the 19th and early 20th centuries. The burro travels faster when driven rather than led, which made it the perfect animal to pull wagons. Smaller than horses, burros were more commonly used as a means of transportation by women. With the advent of the automobile, burros transformed from pack animals to pets. This 1867 photograph shows a woman entering town in her cart pulled by burro. (Photograph by Nicolas Brown, courtesy Palace of the Governors [NMHM/DCA], No. 011832.)

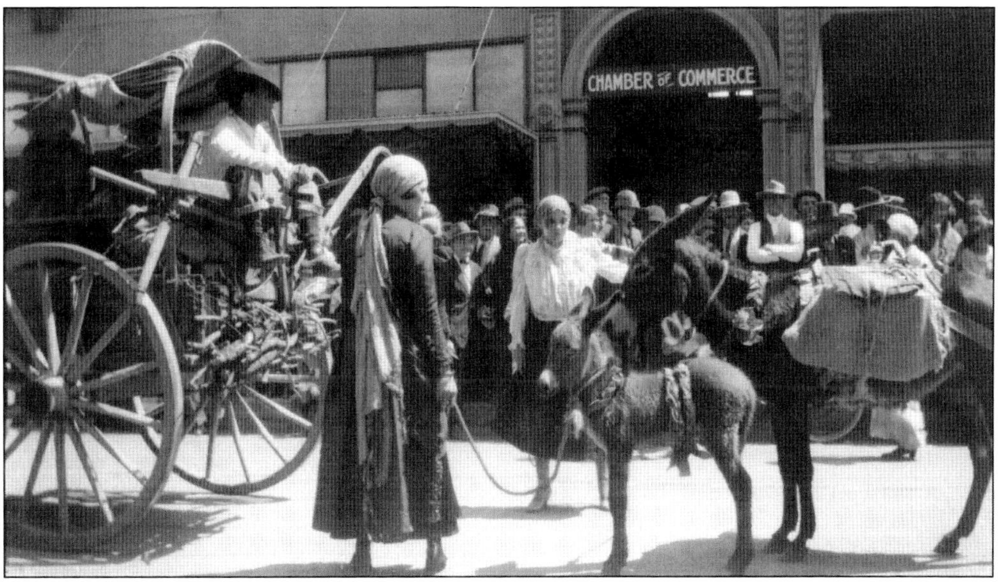

A women and daughter, pictured in front of the chamber of commerce, lead their pet donkeys. Through the 1950s, burros were often used during the Fiesta de Santa Fe parade. (Courtesy Palace of the Governors [NMHM/DCA], No. HP.2016.24.5.)

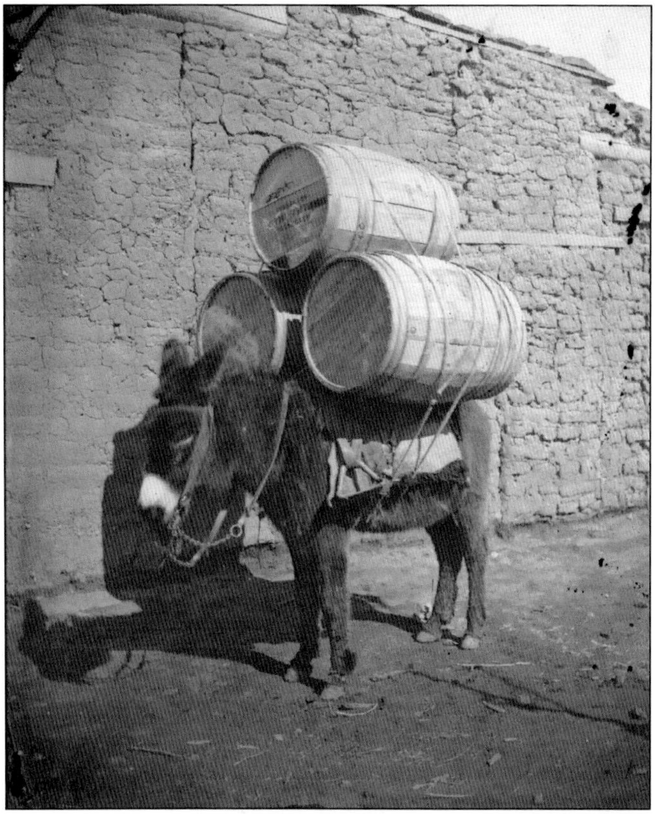

Throughout the world, burros are known for their endurance at high altitudes and in arid climates. Their ability to adapt to the climate of the Southwest proved to be instrumental in the development of Santa Fe and the region. The explorer Juan de Oñate introduced the first burros to the Southwest on his 1598 trek up the Camino Real from Mexico City. Burros were also used to haul goods in 1821 along the Santa Fe Trail from Missouri. In 1872, a burro hauls water barrels near the Santa Fe Plaza. (Photograph by Henry T. Hiester, courtesy Palace of the Governors [NMHM/DCA], No. 037967.)

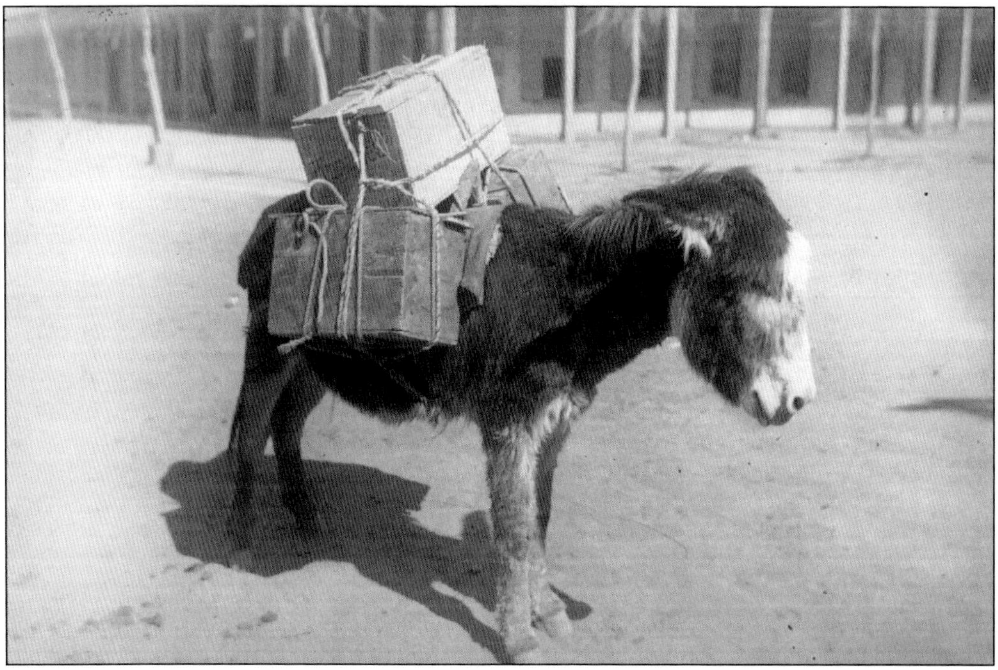

Burros were also used locally to deliver fruit and other perishable items in town around 1884. (Photograph by Dana B. Chase, courtesy Palace of the Governors [NMHM/DCA], No. 050311.)

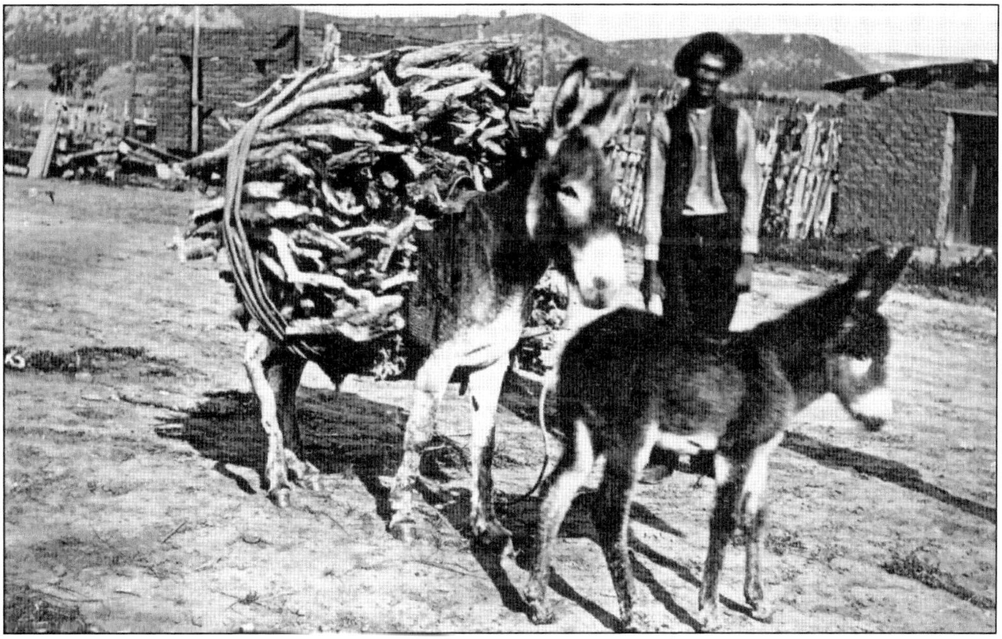

During the 19th century, *varilleros* (traveling salesmen) roamed the countryside sellıng wood, thread, dishes, and pots and pans to housewives out on the prairie. This one is pictured around 1878. (Courtesy Palace of the Governors [NMHM/DCA], No. 086965.)

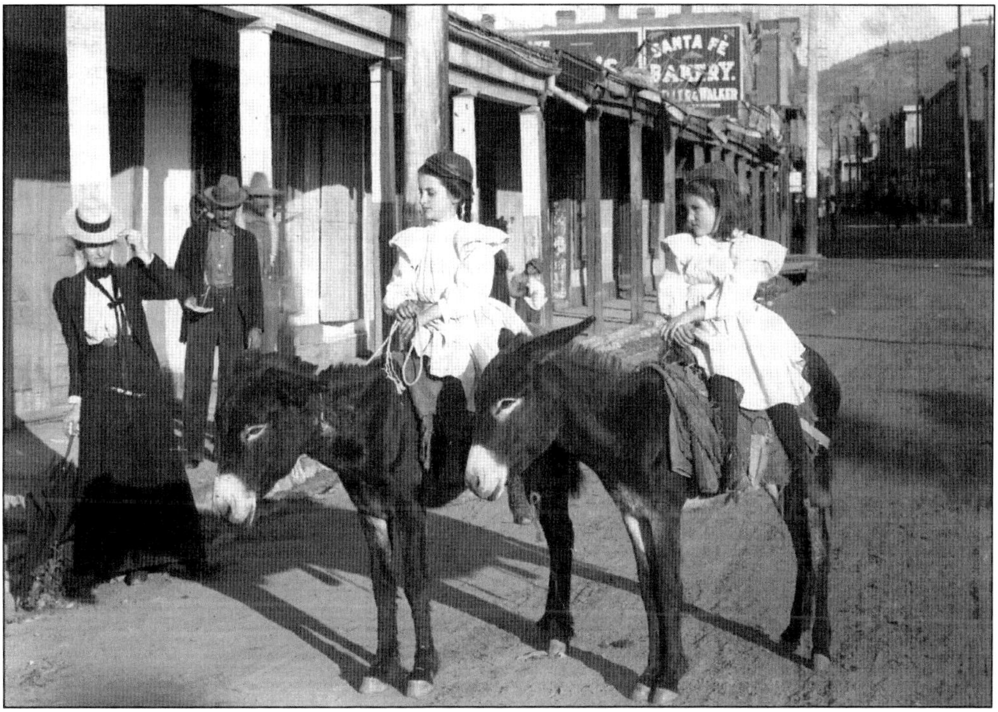

Genevieve Harrison Dunlavy (left) and Helen Harrison Fiske ride burros on West San Francisco Street around 1895. (Photograph by Christian G. Kaadt, courtesy Palace of the Governors [NMHM/DCA], No. 011341.)

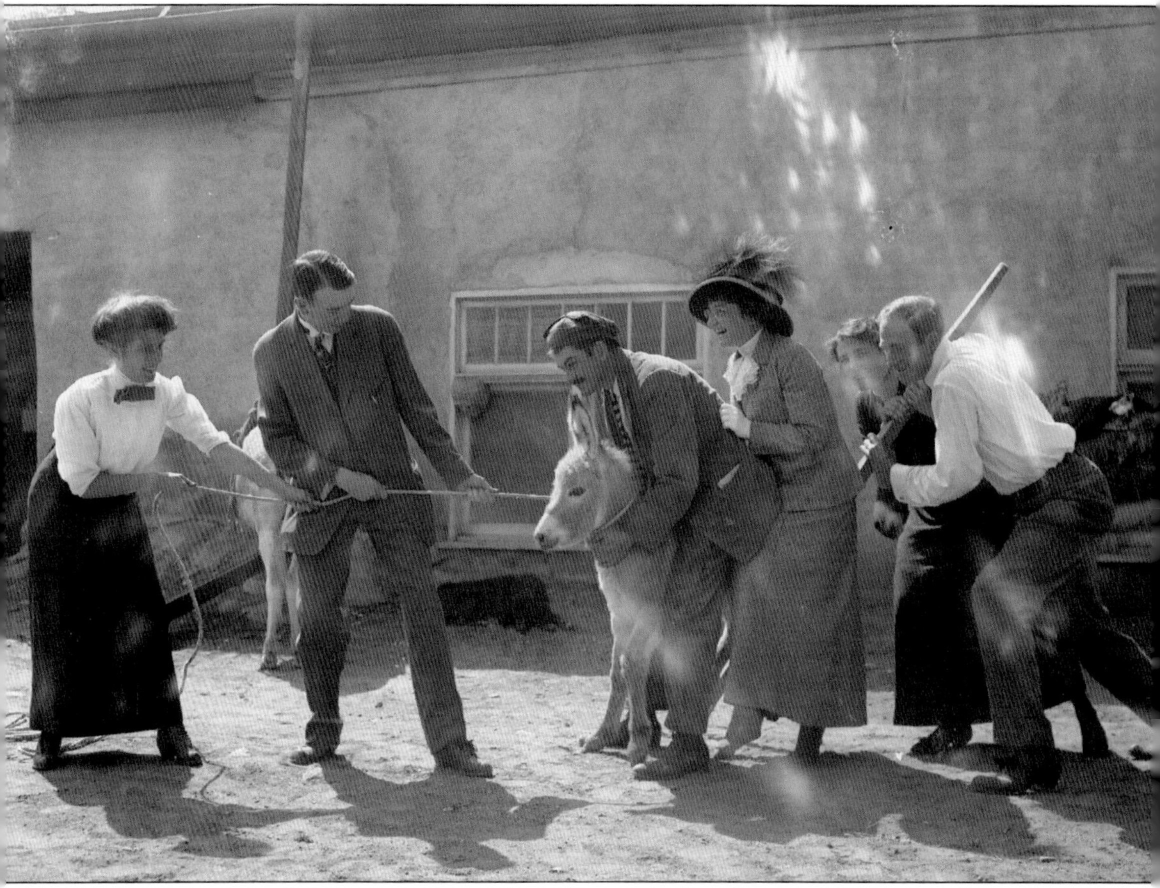

Even in 1912, when New Mexico achieved statehood and automobiles were becoming more popular, burros were a commonplace sight on Santa Fe streets. (Photograph by Jesse Nusbaum, courtesy Palace of the Governors [NMHM/DCA], No. 022310.)

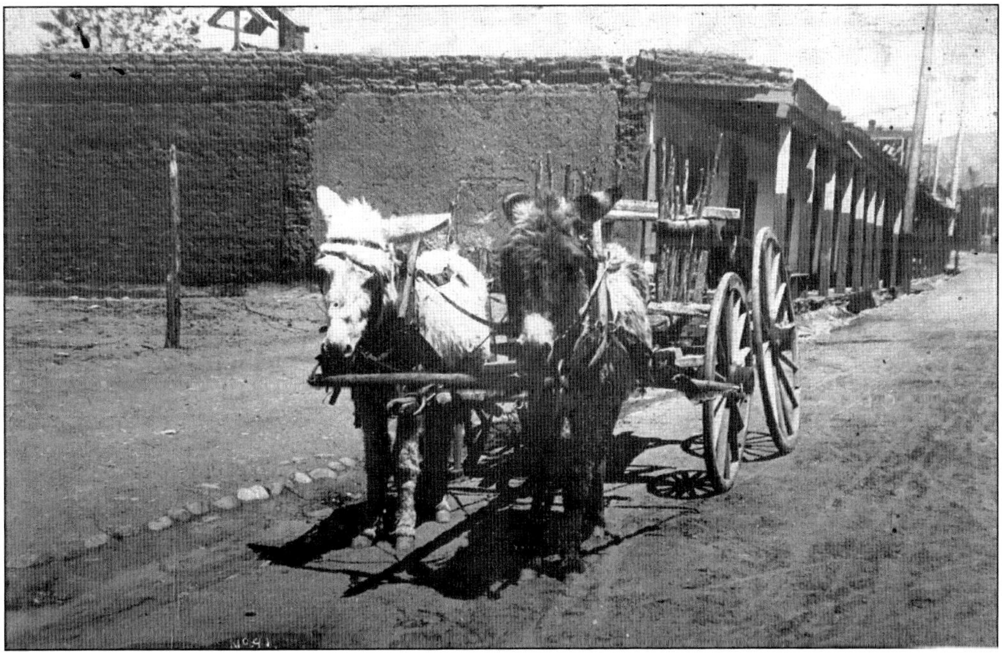

Through the end of the 1800s, Mexican *carretas* were used by Hispanics and Pueblo Indians to transport freight. Burros were typically used to pull the wooden carts around the plaza's business district on San Francisco Street. (Photograph by Christian G. Kaadt, courtesy Palace of the Governors [NMHM/DCA], No. 030200.)

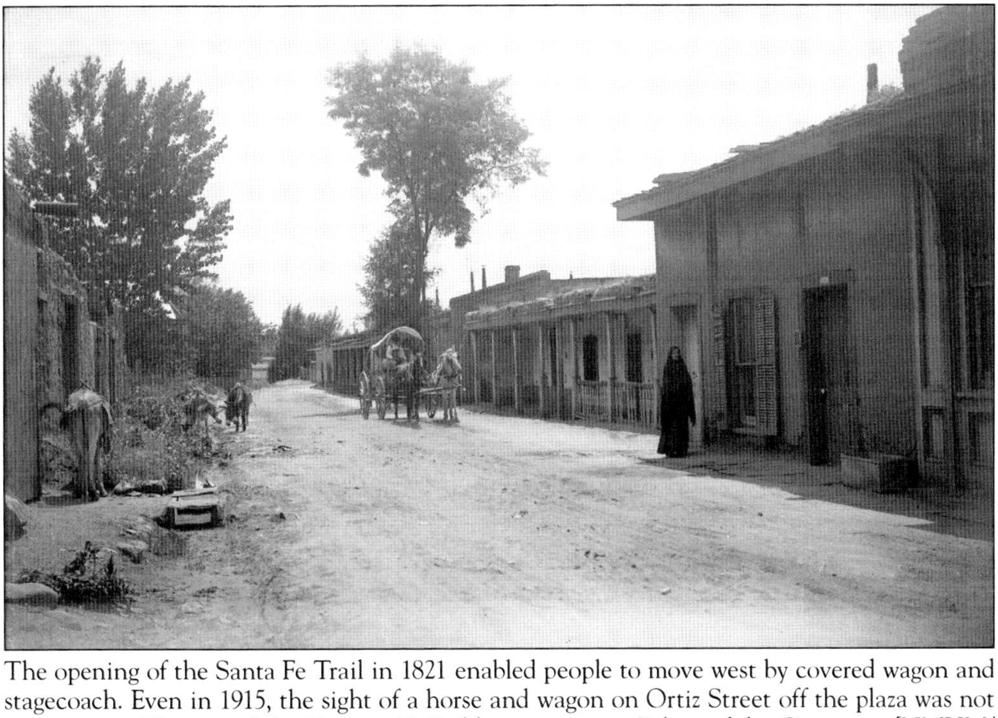

The opening of the Santa Fe Trail in 1821 enabled people to move west by covered wagon and stagecoach. Even in 1915, the sight of a horse and wagon on Ortiz Street off the plaza was not uncommon. (Photograph by Harmon T. Parkhurst, courtesy Palace of the Governors [NMHM/DCA], No. 144777.)

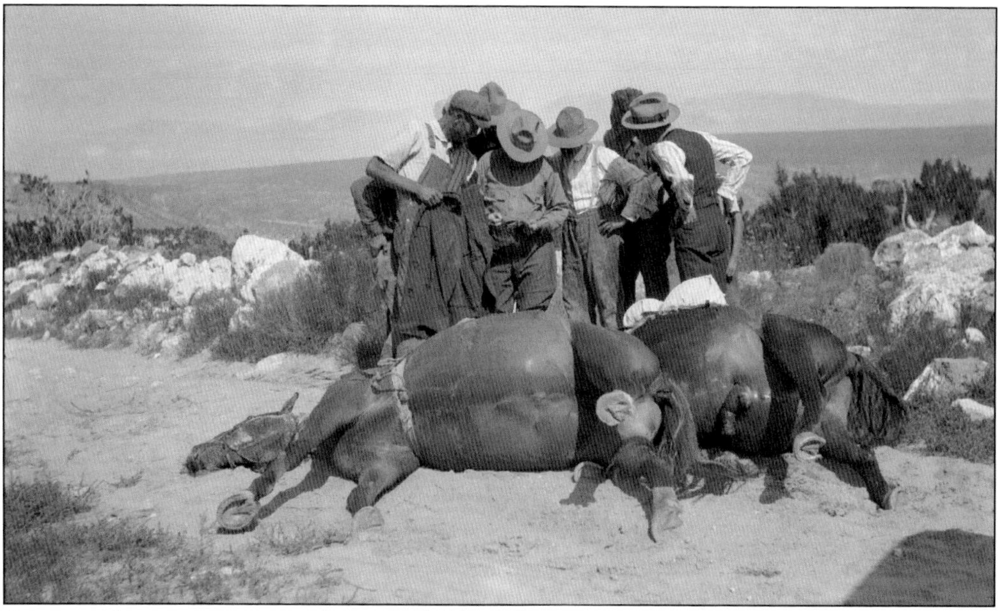

A group of men examine two horses killed by lightning with the Sangre de Cristo Mountains in the background. Lightning deaths are a common occurrence in New Mexico. (Photograph by William H. Roberts, courtesy Palace of the Governors [NMHM/DCA], No. 163214.)

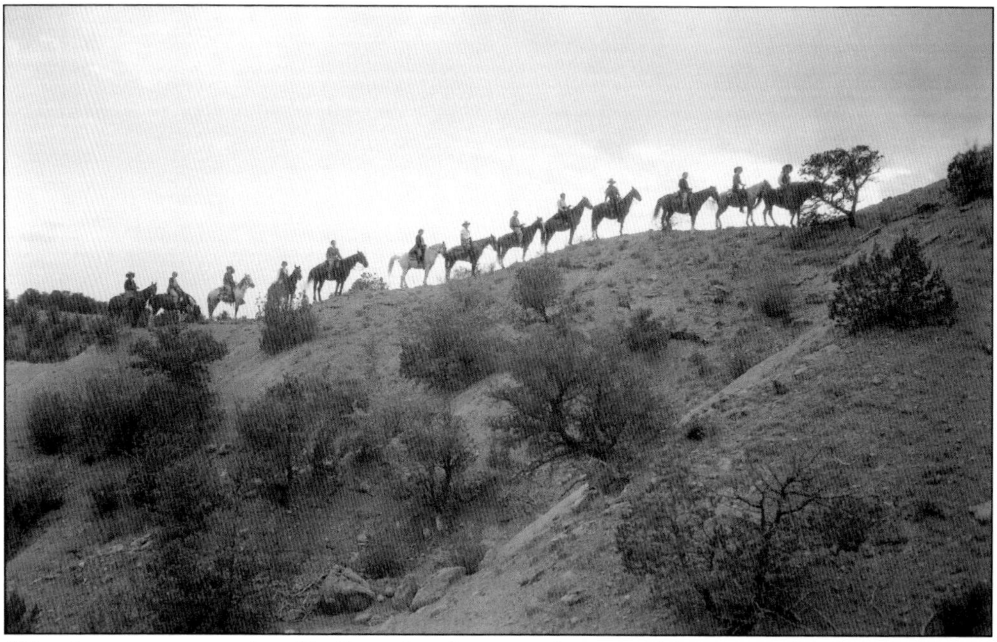

When horses were introduced by Spanish colonists in the early 16th century, they forever changed the landscape of the American Southwest. With their ease of mobility and endurance, they transported people near and far. With the 20th century and the advent of the automobile, horses continued to be used to access mountainous terrain. In 1939, a group on horseback traverses the ridge at Bishop's Lodge. (Photograph by Harmon T. Parkhurst, courtesy Palace of the Governors [NMHM/DCA], No. 051472.)

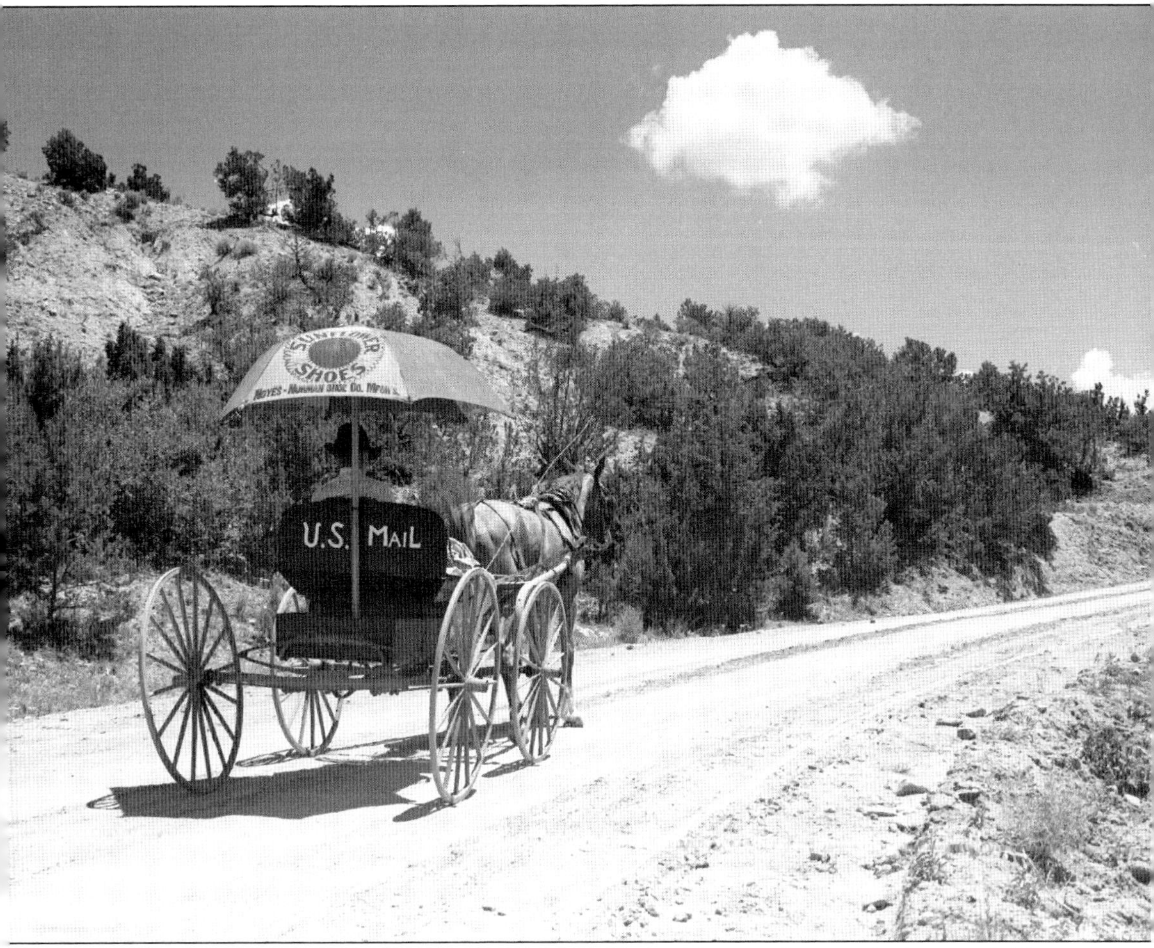

The US Postal Service delivered in all types of weather on winding roads using the best available transportation. This horse-and-buggy carrier in 1940 made sure that remote areas in northern New Mexico did not miss their daily mail. (Photograph by John Candelario, courtesy Palace of the Governors [NMHM/DCA], No. 165854.)

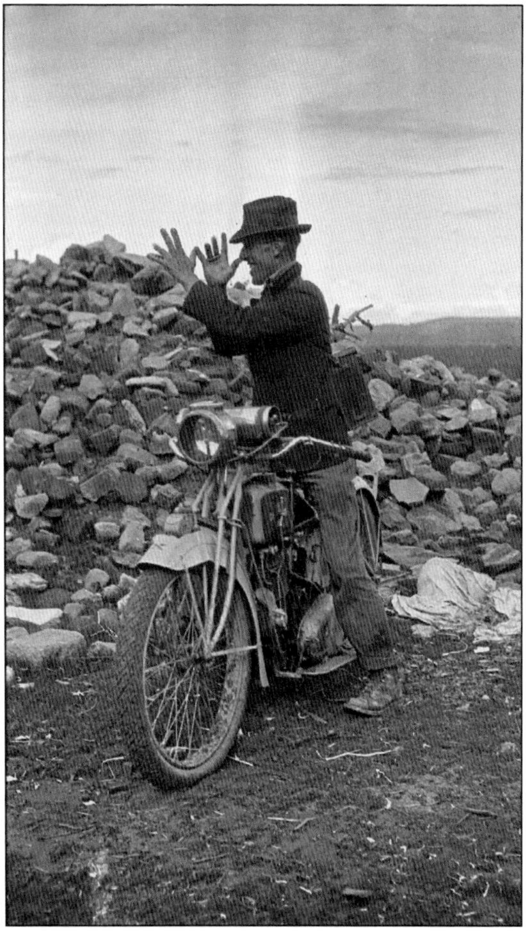

In 1910, Jess Nusbaum was working as an anthropologist at the School of American Research and the Museum of New Mexico. When he needed time to unwind, he took to the unpaved streets in Santa Fe to fool around on his motorcycle. (Courtesy Palace of the Governors [NMHM/DCA], No. 158088.)

In 1877, high-wheel bicycles were being imported to the United States from Europe. They became a sensation when they were brought to Santa Fe in 1884. Until that time, four-legged mammals had been the preferred mode of transportation, but not after people witnessed these six bicycle riders carousing on the plaza. (Photograph by Dana B. Chase, courtesy Palace of the Governors [NMHM/DCA], No. 002267.)

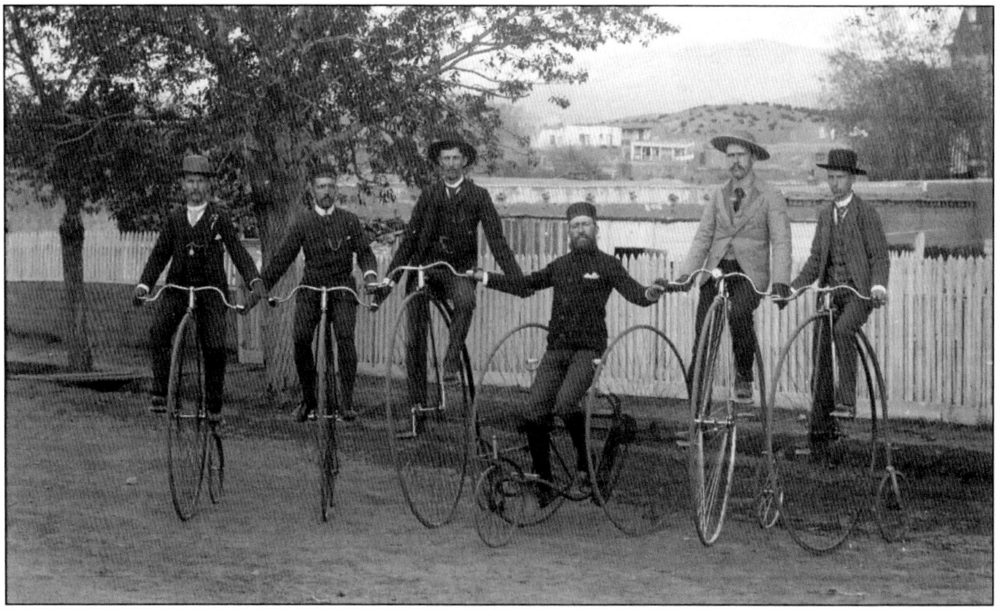

Three

FIESTA DE SANTA FE

The Fiesta de Santa Fe is intrinsic to America's history, not only for being the oldest continuous community celebration in the country but also because it highlights the legacy of three centuries of Catholicism.

The fiesta began with the re-conquest of Santa Fe in 1692. After years of oppression under Spanish rule, the surrounding Pueblos successfully drove the Spanish colonists out of New Mexico in 1680. The mastermind of the revolt was Po'pay, a medicine man from Ohkay Owingeh (formerly San Juan) Pueblo who served the Tewa people. For the next 12 years, the colonists lived in El Paso del Norte, which is now a part of Ciudad Juárez and El Paso, until Don Diego de Vargas reclaimed Santa Fe. When Don Diego died in 1712, Don Juan Páez Hurtado, who had served as his lieutenant governor, drafted a resolution that a fiesta was to be held each year in commemoration of de Vargas and La Conquistadora.

As a US territory after 1848, the Anglo population grew, and the fiesta was gradually transformed. In July 1883, Santa Fe hosted the Tertio-Millennial Celebration and Exposition, and the fiesta was combined with the Fourth of July. This was most likely the first time that Native Americans participated in a community celebration, and it led to subsequent fiesta events. The fiesta was suspended from 1913 through 1918. In 1926, artist Will Shuster created Zozobra, the oversized puppet that was burned as a means of banishing gloom, and in 1927, Amalia Sena Sánchez became Santa Fe's first Fiesta Queen. Since the 1920s, the Fiesta de Santa Fe has evolved into a collective synergy, with its origin as a religious celebration intact.

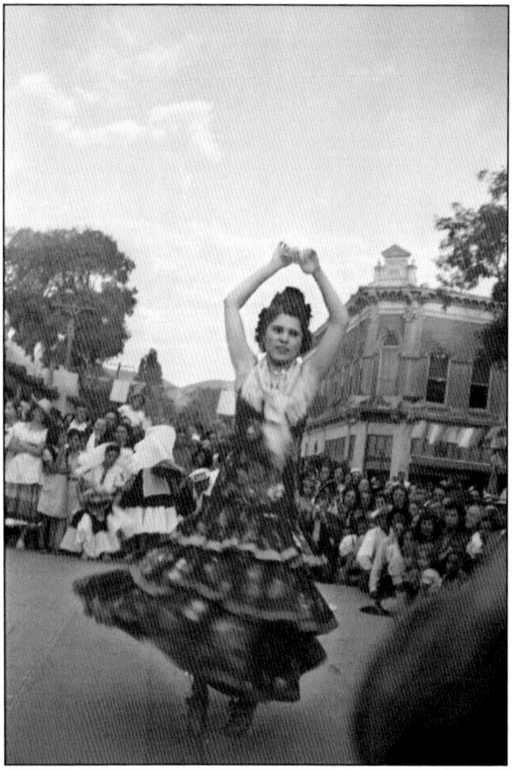

The Fiesta de Santa Fe has always incorporated early Spanish traditions. In this 1936 photograph, Olinda Rodríguez performs a Spanish dance on the plaza. (Courtesy Palace of the Governors [NMHM/DCA], No. HP.2010.02.2.)

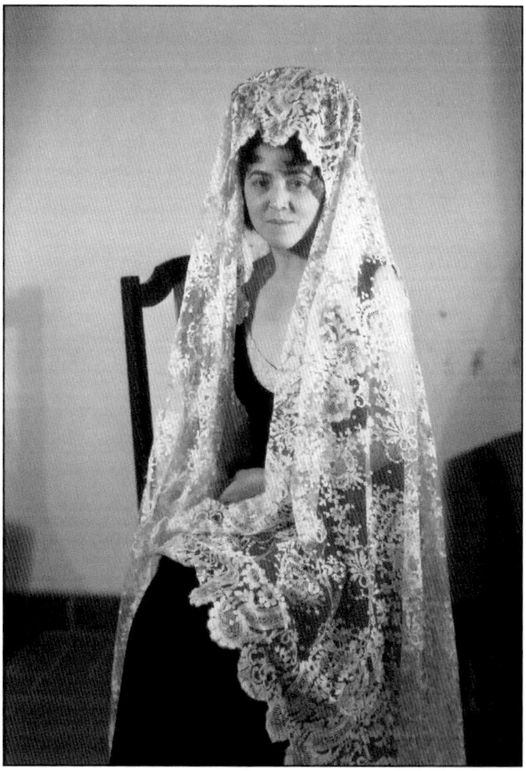

In 1930, Carmen Espinosa studied fashion at El Colegio de los Pirineos in Barcelona. When she returned in 1936, she wrote extensively for the local media on Spanish fashion. Espinosa was photographed as she modeled an 1876 Spanish mantilla for her exposé on fashion. Each year at the Fiesta de Santa Fe, people added to the festive atmosphere by dressing in Spanish and Mexican outfits. (Photograph by Wyatt Davis, courtesy Palace of the Governors [NMHM/DCA], No. 007187.)

Santa Fe Fiesta Queen Consuelo "Peaches" Alarid and her court walk past the Basilica Cathedral of St. Francis of Assisi in 1944. In the 1960s, the use of female pages for the queen's court was eliminated, but around that time, the inclusion of an Indian princess was added. (Photograph by Robert H. Martin, courtesy Palace of the Governors [NMHM/DCA], No. 041384.)

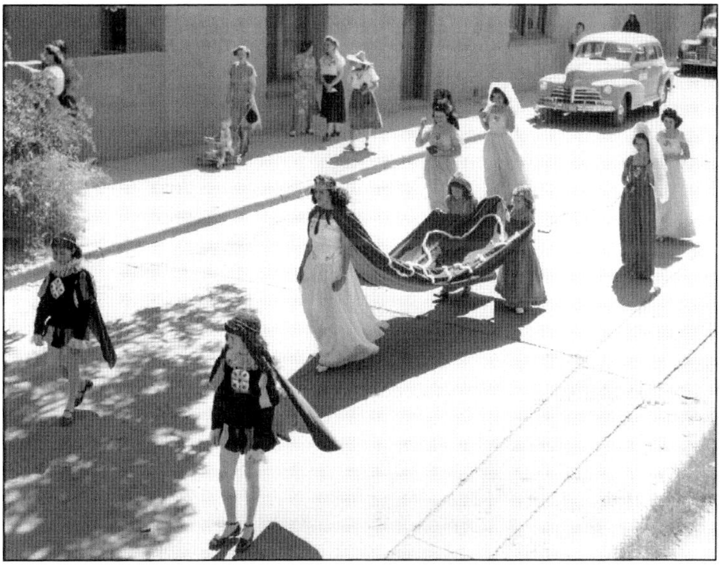

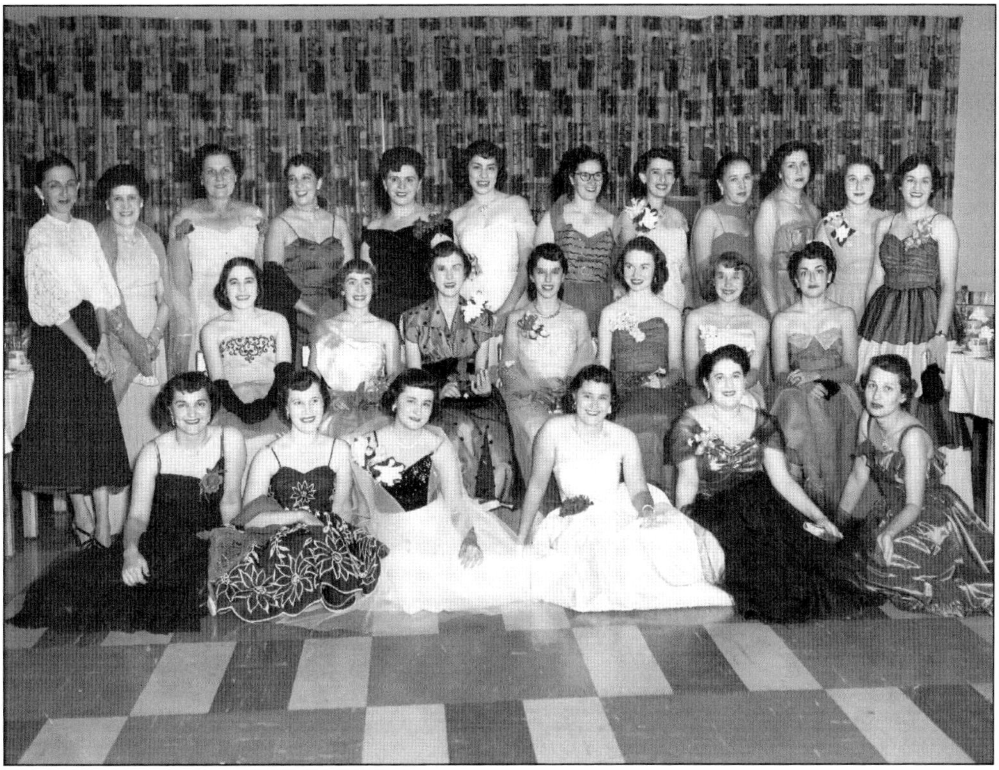

In 1944, the Club Real (Royal Court) was formed as a way to keep the Fiesta Queens and princesses involved for future celebrations. The women set rules and elected officers. All of their meetings were conducted in Spanish. They acted as scouts for the council to recruit potential courts and raised money to purchase a new crown and robe for the queen. They also had a float for the former courts in the fiesta parade. After each fiesta, they sponsored a gala dinner and dance, and the new court was inducted into the organization. Because of a lack of interest and the changing times, the group was disbanded in the 1960s. (Author's collection.)

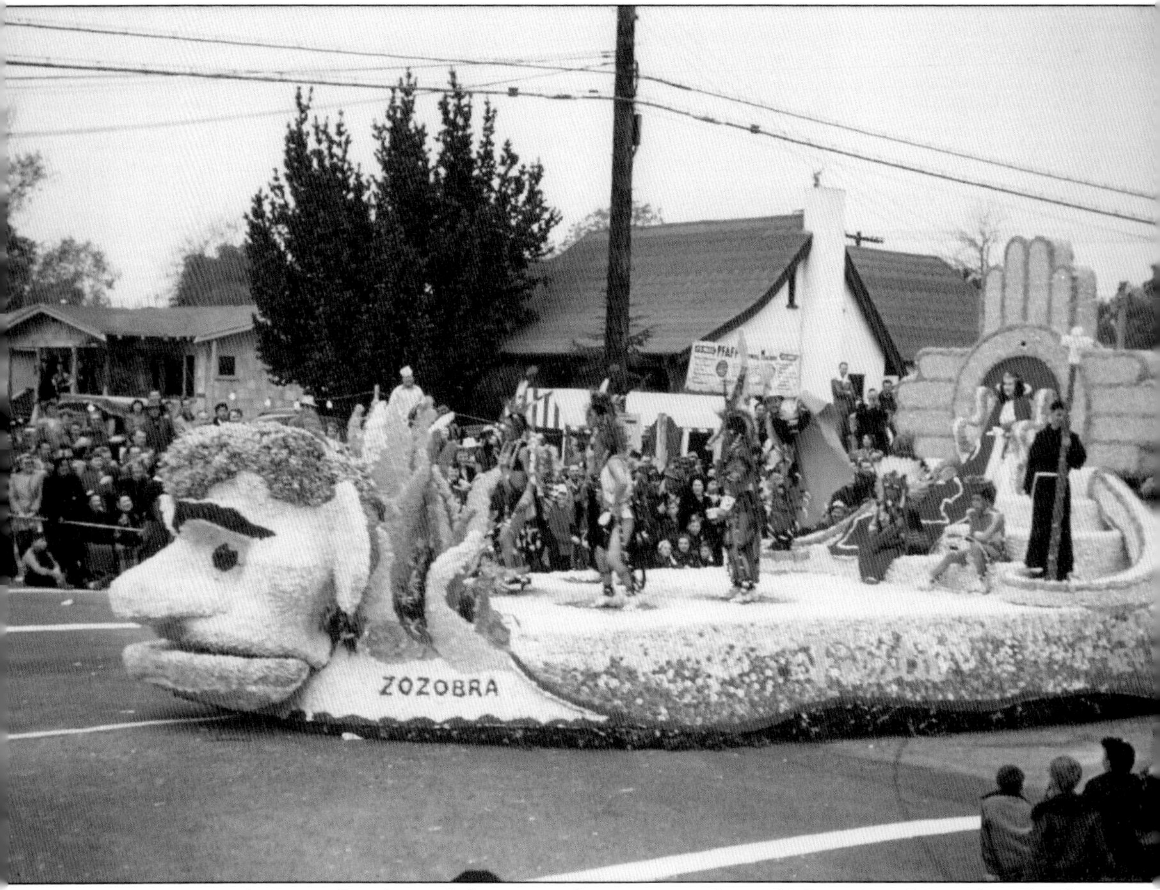

This Fiesta de Santa Fe–themed float won first prize at the 1950 Rose Bowl Parade. The float was designed in the shape of Zozobra by its creator, Will Shuster. It was decorated with more than a million flowers, with New Mexico's Zia symbol bringing up the rear. Fiesta Queen Anita Romero and historian Fray Angélico Chávez rode in the parade, along with de Vargas and hoop dancers from Taos Pueblo. The head of the float had rolling eyes and a working jaw, with smoke and groans coming from its mouth. It was an exact replica of the Zozobra puppet featured at the annual Fiesta de Santa Fe. (Photograph by Henry Dendhal, courtesy Palace of the Governors [NMHM/DCA], No. 055954.)

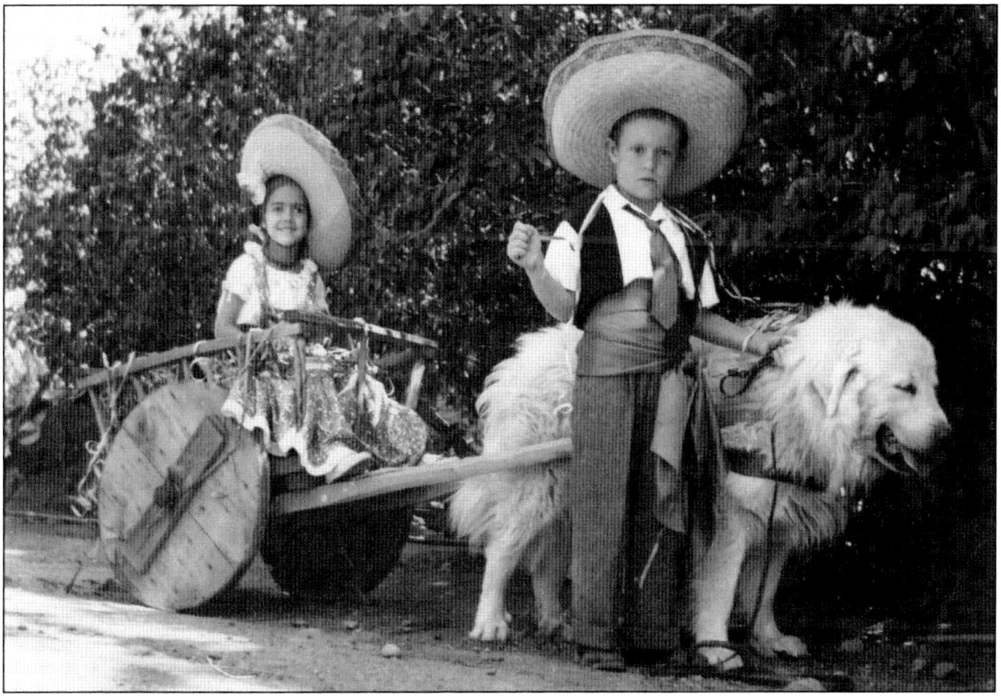

The Pet Parade at the Fiesta de Santa Fe has become one of the most beloved events during the three-day festival. Featured in this 1940s photograph are Donna Margaret Clausor and her brother Donald with their pet dog. (Courtesy Palace of the Governors [NMHM/DCA], No. HP.2007.20.325.)

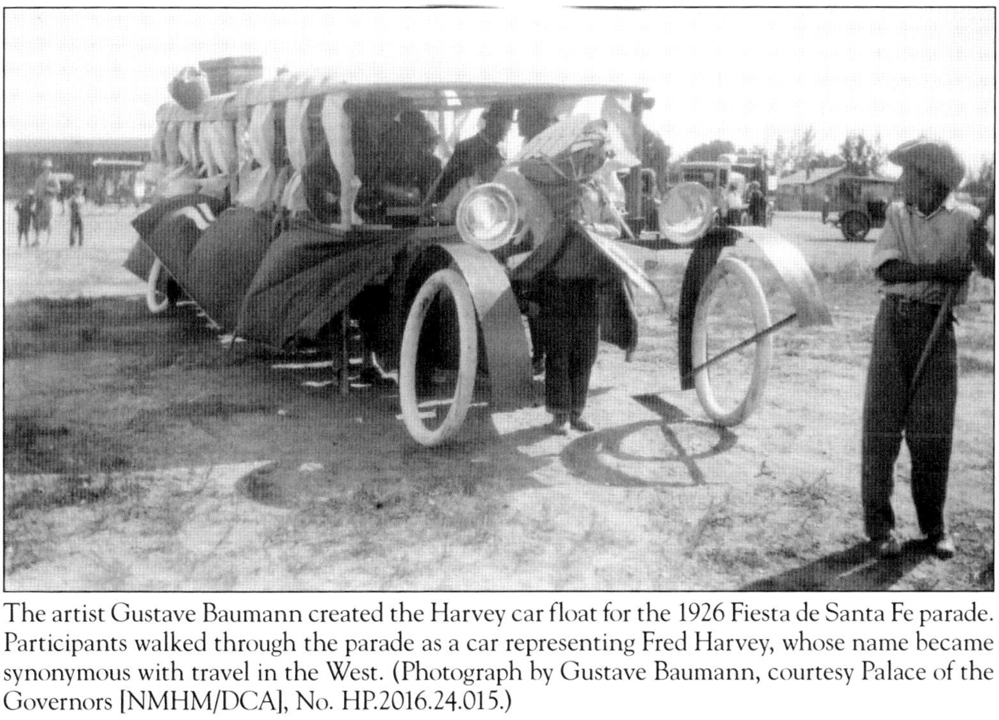

The artist Gustave Baumann created the Harvey car float for the 1926 Fiesta de Santa Fe parade. Participants walked through the parade as a car representing Fred Harvey, whose name became synonymous with travel in the West. (Photograph by Gustave Baumann, courtesy Palace of the Governors [NMHM/DCA], No. HP.2016.24.015.)

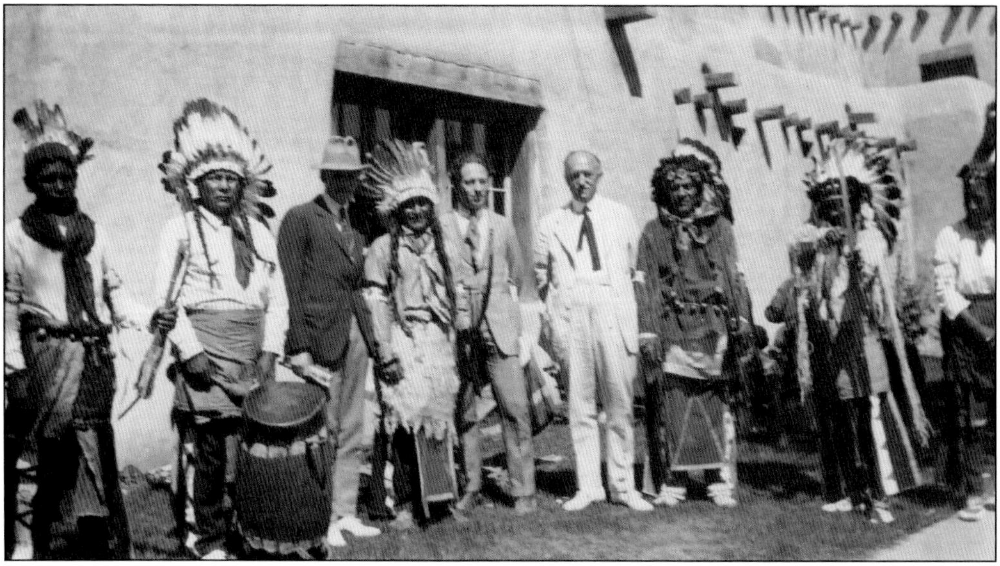

The anthropologist and archaeologist Edgar L. Hewett (in white suit) founded the School of American Archaeology in 1907. He also founded the Museum of New Mexico in 1909. Throughout his career, he established a strong rapport with the Native American community. Pictured here in 1921, he meets with native dancers at the Fiesta de Santa Fe. (Courtesy Palace of the Governors [NMHM/DCA], No. 007028.)

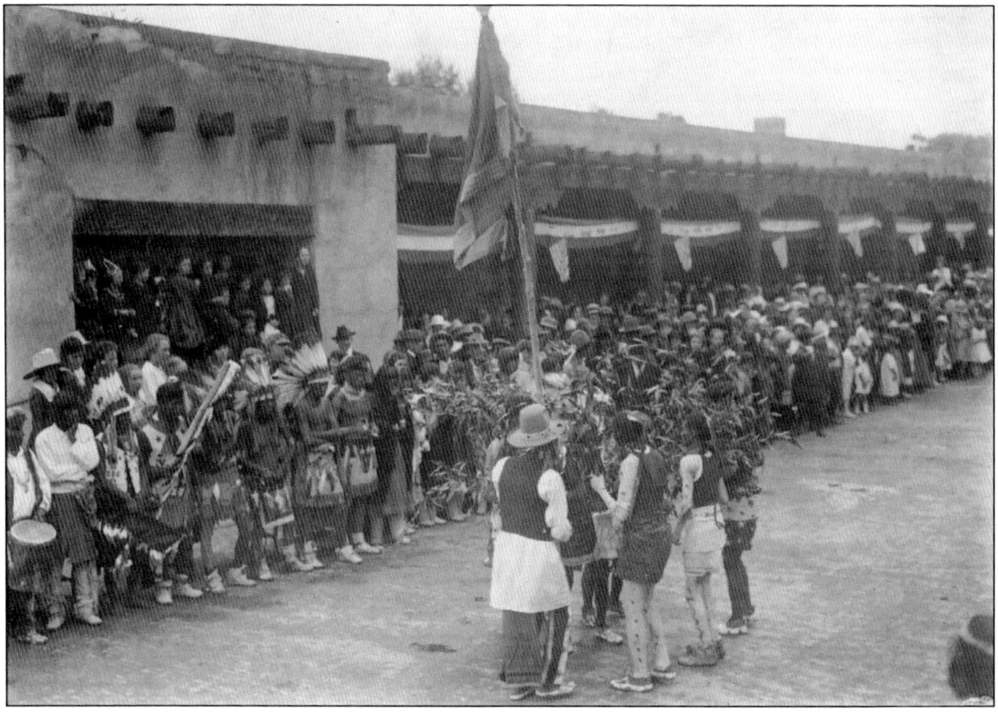

In 1919, the fiesta was combined with a celebration sponsored by the Museum of New Mexico. That year, a footrace was organized by the museum with members of Santa Clara Pueblo on Palace Avenue in front of the Palace of the Governors. (Photograph by Wesley Bradfield, courtesy Palace of the Governors [NMHM/DCA], No. 052366.)

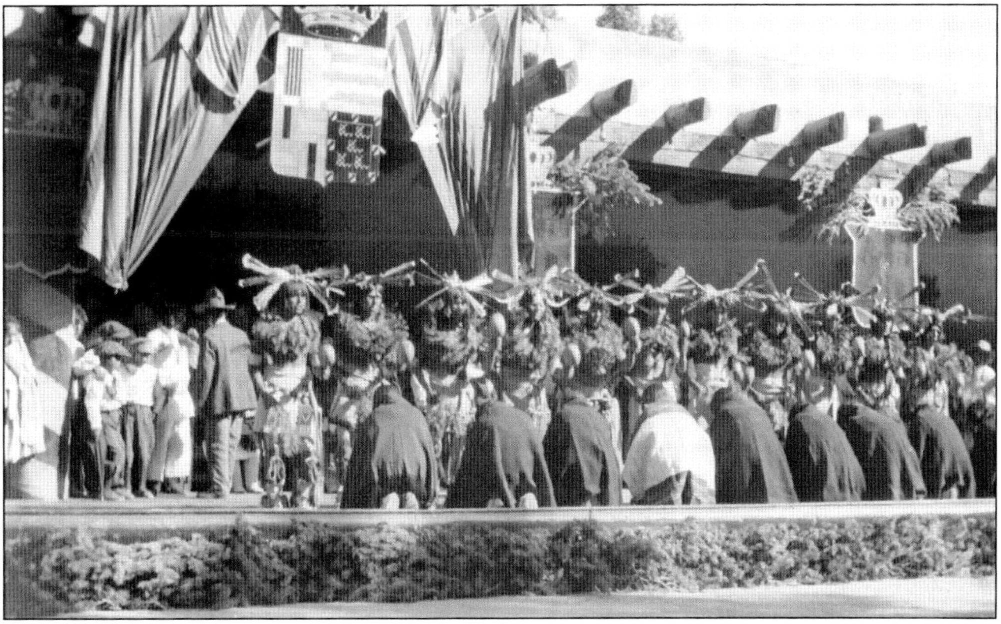

The traditional Pueblo fertility dance is one of the most popular dances performed for the public. This dance took place in front of the Palace of the Governors during the 1921 Fiesta de Santa Fe. (Courtesy Palace of the Governors [NMHM/DCA], No. LS.2164.)

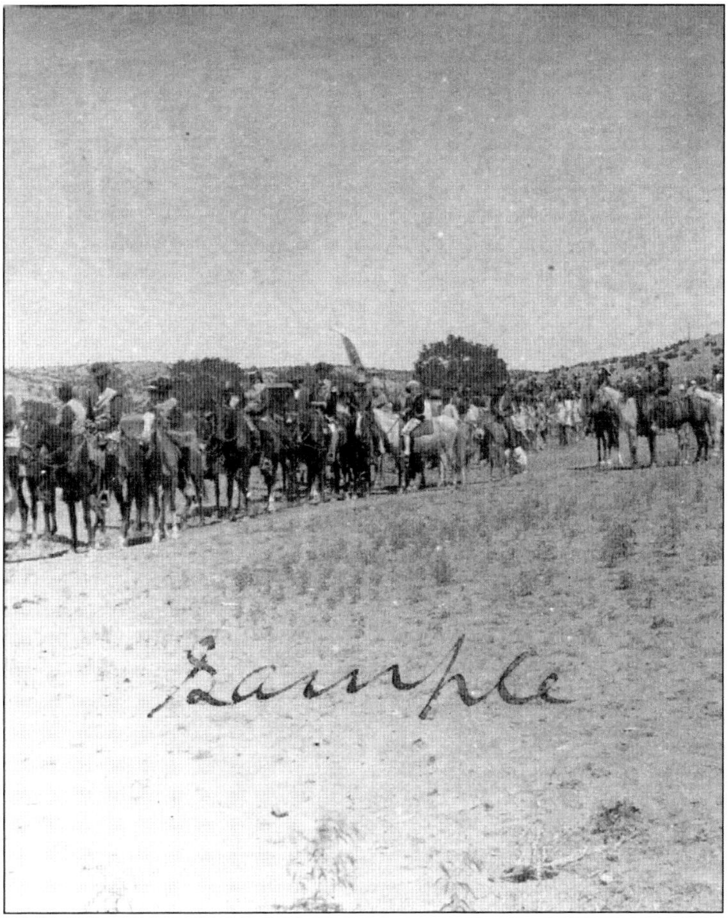

Although New Mexico had become a US territory in 1846, the Fiesta de Santa Fe continued to highlight Spanish culture and history. This reenactment of Francisco Vásquez de Coronado's exploration of New Mexico in 1540 was celebrated in 1880. (Photograph by Bennet and Brown, courtesy Palace of the Governors [NMHM/DCA], No. 015258.)

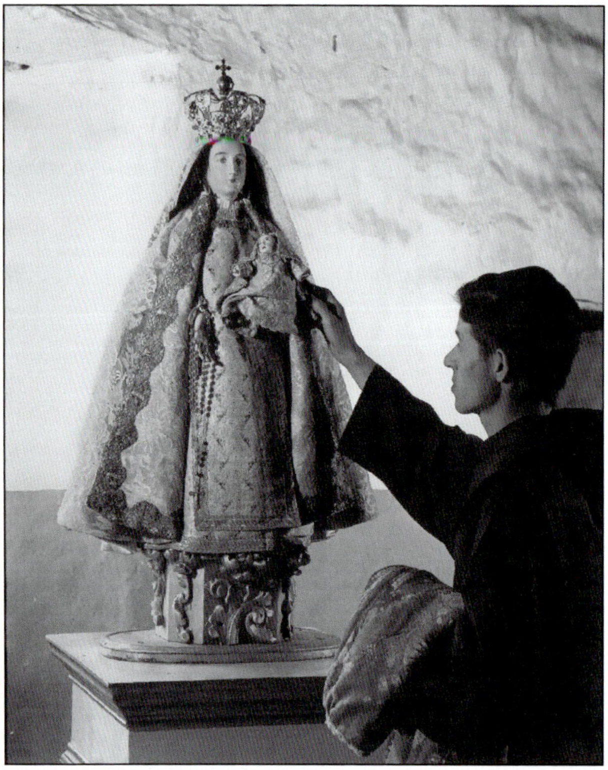

Fray Angélico Chávez, a historian, author, and Franciscan priest, wrote a book on the history of La Conquistadora in 1956. Brought to Santa Fe in 1625, La Conquistadora is the oldest Marian icon in the United States. (Photograph by Laura Gilpin, courtesy Amon Carter Museum, No. P1979.109.59.)

Santa Fe's leading musical ensemble during the 1930s was Los Villeros Alegres. The group provided Mariachi music for the Fiesta de Santa Fe and performed weekly on the Santa Fe Plaza. (Courtesy Ben Muñiz photograph collection.)

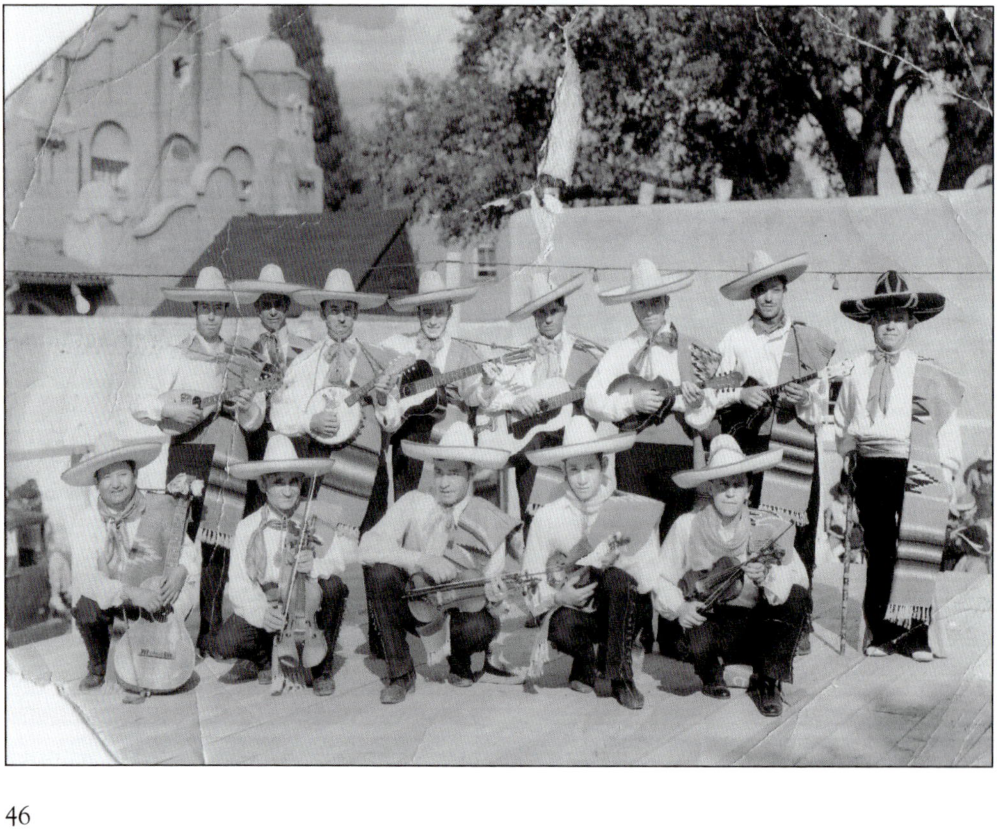

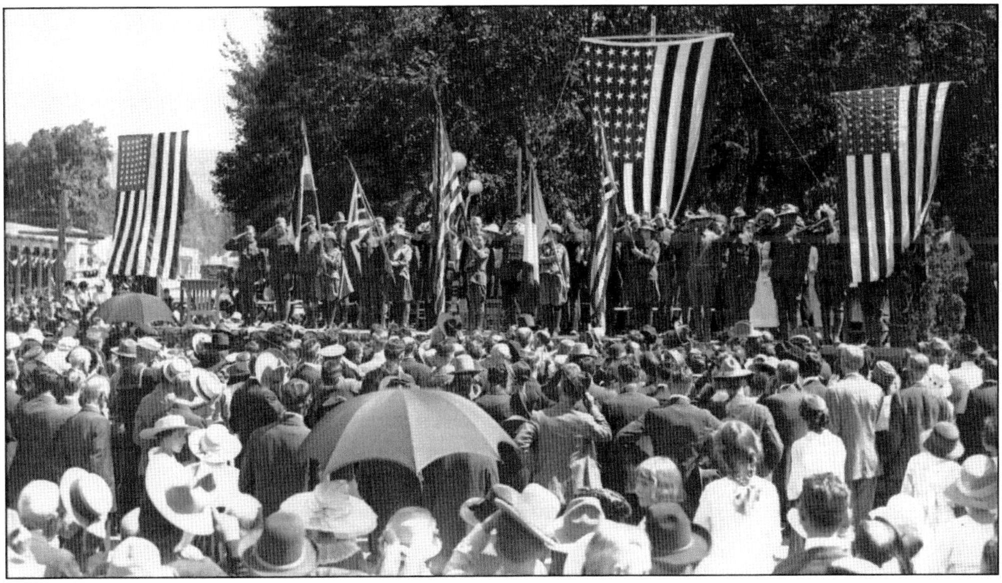

In 1912, New Mexico became the 47th state of the Union. By 1919, displays of American patriotism had become a regular part of fiesta festivities. (Photograph by Wesley Bradfield, courtesy Palace of the Governors [NMHM/DCA], No. 052394.)

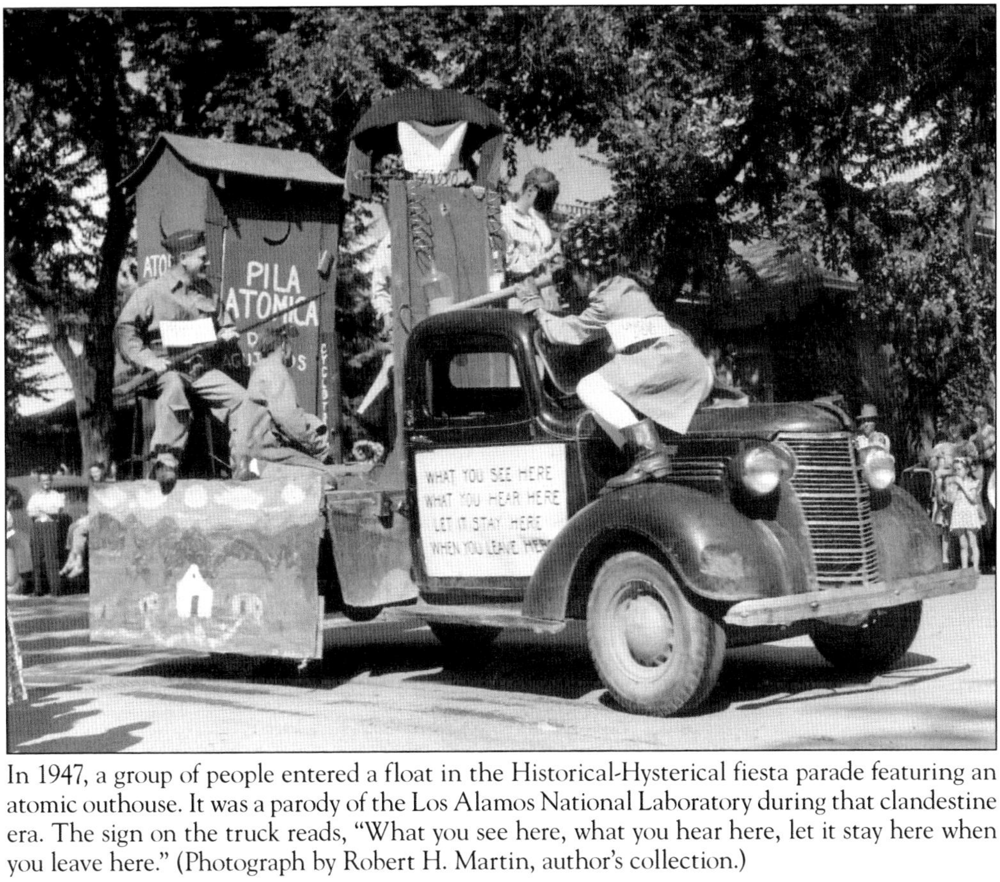

In 1947, a group of people entered a float in the Historical-Hysterical fiesta parade featuring an atomic outhouse. It was a parody of the Los Alamos National Laboratory during that clandestine era. The sign on the truck reads, "What you see here, what you hear here, let it stay here when you leave here." (Photograph by Robert H. Martin, author's collection.)

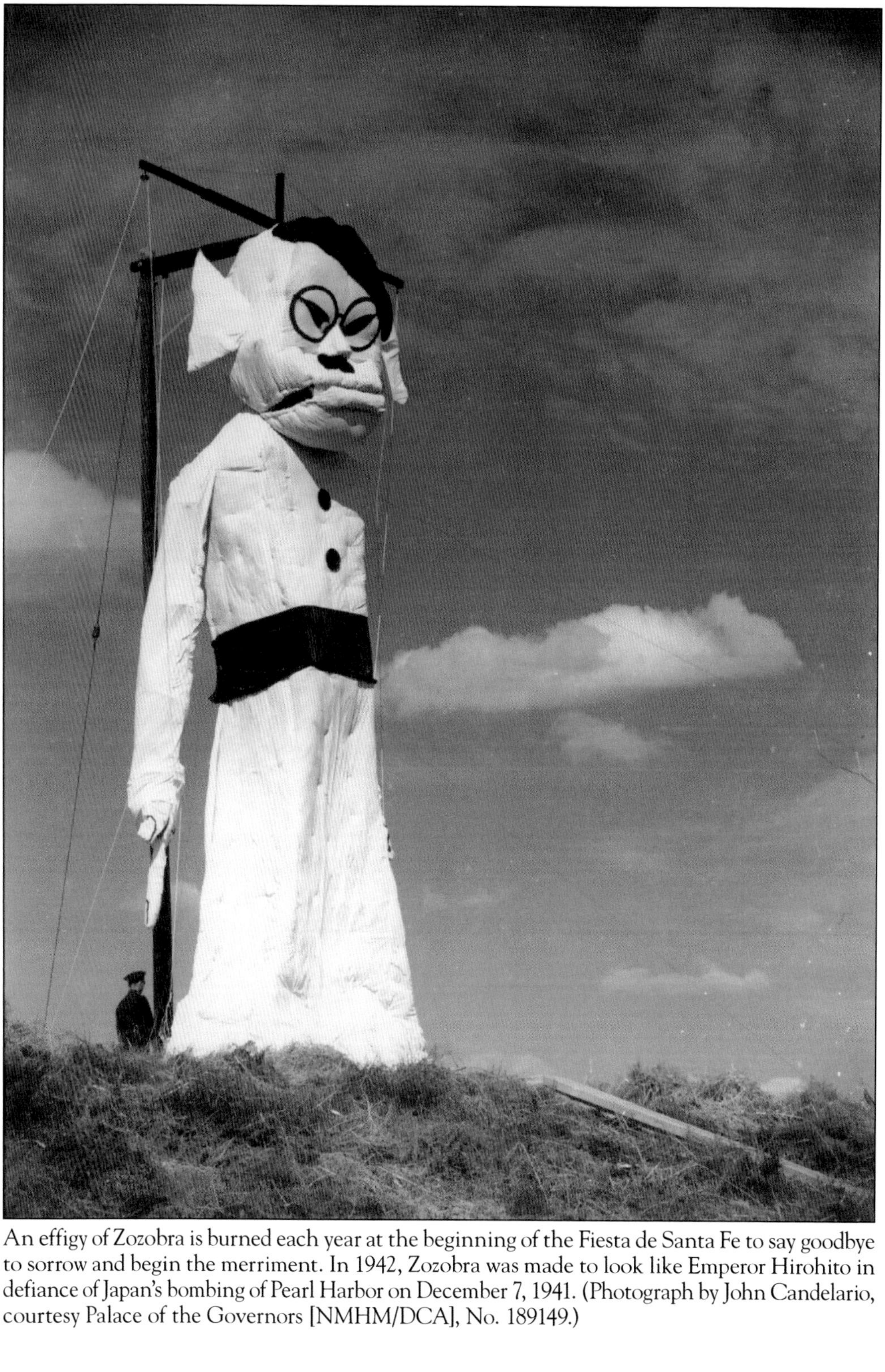

An effigy of Zozobra is burned each year at the beginning of the Fiesta de Santa Fe to say goodbye to sorrow and begin the merriment. In 1942, Zozobra was made to look like Emperor Hirohito in defiance of Japan's bombing of Pearl Harbor on December 7, 1941. (Photograph by John Candelario, courtesy Palace of the Governors [NMHM/DCA], No. 189149.)

Four

LIFE ON PARADE

The custom of processions in Santa Fe began in 1598 when Don Juan de Oñate and the founding families settled the region for the Spanish crown. For centuries, processions were a part of daily life in Europe. It was an inherited tradition that began with St. James, the patron saint of Spain. When St. Peter became the first pope, it was the duty of St. James to spread the teachings of Christianity. He was martyred for his efforts by King Herod. Each year on October 12, Spain honors his legacy with an elaborate procession. During the first 200 years, when Santa Fe was under Spanish and Mexican rule, Catholicism was the only religion practiced. In fact, the Mexican constitution of October 4, 1824, stated, "The religion of the Mexican nation is and will permanently be the Roman Catholic, Apostolic religion." Through the mid-20th century, many Catholic processions took place in and around the Santa Fe Plaza. Today there are fewer of these public showings of devotion, but the procession of La Conquistadora, the nation's oldest Madonna, continues to be held each year in June.

The first nonreligious procession of people walking in unity most likely took place on August 8, 1846, when Gen. Stephen W. Kearny and his army entered Santa Fe. By the following morning, the American flag flew atop the Palace of the Governors, declaring a new government. Since that time, both ceremonial and festive parades have continued around the Santa Fe Plaza as people parade in one form of solidarity or another.

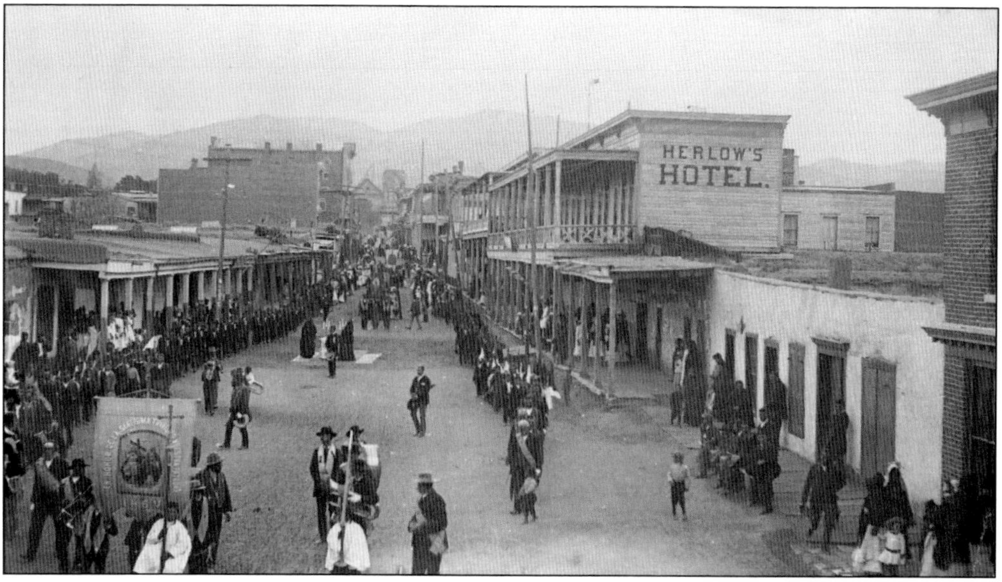

Corpus Christi has been celebrated by Catholics in honor of the Holy Eucharist since 1224. The name is Latin for "Body of Christ." Corpus Christi, or the Feast of the Most Holy Body of Christ, is a moveable feast day on which the consecrated host is carried in a monstrance during procession. During the Middle Ages, elaborate wreaths were laid along the procession route, so the feast day also became known as the Day of the Wreaths. (Courtesy Palace of the Governors [NMHM/DCA], No. 117450.)

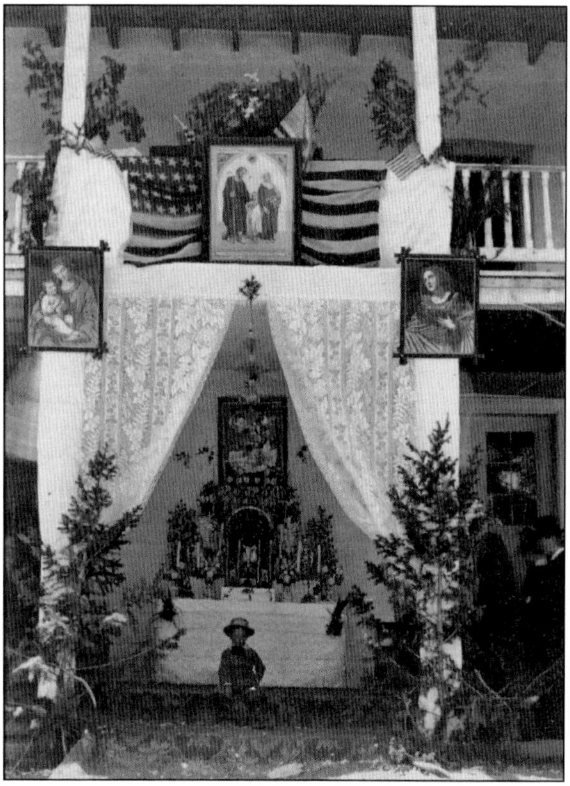

This altar built in 1880 for Corpus Christi on the Santa Fe Plaza shows the progression of time. As an American territory since 1848, the US flag adorns the Catholic altar of saints, which had previously been a Spanish tradition. (Photograph by Bennet and Brown, courtesy Palace of the Governors [NMHM/DCA], No. 146449.)

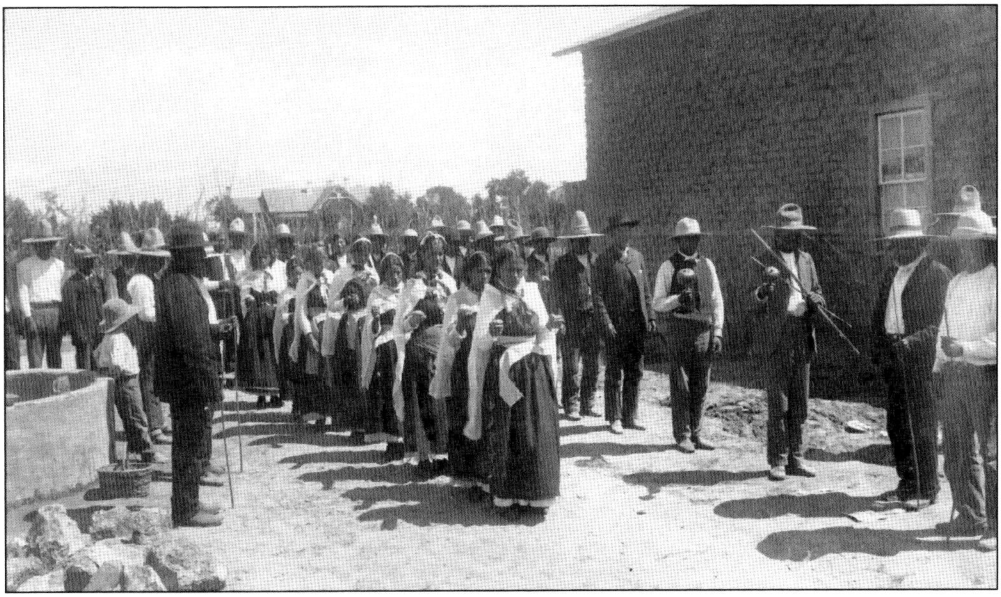

The religious brotherhood of the Penitentes can be traced to the medieval *cofradías* (confraternities) of Spain. The beliefs of these *penitentes*, or penitents, are rooted in Spanish and Roman Catholic tradition. From the 16th century until the mid-19th century, the Spanish people of New Mexico were isolated from the guiding hand of the church, and these confraternities helped preserve religious devotion. The Penitente processions held in Spain during Holy Week also took place in Santa Fe in 1884. (Photograph by Dana B. Chase, courtesy Palace of the Governors [NMHM/DCA], No. 004844.)

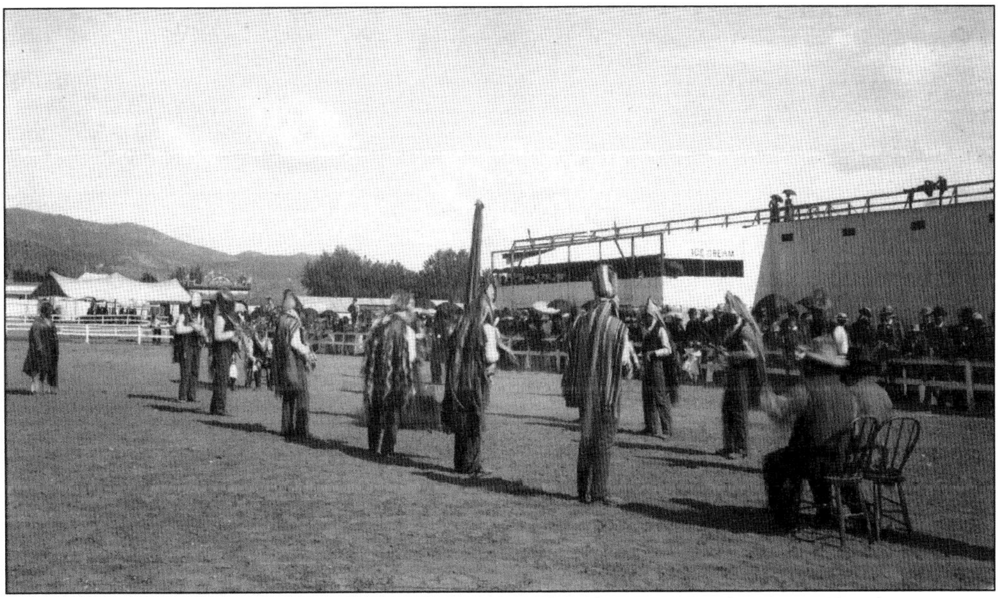

The tradition of the Matachine dancers is believed to have Moorish roots. The dances were used by the Franciscan missionaries in the 17th century as a way of converting the Indians to Catholicism. (Courtesy Palace of the Governors [NMHM/DCA], No. 010995.)

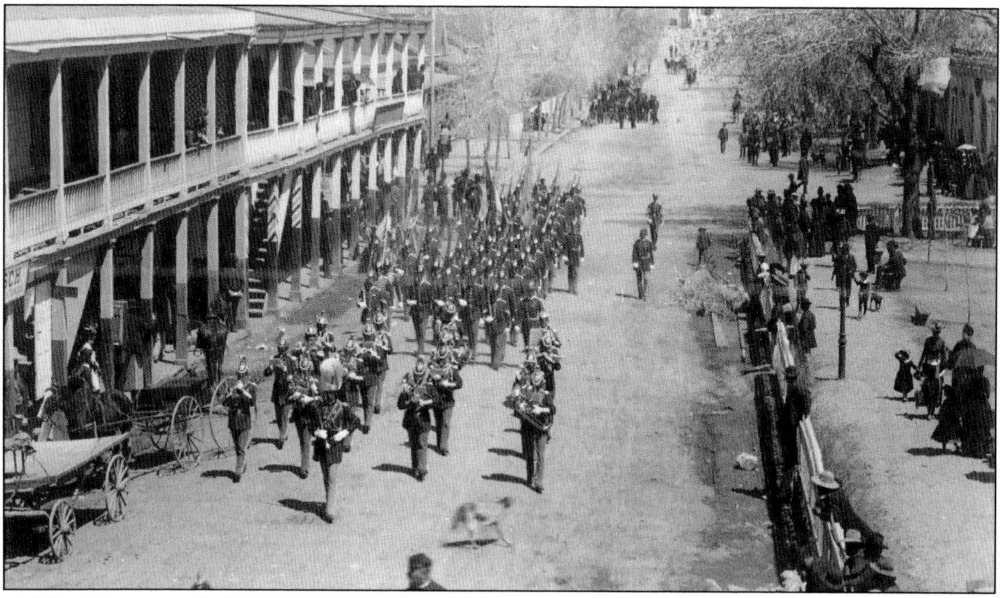

As New Mexico worked toward statehood in the latter part of the 19th century, the fervor of American patriotism grew. On July 4, 1884, this military parade took place on Lincoln Avenue. (Photograph by Dana B. Chase, courtesy Palace of the Governors [NMHM/DCA], No. 056997.)

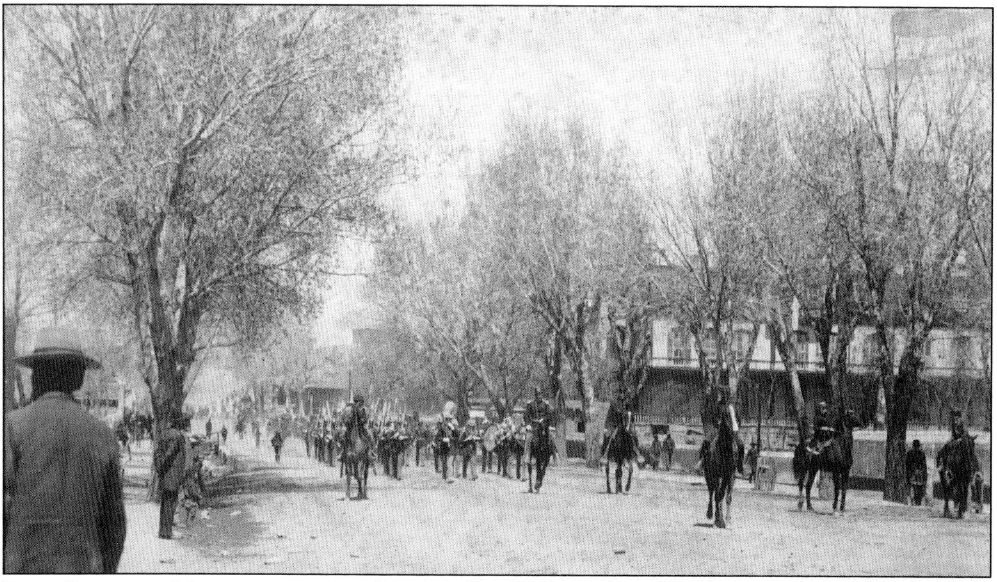

Pres. Benjamin Harrison appointed L. Bradford Prince governor of New Mexico in 1889. A parade was held in honor of the one-term governor. In 1909, he was a member of the New Mexico Territorial Council and president of the Spanish-American Normal School. (Photograph by Dana B. Chase, courtesy Palace of the Governors [NMHM/DCA], No. 056984.)

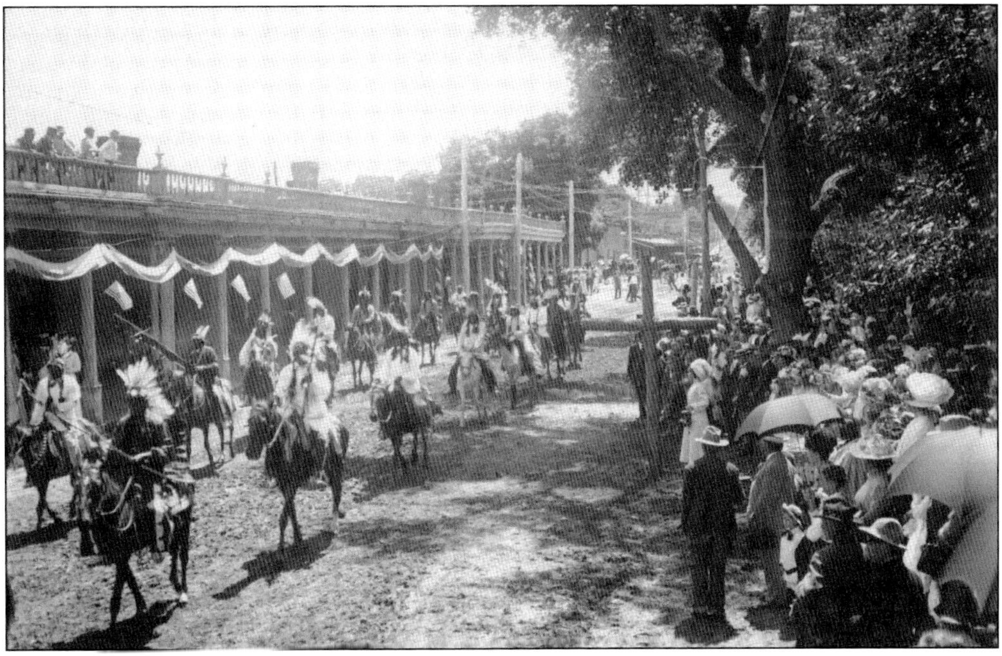

Native Americans from the surrounding pueblos and the region began to participate in the Fiesta de Santa Fe most likely in 1883. That year, Santa Fe hosted the Tertio-Millennial Celebration and Exposition, and the fiesta was combined with the Fourth of July. The railroad was a catalyst in making way for the celebration of the founding of the city. Here, Pueblo Indians on horseback take part in the 1911 de Vargas pageant in front of the Palace of the Governors. (Photograph by Jesse Nusbaum, courtesy Palace of the Governors [NMHM/DCA], No. 158206.)

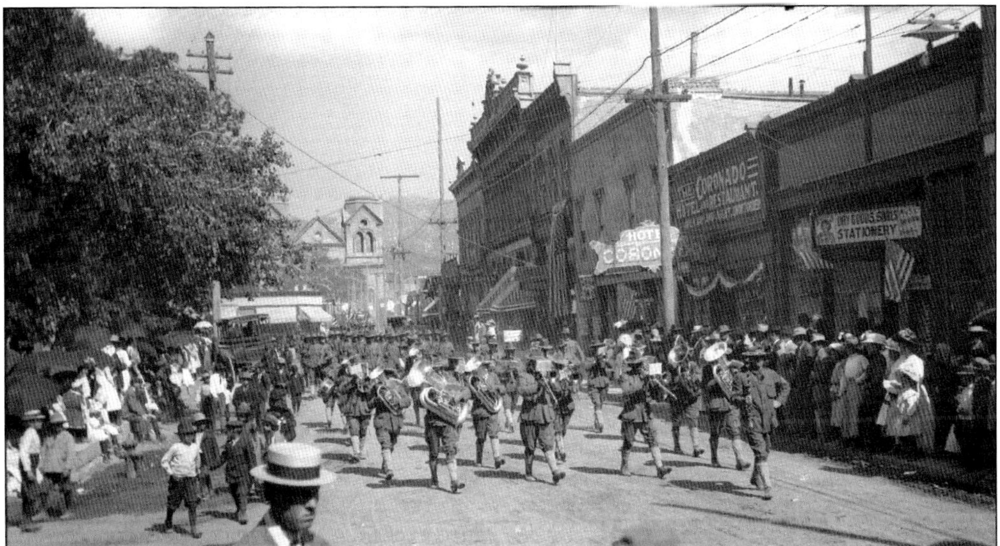

The Santa Fe Plaza is adorned with US flags in 1912 for the Fiesta de Santa Fe parade on San Francisco Street. Both New Mexico and Arizona were granted statehood in 1912. New Mexico became the 47th state on January 6, 1912, followed by Arizona on February 14. (Photograph by Jesse Nusbaum, courtesy Palace of the Governors [NMHM/DCA], No. 118350.)

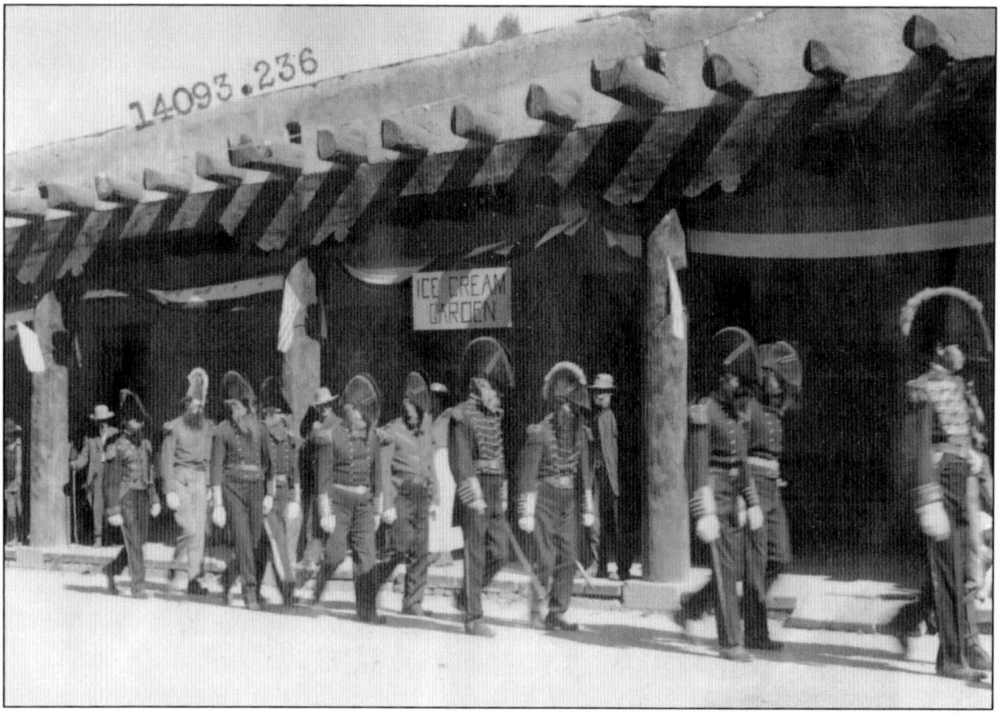

On August 8, 1846, the US Army took control of Santa Fe, proclaiming New Mexico a US territory. This 1919 re-enactment of the 1846 event depicts Gen. Stephen Kearny with his army in front of the Palace of the Governors during the Fiesta de Santa Fe. (Courtesy Palace of the Governors [NMHM/DCA], No. 052418.)

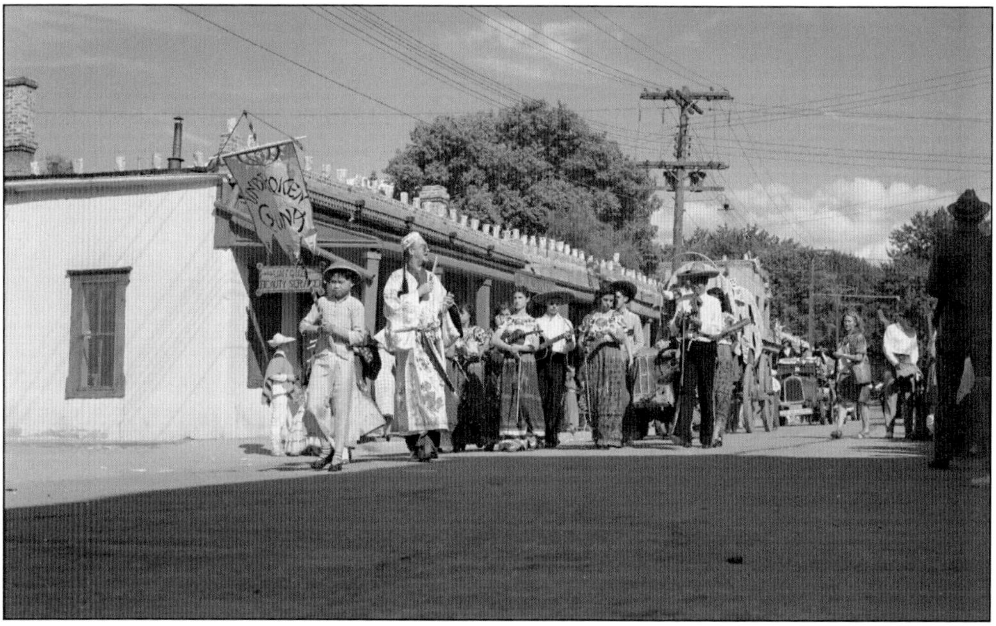

The author Witter Bynner leads the fiesta parade dressed in Oriental garb. By the 1920s, many artists and writers began to take part in the annual fiesta. (Photograph by John Candelario, courtesy Palace of the Governors [NMHM/DCA], No. 177044.)

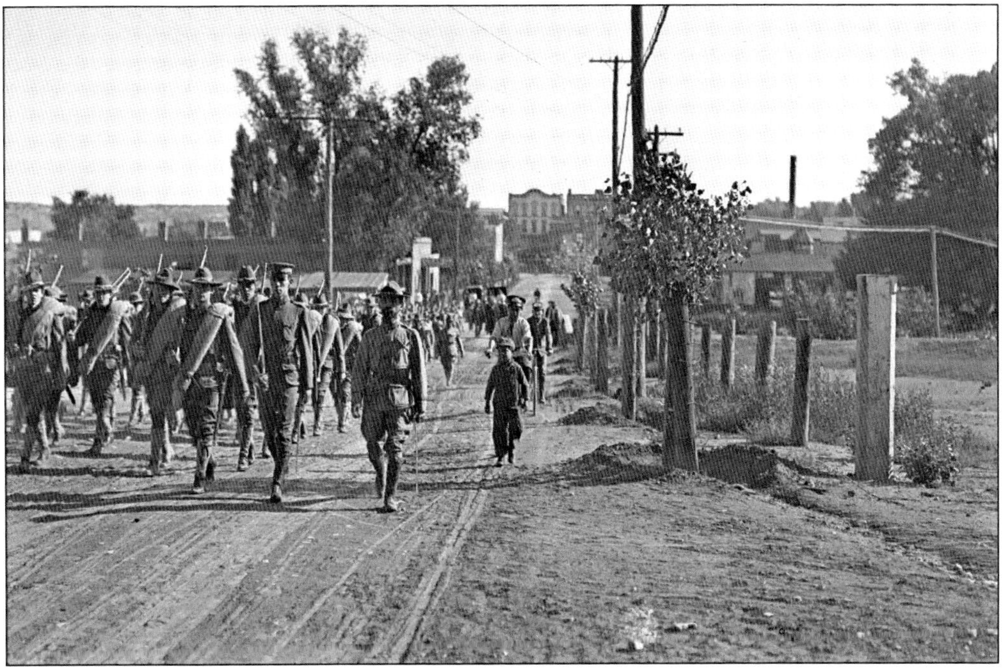

The New Mexico National Guard held a celebratory march on Don Gaspar Street in 1912. One of the guard's first missions under statehood was to guard the border with Mexico. (Photograph by Jesse Nusbaum, courtesy Palace of the Governors [NMHM/DCA], No. 061403.)

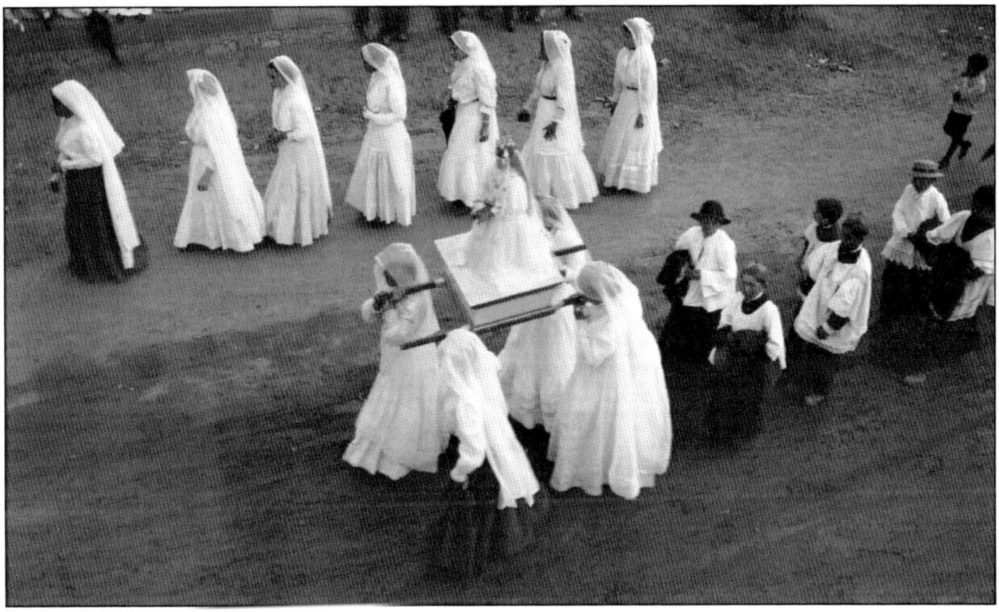

This 1912 photograph shows the procession of La Conquistadora, the nation's oldest Madonna. For over three centuries, the Marian icon has been carried in procession from her chapel at the Basilica Cathedral of St. Francis of Assisi to Rosario Chapel annually. She resides at the chapel for the coming week, where a double novena is prayed to her in the morning and evening. At the end of the novena, she is carried in procession back to her chapel at the cathedral. (Photograph by Jesse Nusbaum, courtesy Palace of the Governors [NMHM/DCA], No. 118367.)

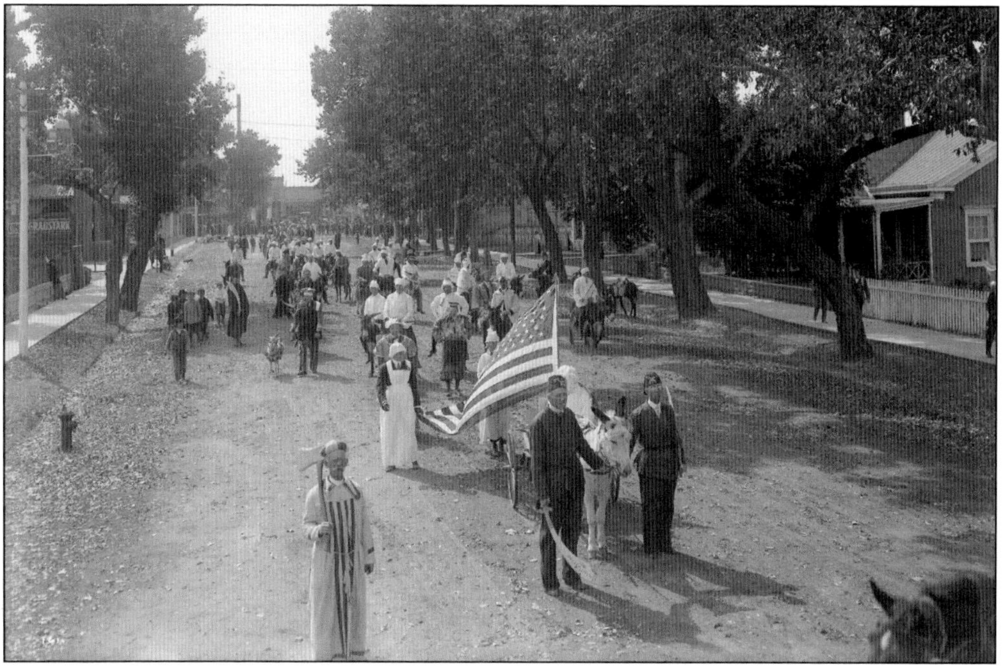

The Shriner's Parade on Lincoln Avenue celebrates statehood in 1912. The fraternal brotherhood of the Shriners came to Santa Fe during the first decade of the 20th century along with the Masons. (Photograph by Jesse Nusbaum, courtesy Palace of the Governors [NMHM/DCA], No. 139021.)

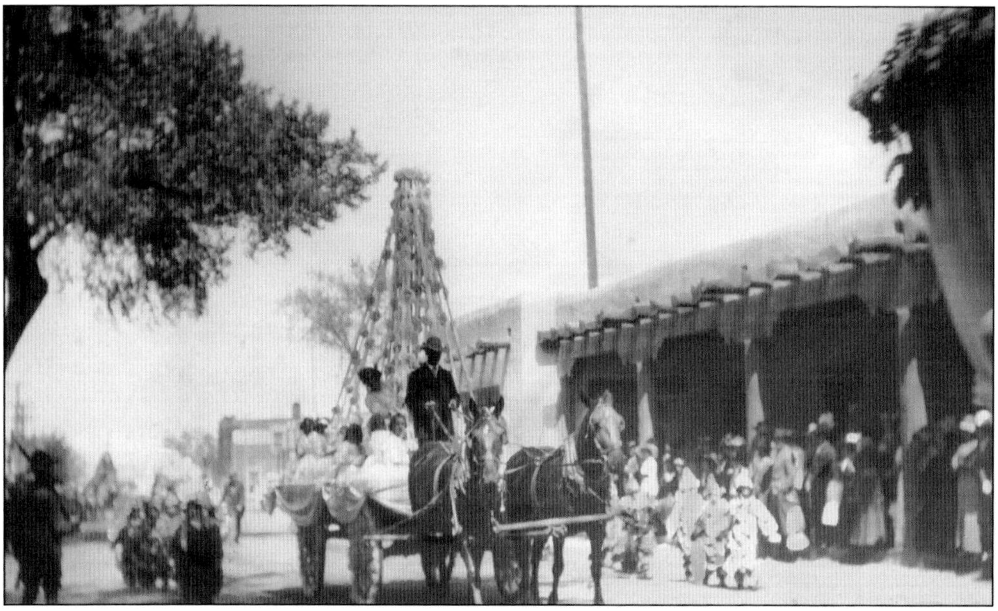

May Day, celebrated throughout the world on May 1, pays tribute to all workers. The holiday began in the late 19th century to protest unsafe working conditions and 16-hour workdays. St. Joseph is venerated on this day as the patron saint of laborers. This May Day parade float stops in front of the Palace of the Governors in 1914. (Courtesy Palace of the Governors [NMHM/DCA], No. 117450.)

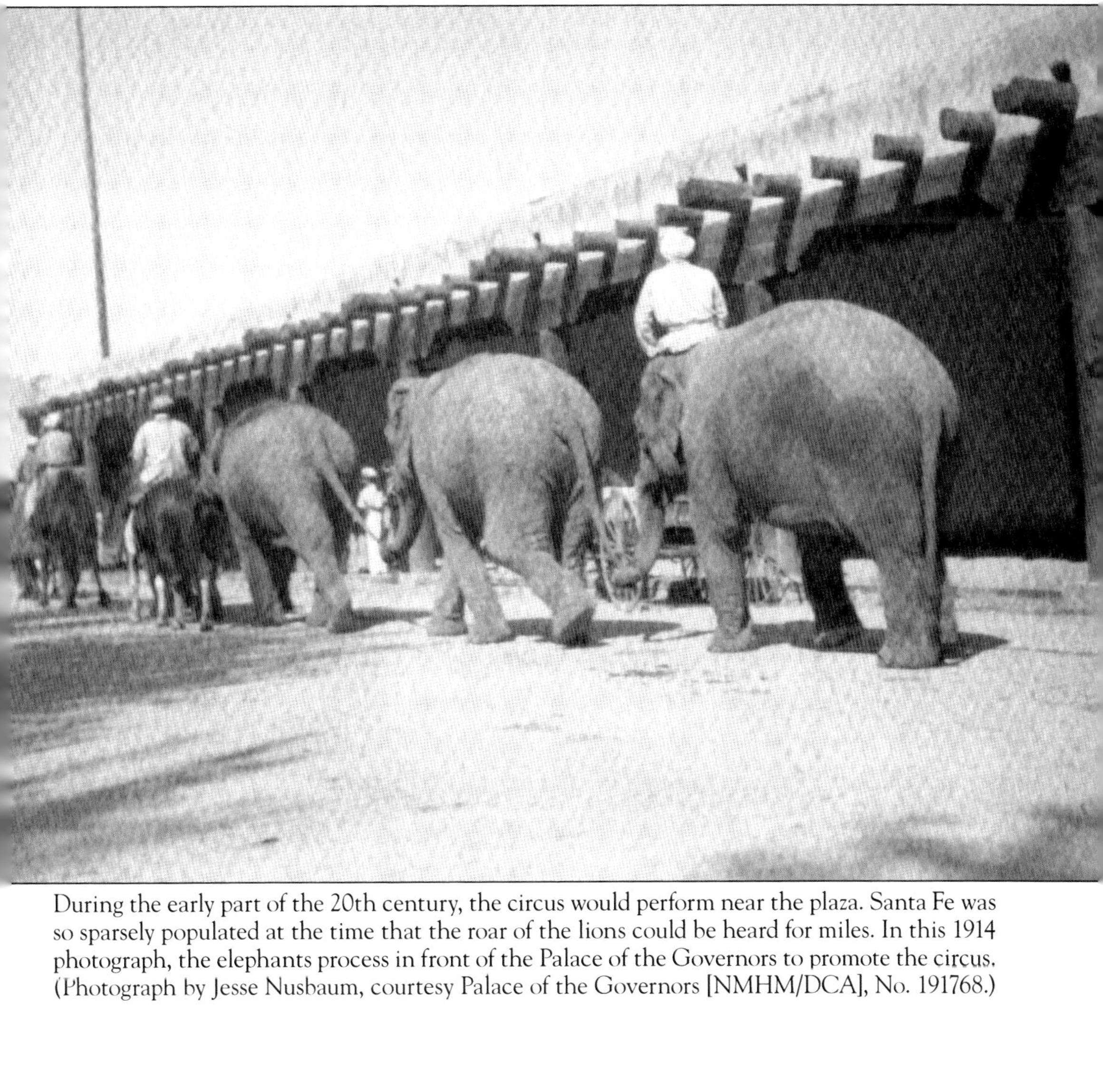

During the early part of the 20th century, the circus would perform near the plaza. Santa Fe was so sparsely populated at the time that the roar of the lions could be heard for miles. In this 1914 photograph, the elephants process in front of the Palace of the Governors to promote the circus. (Photograph by Jesse Nusbaum, courtesy Palace of the Governors [NMHM/DCA], No. 191768.)

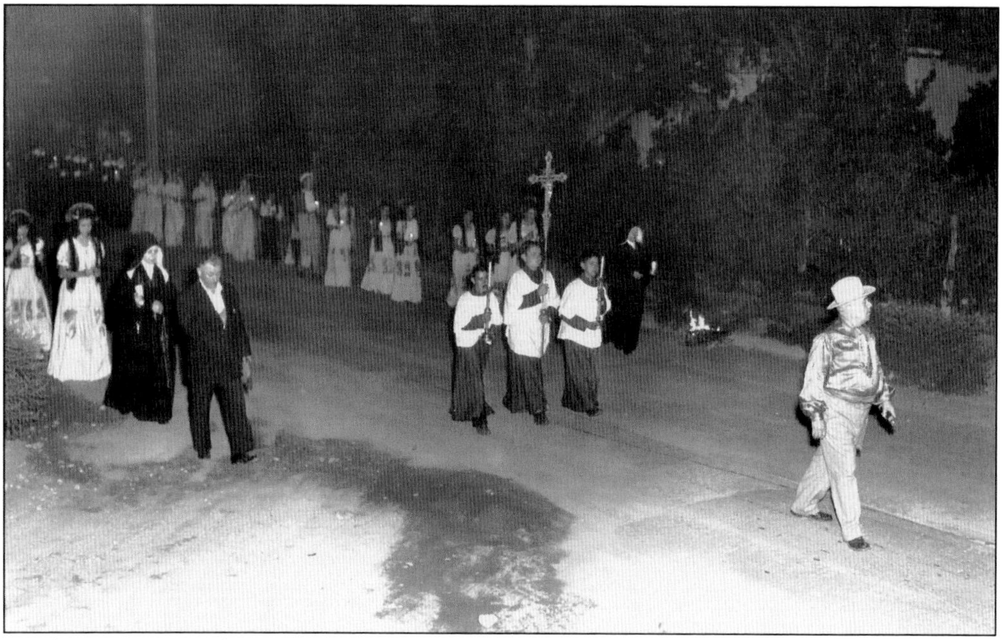

For three centuries, the Fiesta de Santa Fe has been a religious celebration of Catholicism. The candlelight procession to the Cross of the Martyrs is the concluding ceremony of the festivities, seen here around 1946. (Photograph by Robert H. Martin, courtesy Palace of the Governors [NMHM/DCA], No. 041278.)

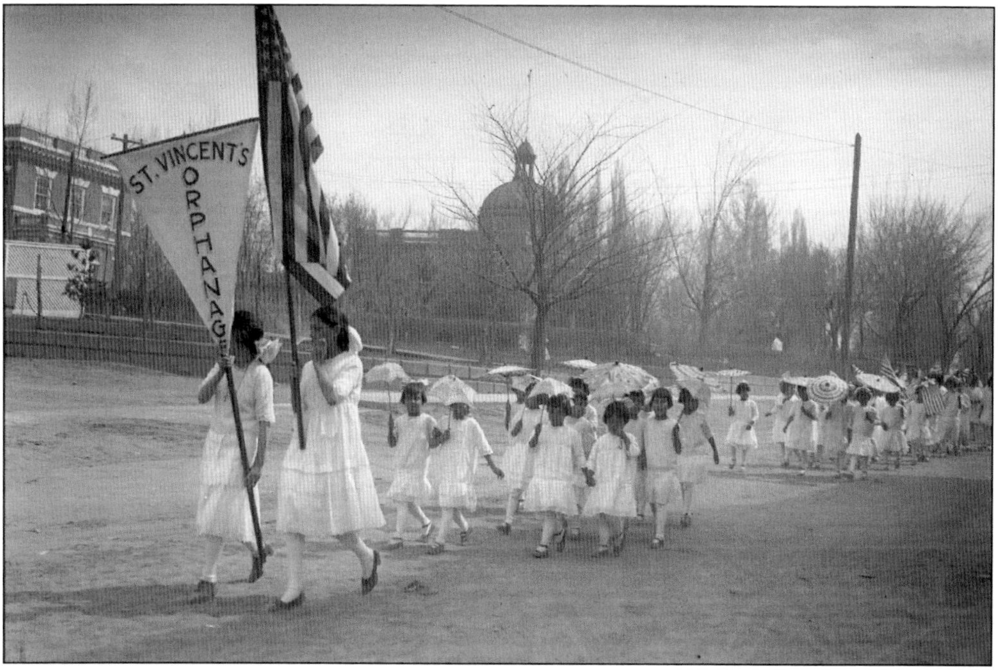

Four nuns of the Sisters of Charity founded the St. Vincent Orphanage Asylum at the end of the 19th century. Children were cared for at the orphanage through the 1950s and regularly took part in Santa Fe's religious processions. (Photograph by Wesley Bradfield, courtesy Palace of the Governors [NMHM/DCA], No. 051990.)

Five

Personalities

Santa Fe has always been a small town with a big reputation, attracting people from all walks of life. Many are drawn to the physical beauty of its high-mountain desert. The quaint adobe architecture and temperate weather are also enticing, but mostly it is the muddle of humanity that keeps life interesting. Long before Santa Fe was dubbed the "City Different" during the middle of the 20th century, its small population was already a microcosm of a bigger reality.

The first serendipitous discovery that anthropologists and archaeologists made during their early-20th-century arrival was a town with a railroad and telegraph just minutes away from Indian pueblos and ancient ruins; it was almost too good to be true! Artists and writers soon followed, finding inspiration in the landscape and light. There were the civic-minded people who came with a yearning to be of service, and businesspeople who sought their fortunes. Others, like soldiers, came in search of respite and found a place to heal from the pain of their past. And then there were those with no direction at all, just in need of a place to set stakes.

Even before the advent of telecommunications, Santa Fe was on the radar screen. US presidents, international royalty, millionaires, aviators, movie stars, the famous, and the infamous passed through Santa Fe. Perhaps they sought adventure, or just a change of pace. What they found here differed for all, but they were left with an indelible mark of being a part of something out of the ordinary. Those who chose to stay continued to make the City Different all the more different.

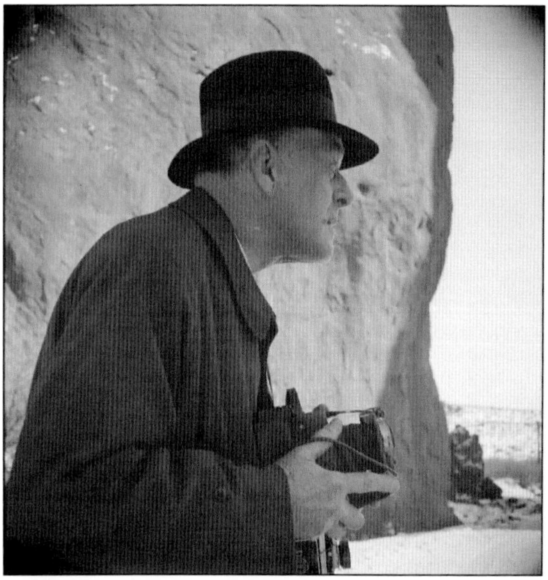

The British photographer J. Dudley Johnston was born in Liverpool in 1868. He was the curator of the Royal Photography Society for 30 years and was twice elected president of the organization. A man of many talents, Johnston was also the director of the Liverpool Philharmonic Orchestra. He specialized in landscape photography and found his way in the 1940s to America, where he captured the spirit of the Southwest. He died in England in 1955. (Photograph by Laura Gilpin, courtesy Amon Carter Museum, No. P1979.230.3694.)

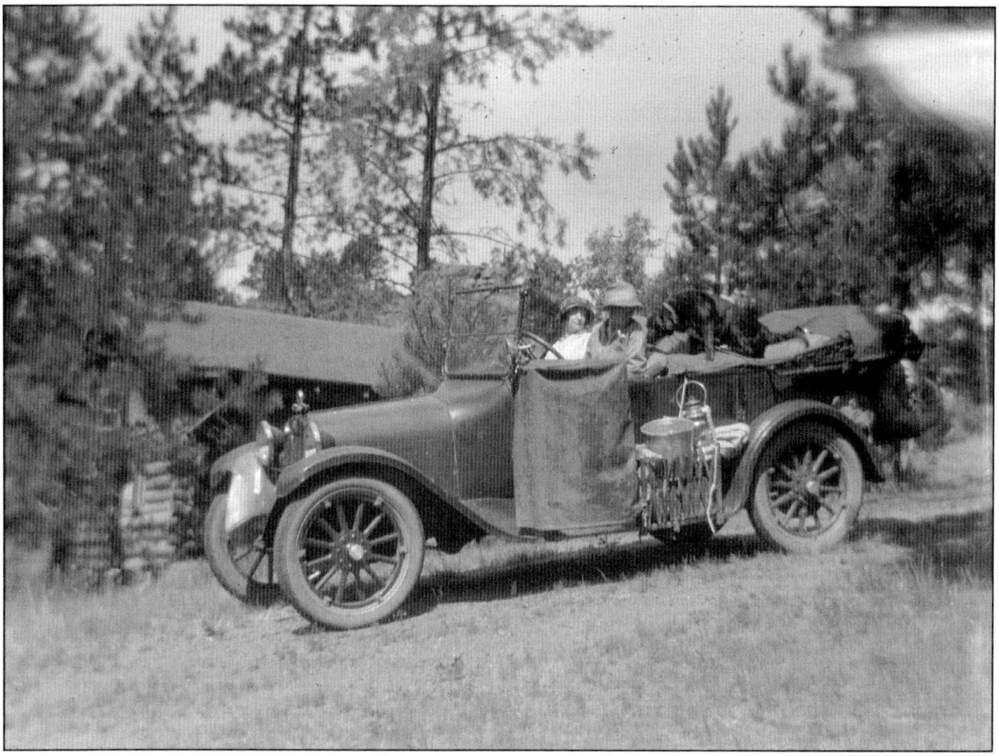

Elizabeth Forster drove her friend, Brenda Putnam, on a camping trip in the Southwest in 1924. Forster was the nurse who cared for photographer Laura Gilpin during the 1918 flu epidemic. As a visiting nurse for the New Mexico Association for Indian Affairs, Forster had befriended many native people. These friendships allowed Gilpin to photograph ceremonial rituals and other aspects of Native American life. Brenda Putnam and Laura Gilpin were roommates in New York in 1916. Putnam went on to become a noted sculptor whose work has been exhibited around the world. (Photograph by Laura Gilpin, courtesy Amon Carter Museum, No. P1979.230.51.)

Benigno Muñiz was born in 1870, and when he was 11, he served as an altar boy for Archbishop Jean-Baptiste Lamy. In 1899, he became the editor of the Spanish-language newspaper *El Nuevo Mexicano*. He also performed with Los Villeros Alegres, a leading musical ensemble, in 1931, and was in charge of the weekly band concerts on the plaza. Muñiz owned several houses that he rented to many of the early artists who came to Santa Fe, like Paul Burlin and Arthur Musgrave. Eventually he sold one of the houses at the corner of College Street to writer and poet Witter Bynner. (Courtesy Benigno Muñiz photograph collection.)

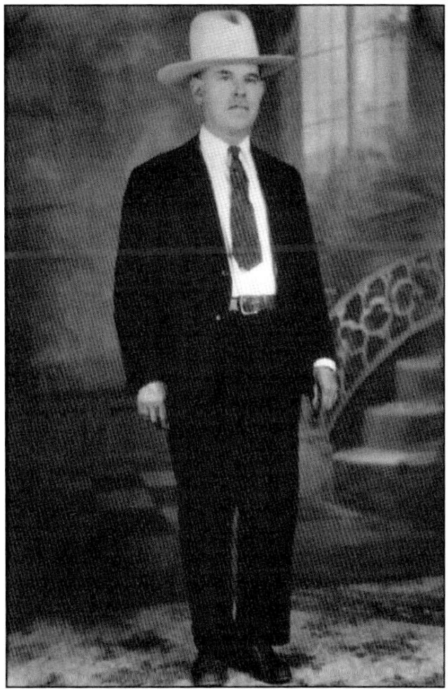

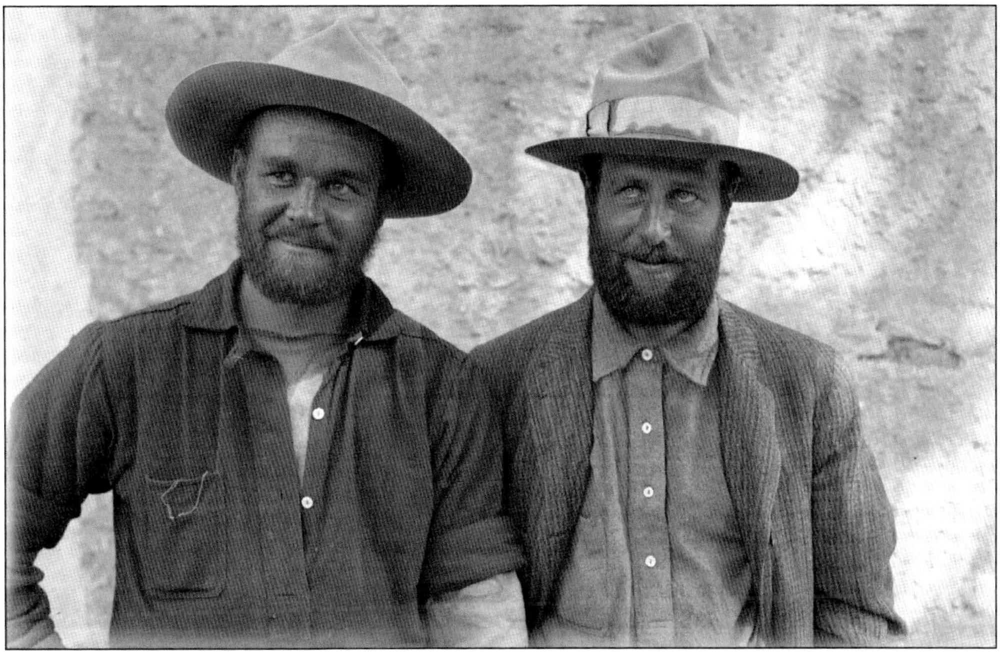

The American archaeologist Alfred Vincent Kidder, seen on the left, did groundbreaking work in the southwestern part of the United States and Mesoamerica. Through his fieldwork he provided the first comprehensive blueprint for American archaeological studies. He became an expert in the ancient Anasazi culture and provided an archaeological timescale that continues to be used by scholars and researchers today. In 1950, the American Anthropological Association instituted the Alfred Vincent Kidder Award for Eminence in the Field of American Anthropology in honor of his contributions. Kidder was born in 1885 and died in 1965. (Photograph by Jesse Nusbaum, courtesy Palace of the Governors [NMHM/DCA], No. 060647.)

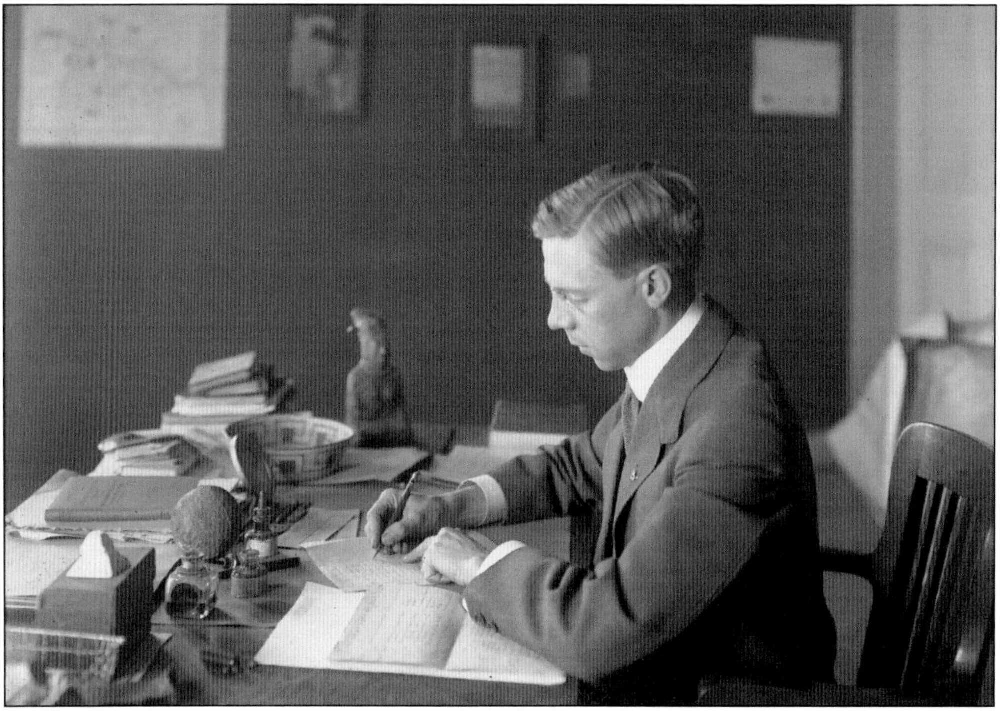

The American archaeologist Sylvanus G. Morley is believed to have been the inspiration for the fictional archaeologist Indiana Jones, created by movie producers George Lucas and Stephen Spielberg. Morley began his lifelong adventures in 1907 in Santa Fe, where he worked for the School of American Archaeology. (Photograph by Jesse Nusbaum, courtesy Palace of the Governors [NMHM/DCA], No. 010313.)

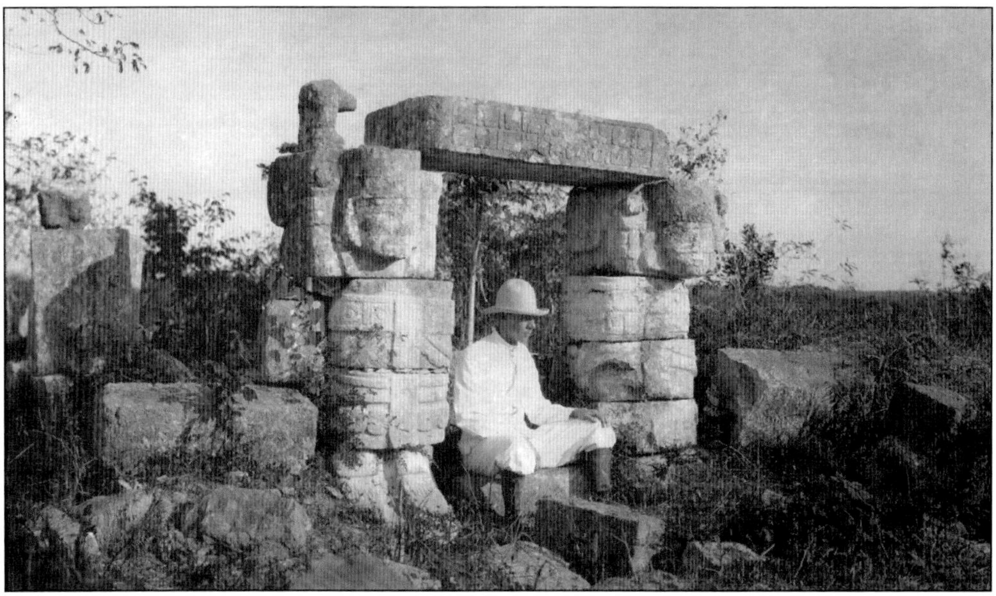

Later in his career, Morley set out to explore the Yucatán Peninsula in Mexico. He is credited with rediscovering and restoring the ceremonial Mayan center known as Chichén Itzá. (Photograph by Jesse Nusbaum, courtesy Palace of the Governors [NMHM/DCA], No. 118269.)

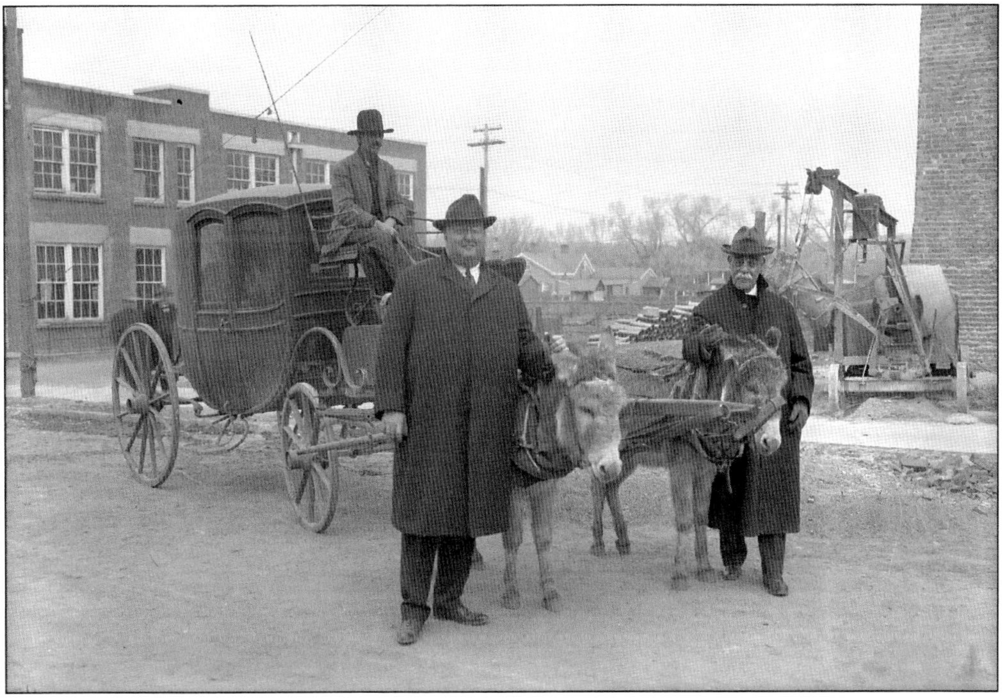

George Heye, standing at left with Harmon Hendricks in this 1907 photograph on Palace Avenue, was a frequent visitor to Santa Fe at the beginning of the 20th century. Heye founded the Museum of the American Indian in New York City in 1916. His interest in Native American artifacts resulted in a collection that spanned 45 years of travel. This collection became the largest and most comprehensive in the world and contains more than a million objects crafted by the indigenous inhabitants of the western hemisphere. Originally the Museum of the American Indian, it was transferred to the Smithsonian Institution in Washington, DC, in 1989 and became the National Museum of the American Indian. (Photograph by Jesse Nusbaum, courtesy Palace of the Governors [NMHM/DCA], No. 061813.)

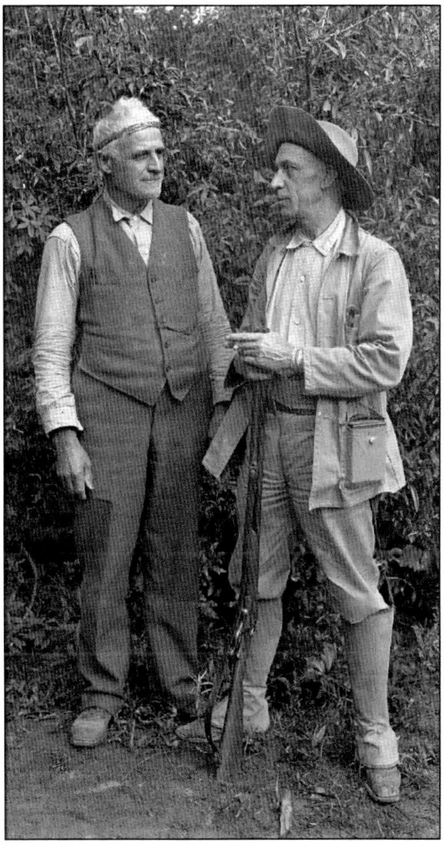

Charles Fletcher Lummis (right) had a storied career as a journalist, archaeologist, ethnographer, poet, photographer, historian, librarian, and activist for the rights of the American Indian. He became a prolific writer who introduced New Mexico to the larger world through magazine articles and books. In 1907, Lummis founded the Southwest Museum in Los Angeles and continued his work in preserving the rights of Native Americans. (Courtesy Palace of the Governors [NMHM/DCA], No. 007745.)

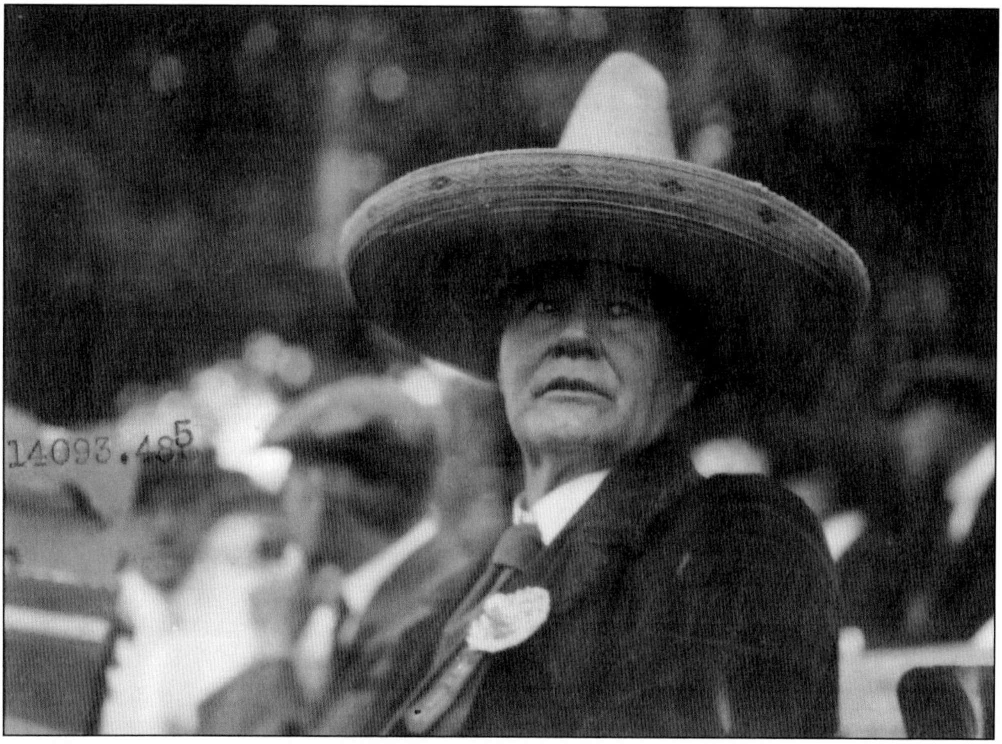

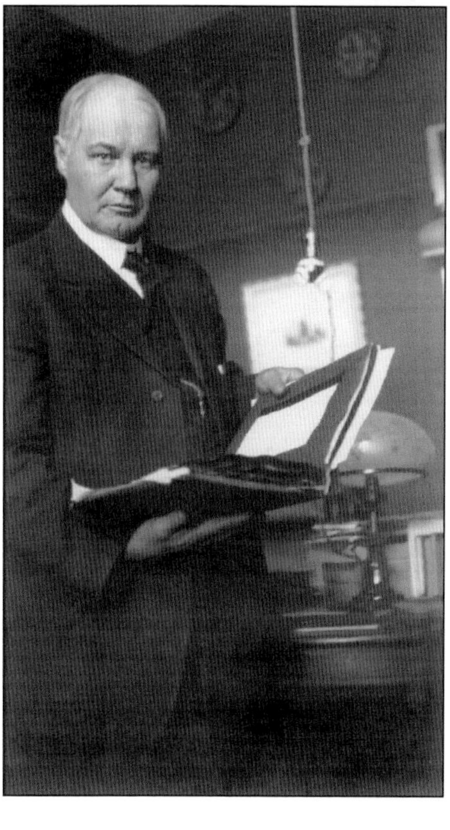

The noted historian Ralph Emerson Twitchell wore many hats during his life in New Mexico. In 1893, he served as the mayor of Santa Fe. He was also the chairman of the International Boundary and Water Commission and Rio Grande Commission. His work on that commission resulted in a treaty between the United States and Mexico, leading to the building of the Elephant Butte Dam in southern New Mexico. An expert in water rights issues, Twitchell helped organize the first National Irrigation Congress in 1891. (Courtesy Palace of the Governors [NMHM/DCA], No. 012554.)

Ralph Emerson Twitchell was a member of the special council for the US Department of the Interior, where he worked with Native American water rights. For 43 years, he was a member of the legal department of the Santa Fe Railroad. During his lengthy career, Twitchell was also a prosecuting attorney for Santa Fe County. (Courtesy Palace of the Governors [NMHM/DCA], No. 007902.)

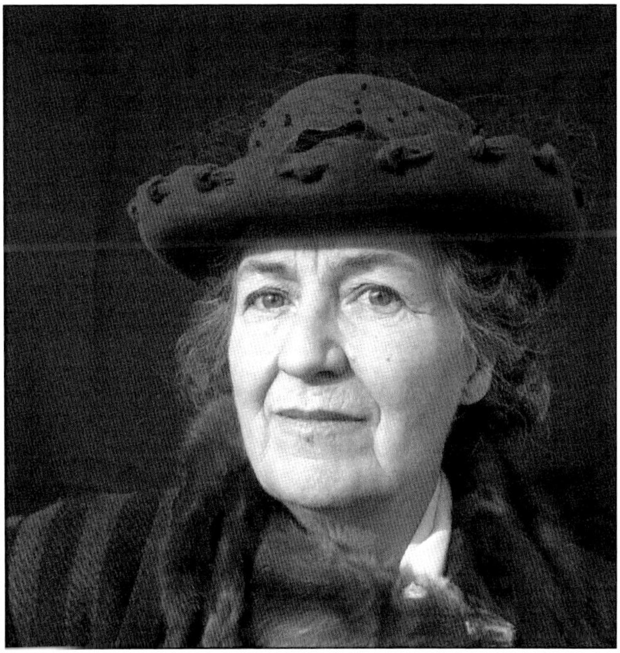

Mabel Dodge Luhan was born in Buffalo, New York, to a family of great wealth and privilege. As a young woman, she lived in Europe and New York, where she became known as a patron of the arts and confidante of the intelligentsia. She moved to Taos, New Mexico, in 1919 and started a literary colony that included D.H. Lawrence. She also befriended artist Georgia O'Keeffe and photographer Ansel Adams, among other well-known artists of the 20th century. When she died in 1962, the Mabel Dodge Luhan home was designated a national historic landmark. (Photograph by John Candelario, courtesy Palace of the Governors [NMHM/DCA], No. 179240.)

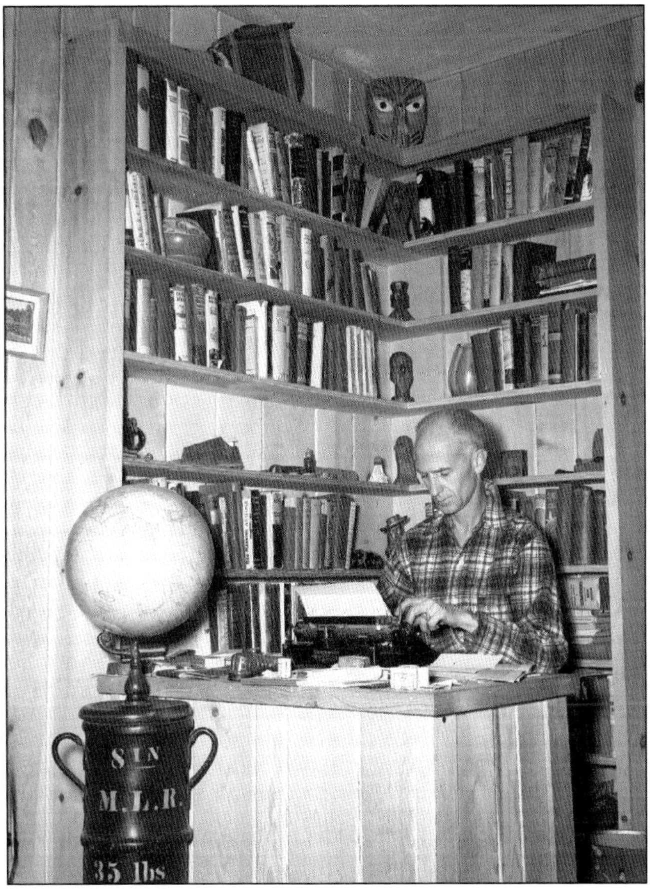

Ernie Pyle was an American journalist and World War II correspondent who was awarded a Pulitzer Prize in 1945 for his column depicting the trials and tribulations of American soldiers, which was syndicated in 300 newspapers throughout the country. He was killed by enemy fire that year during the Battle of Okinawa. After his death, Pres. Henry Truman said, "No man in this war has so well told the story of the American fighting man as American fighting men wanted it told. He deserves the gratitude of all his countrymen." His home in Albuquerque became the first branch library of the Albuquerque–Bernalillo County Library System. (Photograph by John Candelario, courtesy Palace of the Governors [NMHM/DCA], No. 165756.)

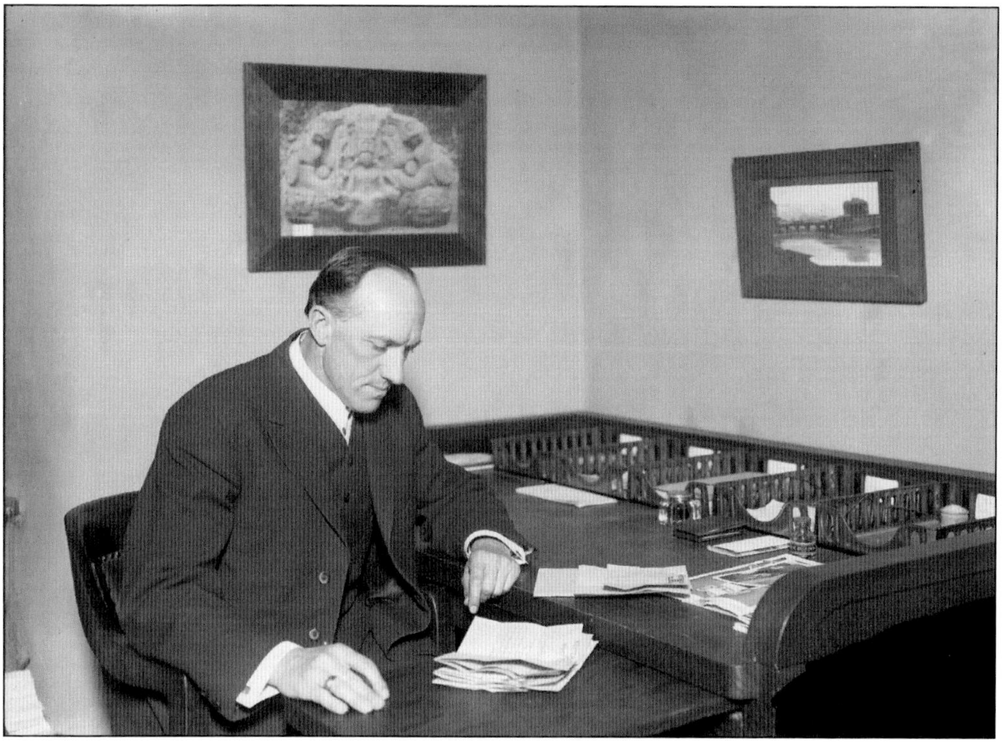

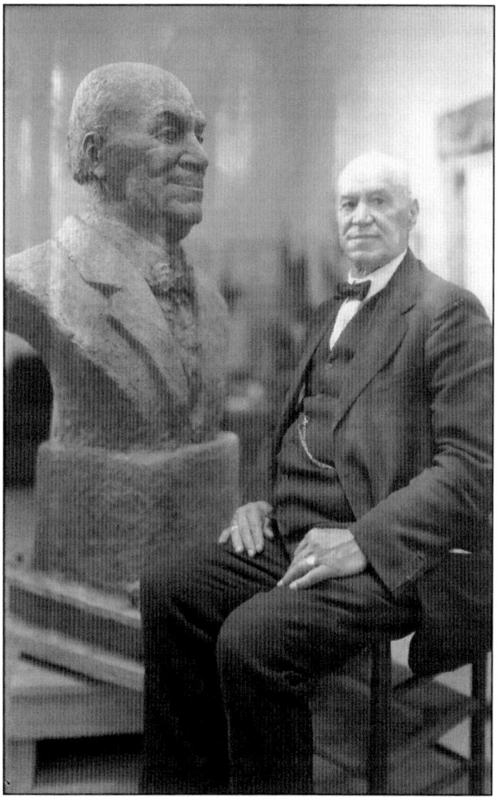

The anthropologist Edgar L. Hewett came to Santa Fe from Greeley, Colorado, in 1893 in search of medical help for his wife, Cora Whitford, who suffered from tuberculosis. In 1906, he secured the support of the US Congress in passing the Antiquities Act, which made it illegal to pillage ancient ruins. In 1907, he founded the School of American Archaeology, which is now called the School of Advanced Research. Two years later, in 1909, he also founded the Museum of New Mexico, where his ashes are interred today. (Photograph by Jesse Nusbaum, courtesy Palace of the Governors [NMHM/DCA], No. 007383.)

In 1927, Miguel Chavez, a wealthy philanthropist, donated $65,000 for construction of a new building at his alma mater, St. Michael's College. When Chavez died in 1928, he left much of his estate to the St. Vincent's Girls Orphanage in Santa Fe and St. Anthony's Boys Orphanage in Albuquerque. (Courtesy Palace of the Governors [NMHM/DCA], No. 050926.)

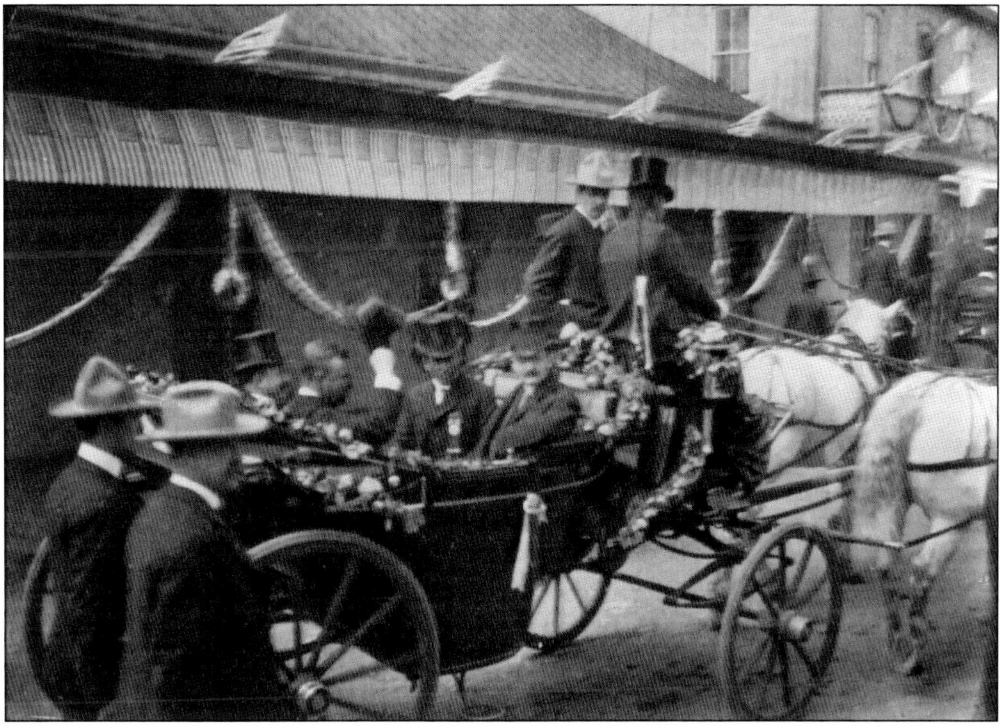

Teddy Roosevelt was the assistant secretary of the Navy in 1898. He left that post to organize the 1st Volunteer Army Cavalry, which was nicknamed "the Rough Riders." This diverse group of men comprised Native Americans, cowboys, miners, gamblers, military veterans, and police officers. Their mission was to fight against Spain in Cuba. This group was chosen from the Southwest in the belief that they would be more acclimated to the hot climate of Cuba. (Courtesy Palace of the Governors [NMHM/DCA], No. 010983.)

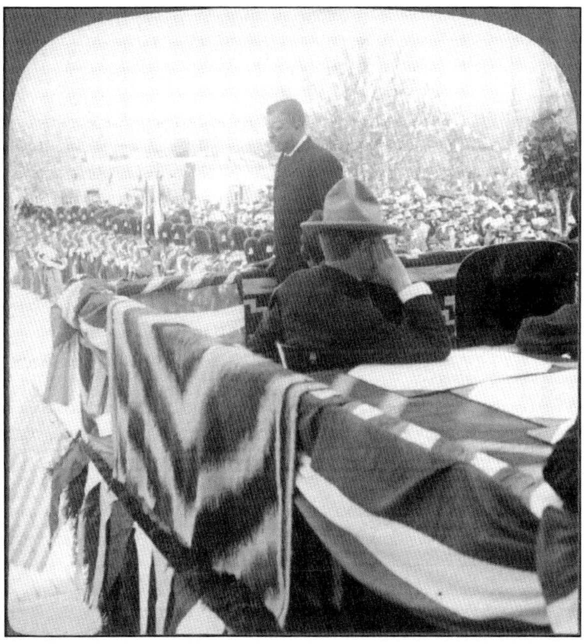

Teddy Roosevelt visited Santa Fe in 1903, and a special ceremony was held on the plaza. Roosevelt served as the US president from 1901 to 1909. (Courtesy Palace of the Governors [NMHM/DCA], No. 139021.)

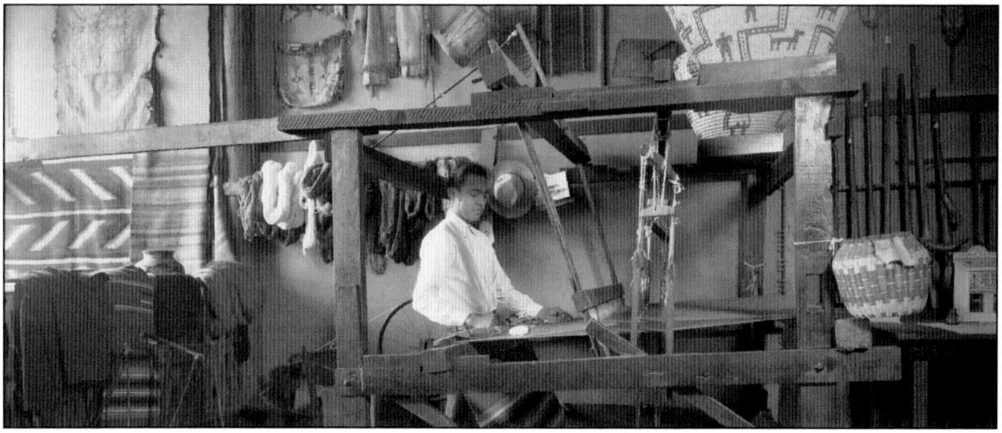

Nicolás Escajeda was born in 1902 in Acensión in the Mexican state of Chihuahua. He came to Santa Fe in 1922 and became a soloist in the choir at the Cathedral Basilica of St. Francis of Assisi. While making a living as a weaver at Gans Store on the Santa Fe Plaza, he often sang the old songs of Mexico, to the delight of customers and tourists. Escajeda was featured in the book *Caballeros, The Romance of Santa Fe and the Southwest*, by Ruth Laughlin. (Photograph by Harmon T. Parkhurst, courtesy Palace of the Governors [NMHM/DCA], No. 006918.)

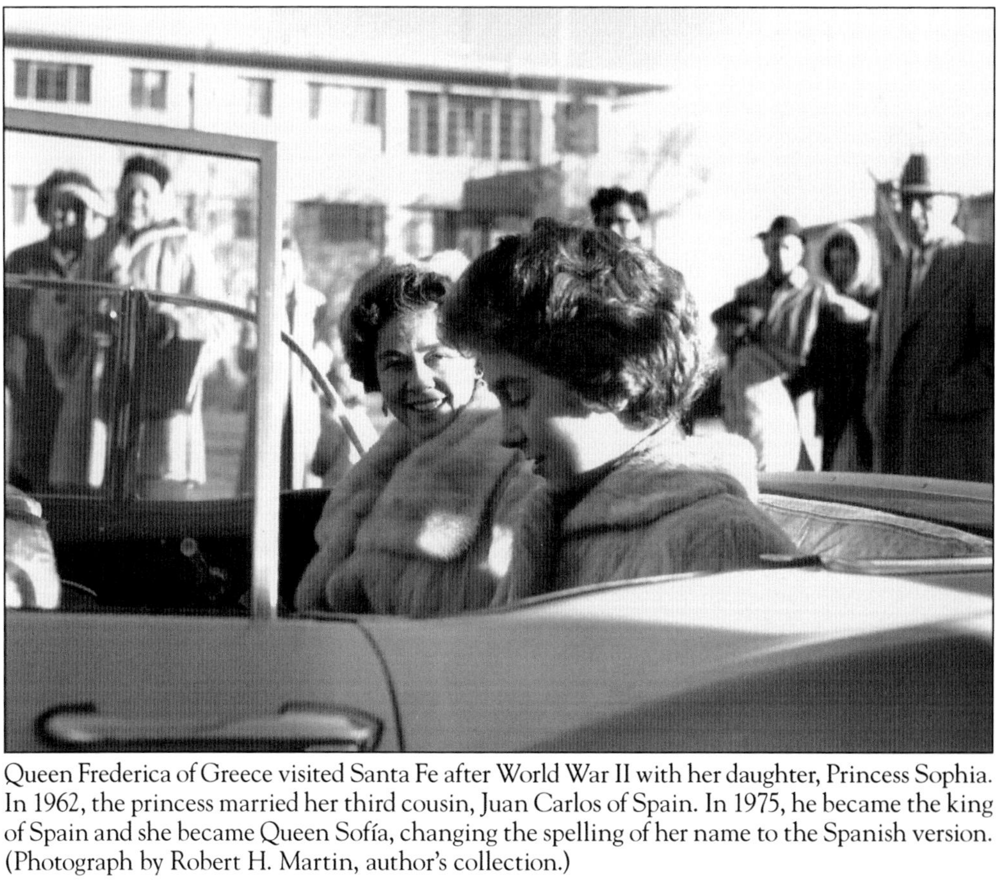

Queen Frederica of Greece visited Santa Fe after World War II with her daughter, Princess Sophia. In 1962, the princess married her third cousin, Juan Carlos of Spain. In 1975, he became the king of Spain and she became Queen Sofía, changing the spelling of her name to the Spanish version. (Photograph by Robert H. Martin, author's collection.)

The architect Frank Lloyd Wright designed more than 1,000 buildings in his lifetime, two of which can be found in New Mexico. In 1948, he constructed a house for Arnold Friedman in Pecos, New Mexico. He was also commissioned by newspaperman Lloyd Burlingham in 1942 to build a house in Santa Fe. The house had not been completed when Wright died in 1959. When it was finished, it became known as the Pottery House. It is located on Hyde Park Road abutting the Sangre de Cristo Mountains. (Photograph by Laura Gilpin, courtesy Amon Carter Museum, No. P1979.230.912.)

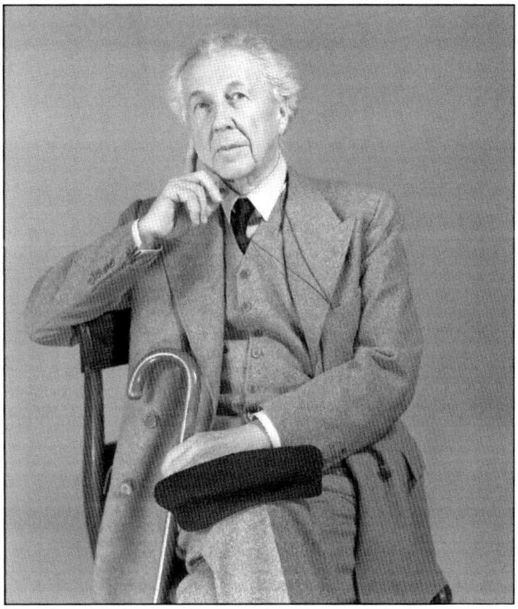

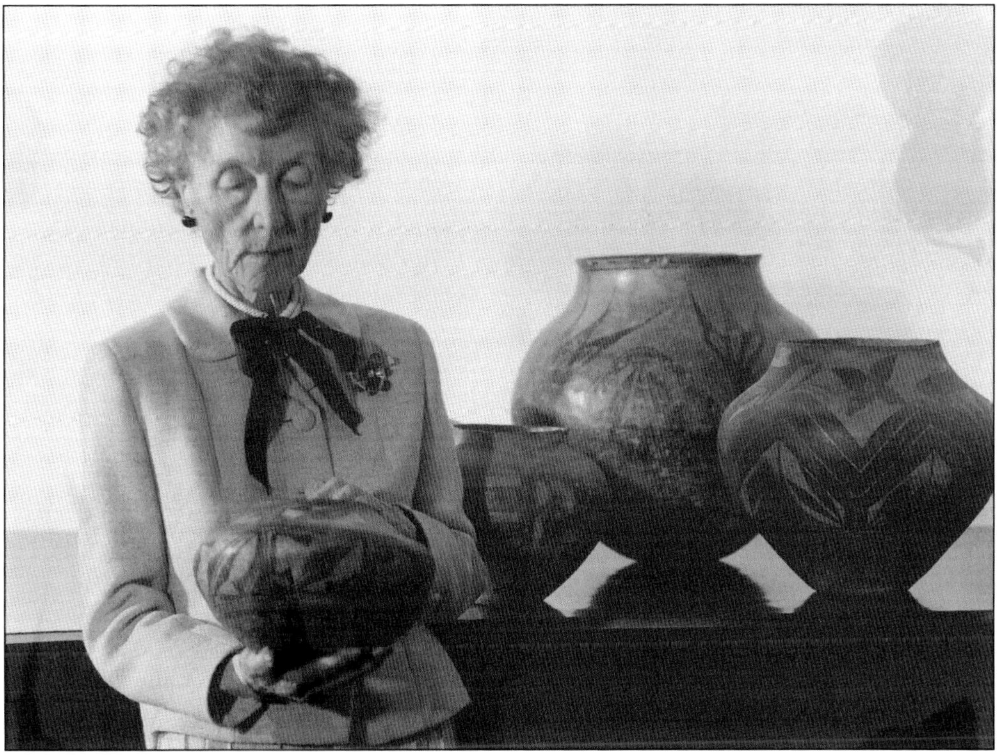

Amelia Elizabeth White and her sister, Martha, came to Santa Fe in 1923. They began the De Vargas Development Company with Sen. Bronson Cutting, and acquired vast amounts of real estate on the north side of Santa Fe. They later donated the land that was developed for the Museum of Indian Arts and Culture and the International Folk Art Museum. Their home on Garcia Street became the headquarters for the School of Advanced Research. (Photograph by Laura Gilpin, courtesy Amon Carter Museum, No. P1979.130.1224.)

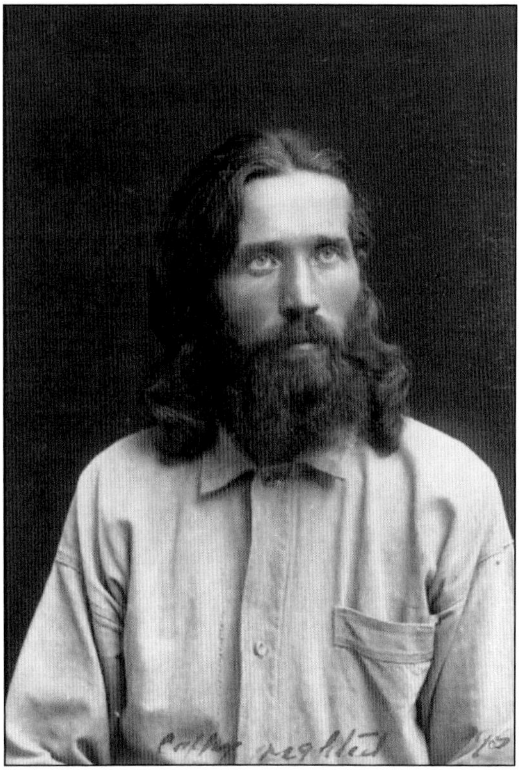

Francis Schlatter immigrated to the United States in 1884 from Alsace, on the border of France, Germany, and Switzerland. A cobbler by trade, he acquired a following and reputation as a healer. Ada Morley, the wife of Santa Fe archaeologist Sylvanus Morley, published the book *The Life of the Harp in the Hand of the Harper*, which told of the healer's three-month stay on their ranch at Dátil, New Mexico. The healer also befriended archaeologist Edgar Lee Hewett in 1895. Hewett recovered Schlatter's healing rod in a grave in Mexico. Today, the healing rod is part of the collection at the New Mexico History Museum in the Palace of the Governors. (Courtesy Palace of the Governors [NMHM/DCA], No. 051264.)

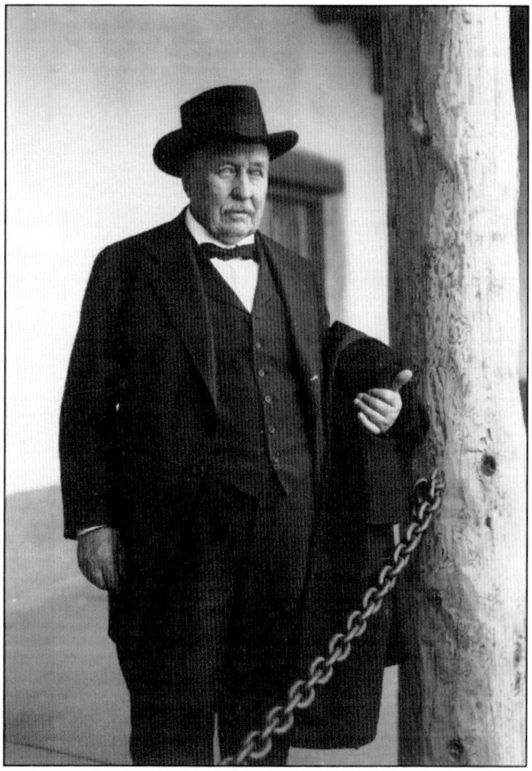

Attorney Thomas B. Catron came to Santa Fe after the Civil War. He and fellow attorney Stephen Elkins formed a group that became known as the Santa Fe Ring. It included prominent businessmen who made their fortunes in oil and real estate. Their shrewd and aggressive tactics angered the townsfolk, but through their wealth they were able to control most of the local politicians, who became their puppets and pawns. Referred to in the local press at the time as an "unholy cabal," the Santa Fe Ring made more than its share of enemies, who opposed its tactics when the railroad bypassed Santa Fe for Las Vegas, New Mexico. (Photograph by Wesley Bradfield, courtesy Palace of the Governors [NMHM/DCA], No. 013309.)

Ruth Laughlin was the author of two seminal books on Santa Fe history. In 1945, she wrote *Caballeros, The Romance of Santa Fe and the Southwest*, which depicted Spanish life at the beginning of the 20th century. In 1951, she wrote *The Wind Leaves No Shadow*, a historical novel about Santa Fe's Doña Tules, who ran a gambling house and brothel in the 1840s. The gambling madam grew wealthy and was well received in society. She is buried under the Cathedral Basilica of St. Francis of Assisi. Laughlin's father, N.B. Laughlin, came to Santa Fe from Texas in 1879 and became a territorial supreme court judge in the early 1900s. (Courtesy Palace of the Governors [NMHM/DCA], No. 050326.)

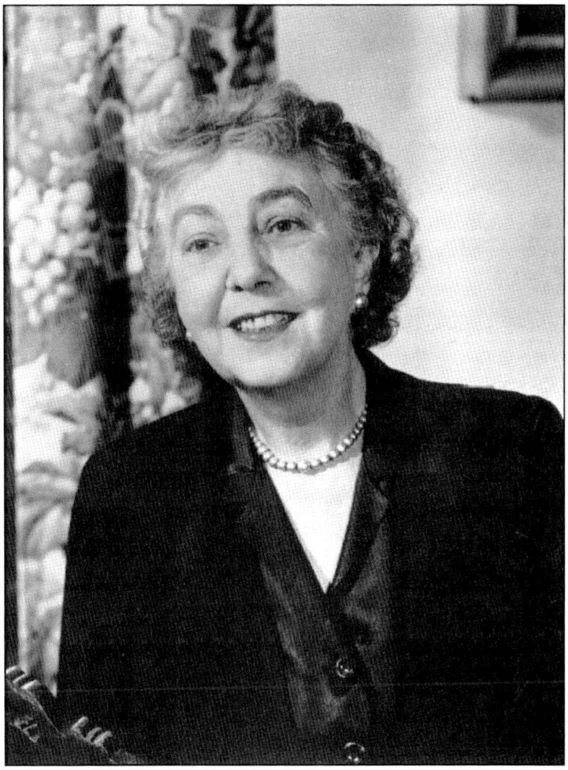

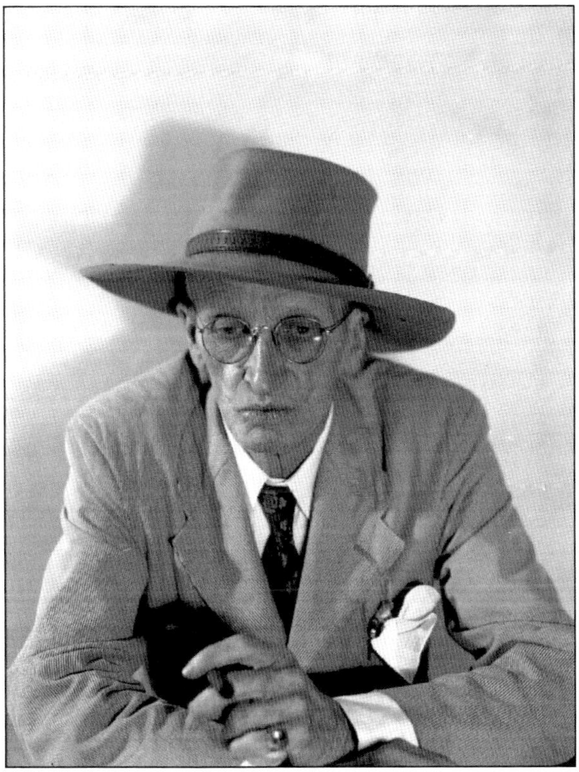

Brian Boru Dunne was a gossip columnist for the *Santa Fe New Mexican* in the 1940s. In his lively column, B.B. Dunne provided Santa Fe with a "Who's Who" of celebrities passing through town. Even when he was not writing about famous people, the prolific writer was able to make the mundane relevant with the motto "There's not much to see in a small town but what you hear makes up for it." (Photograph by Harmon T. Parkhurst, courtesy Palace of the Governors [NMHM/DCA], No. 050926.)

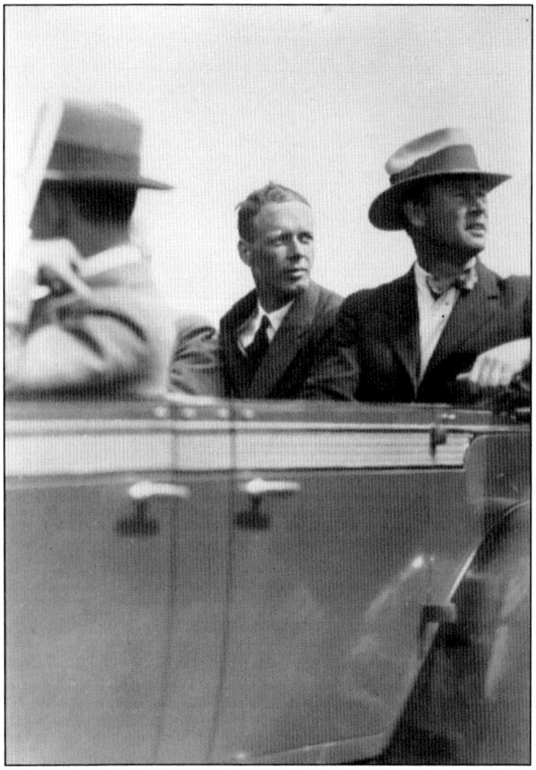

The famed aviator Charles A. Lindbergh (center) visited Santa Fe in 1927, the same year that he made the first solo transatlantic flight from New York to Paris in his plane *The Spirit of St. Louis*. In 1929, he took aerial photographs of Chaco Canyon and other important archaeological sites of the Southwest. (Courtesy Palace of the Governors [NMHM/DCA], No. 168501.)

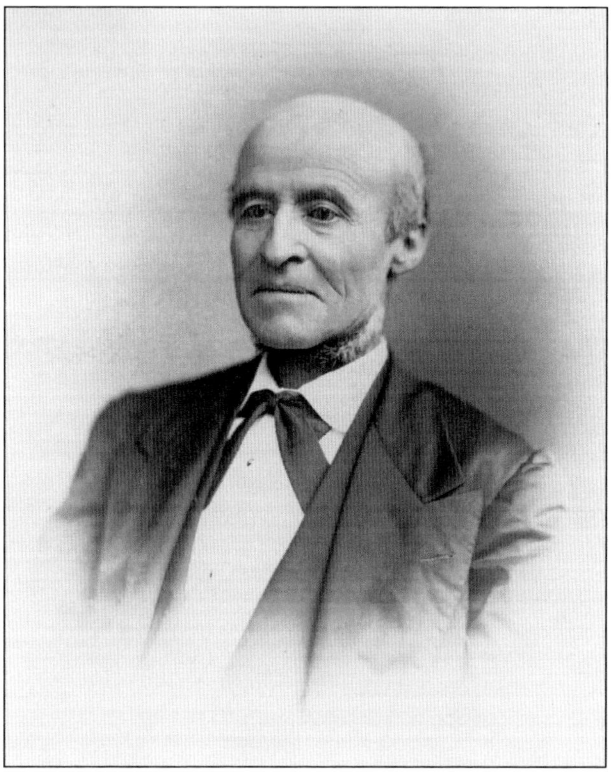

Padre José M. Gallegos became New Mexico's first Hispanic delegate elected to Congress in 1853. The house he built on Washington Avenue in the late 1850s is now home to the popular restaurant Santacafé. In 1914, artist Sheldon Parsons lived in that house, which became a meeting place for the artists of the early 20th century. (Photograph by Frederick Gutekunst, courtesy Palace of the Governors [NMHM/DCA], No. 00982.)

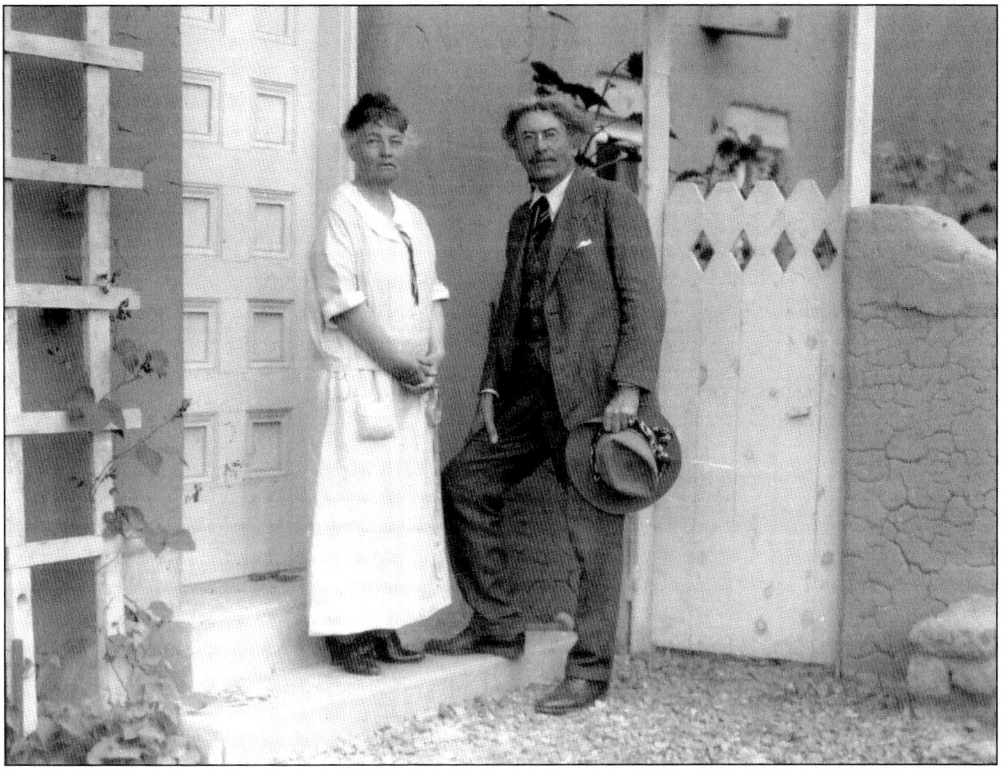

In 1903, Mary Austin wrote the classic *The Land of Little Rain* about the people, terrain, and spirituality of the West. When Austin came to Santa Fe in 1918, she founded the Santa Fe Little Theater. Her friend Ernest Thompson Seton wrote 40 books on wildlife and nature. In 1933, he built Seton Village Castle southeast of Santa Fe, which became a national historic landmark in 2005. (Photograph by Carol Stryker, courtesy Palace of the Governors [NMHM/DCA], No. 014248.)

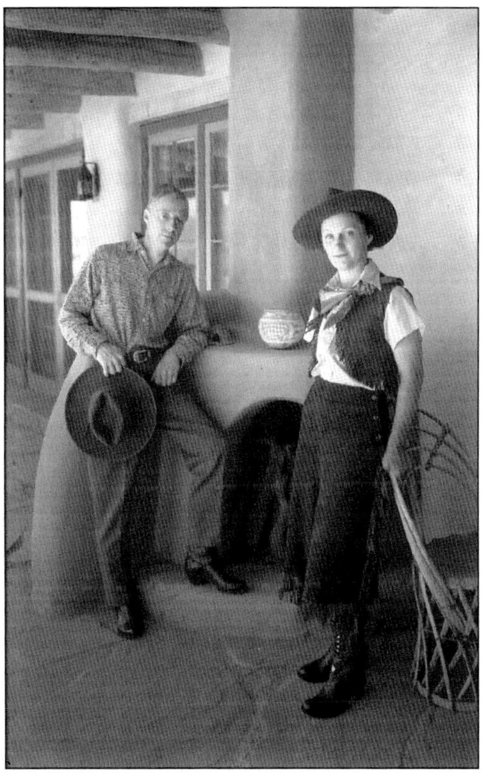

In 1934, Arthur and Phoebe Pack were the owners of Ghost Ranch in northern New Mexico. The couple sold a parcel of land on the ranch to Georgia O'Keeffe in 1940. Fifteen years later, the Packs donated the entire ranch to the Presbyterian Church, which infuriated O'Keeffe, who felt that her privacy would be compromised. Today, Ghost Ranch is a spiritual retreat that is visited by many seeking solace in an area now known as O'Keeffe Country. (Photograph by Harmon T. Parkhurst, courtesy Palace of the Governors [NMHM/DCA], No. 089653.)

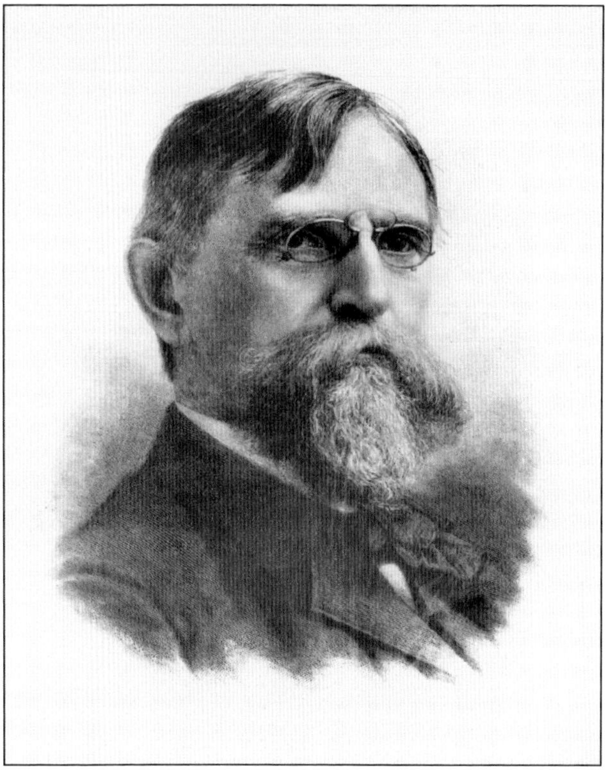

Lew Wallace was the governor of New Mexico from 1878 to 1881. In 1880, he wrote the book *Ben Hur*, considered by some to be the most important Christian book of the 19th century. (Courtesy Palace of the Governors [NMHM/DCA], No. 013123.)

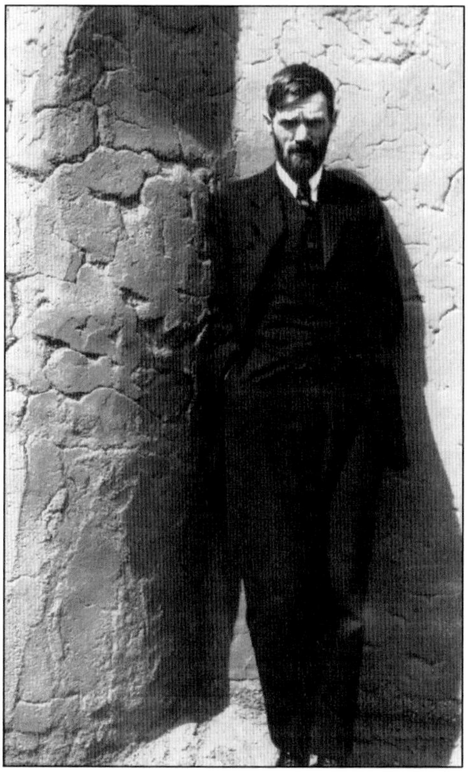

The writer and poet Witter Bynner took this photograph of the English author D.H. Lawrence on a visit to Santa Fe. D.H. Lawrence is best known for his 1913 book *Sons and Lovers*, which was made into a movie in 1960. He and his wife, Frieda, lived in Taos from 1922 to 1925. Lawrence died in 1930 in France at the age of 45. His ashes were later brought to New Mexico, where they are interred at the D.H. Lawrence Ranch, 18 miles northwest of Taos. (Photograph by Witter Bynner, courtesy Palace of the Governors [NMHM/DCA], No. 200135.)

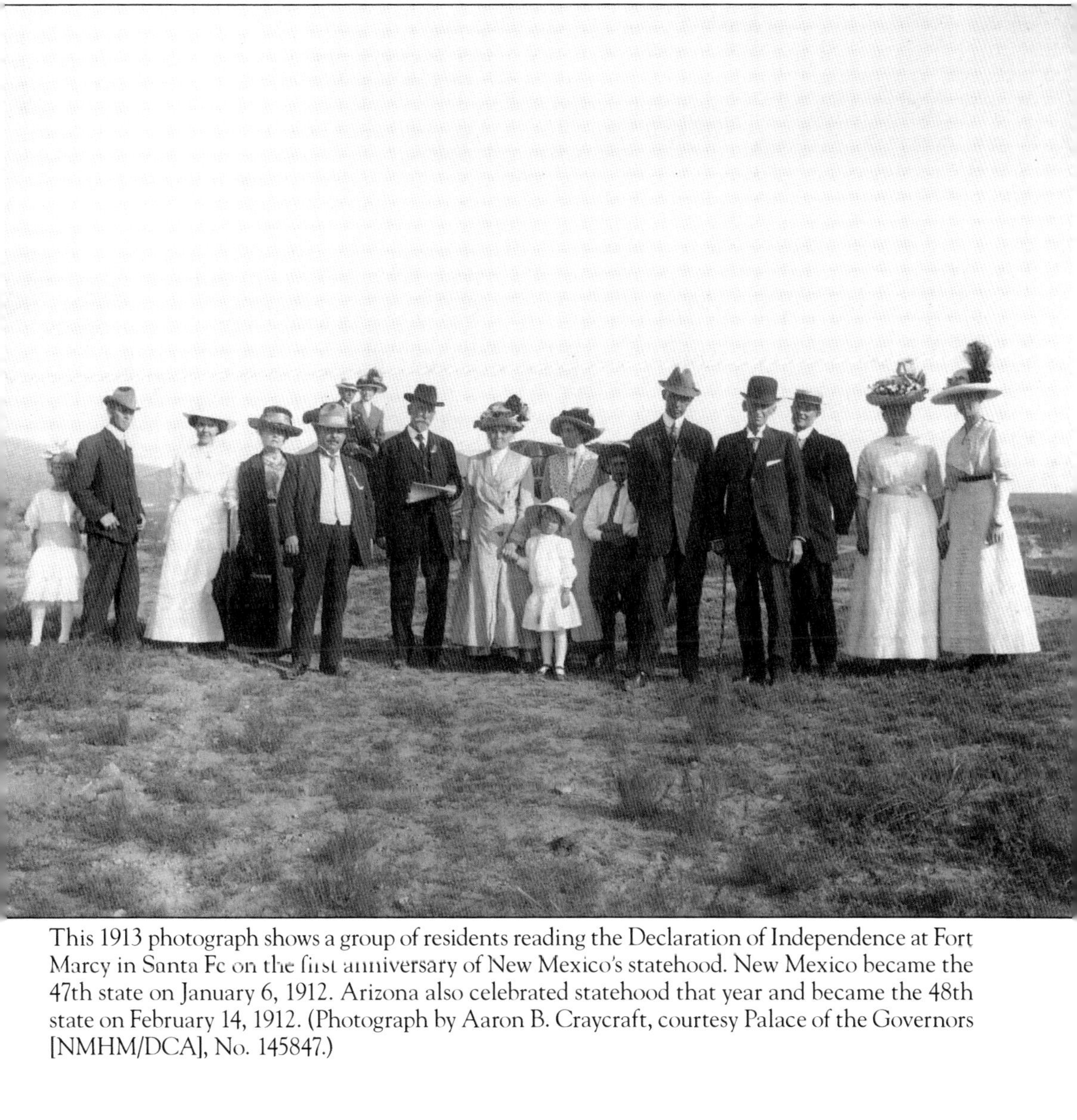

This 1913 photograph shows a group of residents reading the Declaration of Independence at Fort Marcy in Santa Fe on the first anniversary of New Mexico's statehood. New Mexico became the 47th state on January 6, 1912. Arizona also celebrated statehood that year and became the 48th state on February 14, 1912. (Photograph by Aaron B. Craycraft, courtesy Palace of the Governors [NMHM/DCA], No. 145847.)

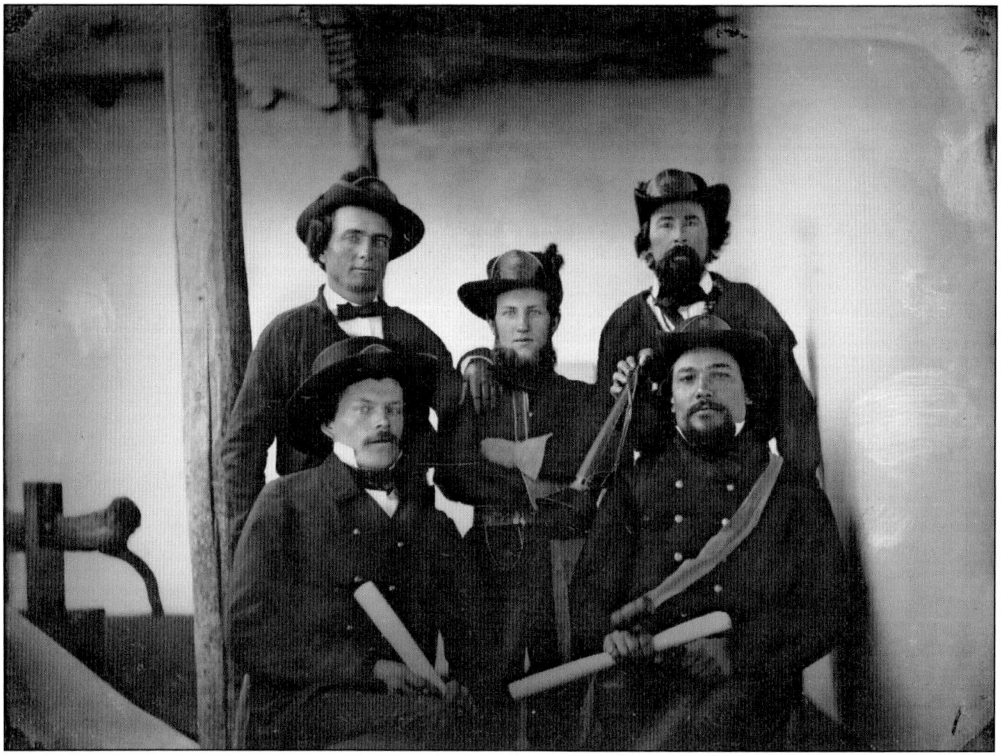

When New Mexico became a US territory in 1848, civil-service organizations began to be established. This is a photograph taken in the early 1860s of the Santa Fe Fire Company. (Courtesy Palace of the Governors [NMHM/DCA]. HP.2014.50.1.)

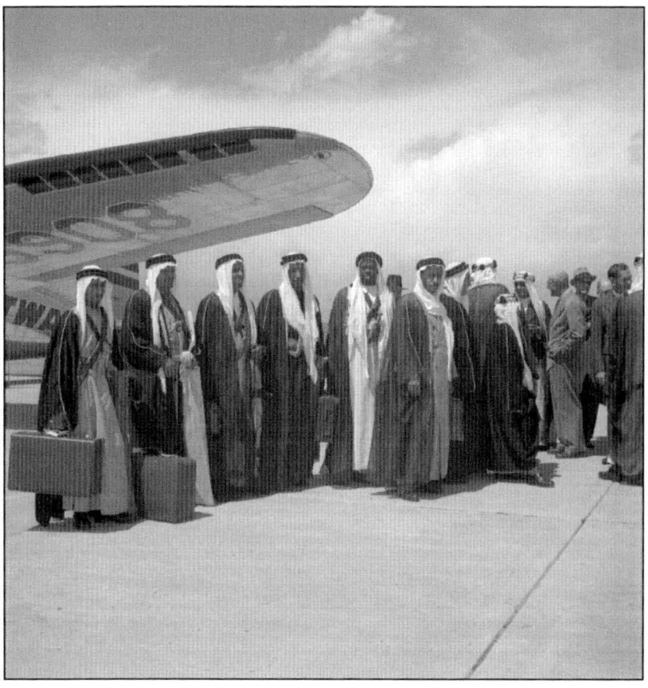

Photographer John Candelario had extensive contacts in both New Mexico and New York, which allowed him access to many prominent people from that era. Seen in this Candelario photograph on April 22, 1945, is the Saudi Arabian delegation at the Santa Fe airport. (Photograph by John Candelario, courtesy Palace of the Governors [NMHM/DCA], No. 165694.)

In the late 19th century, Englishman and entrepreneur Fred Harvey helped define Southwest hospitality with the help of young refined women he hired to work as waitresses at his Harvey House chain of restaurants and hotels along railways from Kansas to California. Known as "Harvey Girls," their legacy became synonymous with the lore and lure of the West. In 1946, MGM studios made the movie *The Harvey Girls*, staring Judy Garland and Angela Lansbury, which forever solidified the fame of legions of young women who helped tame the image of the "Wild West." (Courtesy Palace of the Governors [NMHM/DCA], No. HP.2011.1.8.)

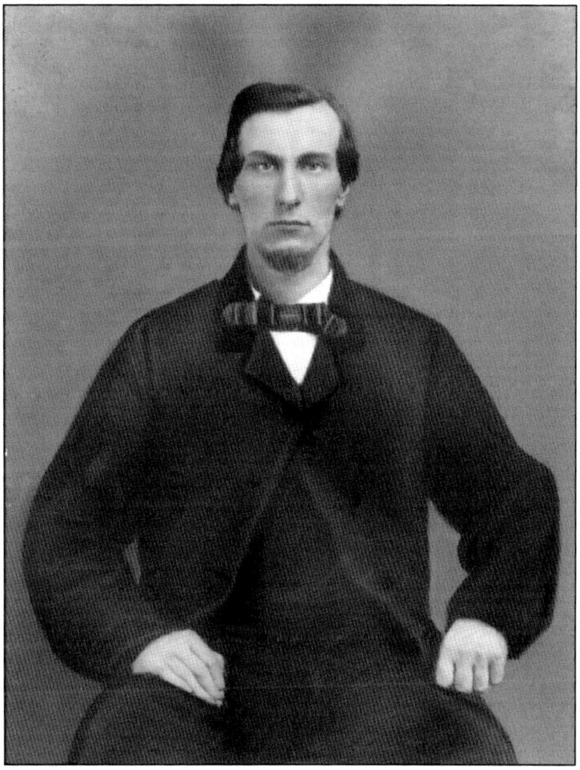

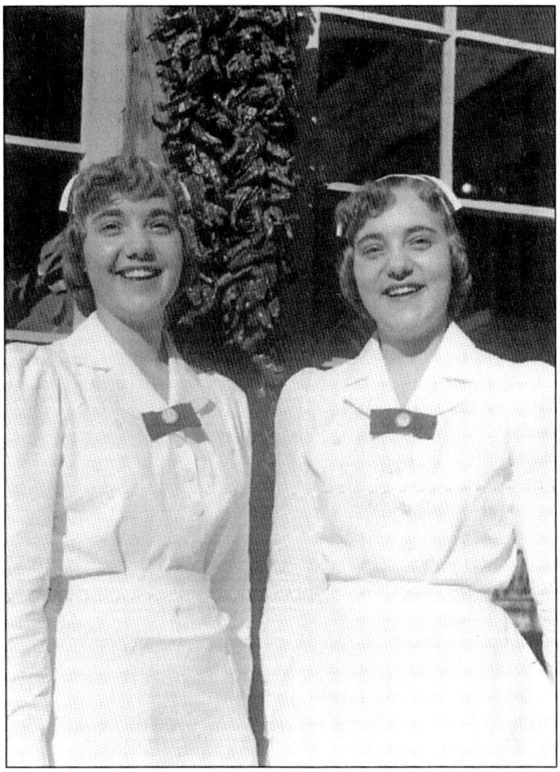

Beverly Ireland and her identical twin sister, Bernette Jarvis, worked as Harvey Girls at La Fonda in 1955. The twins were hired at La Fonda because of their previous experience waitressing at the Jolly Green Giant factory restaurant in Minnesota. As Harvey Girls, the two young sisters got to know all the politicians, writers, and artists who ate there as well as the movie stars who were guests at La Fonda. (Author's collection.)

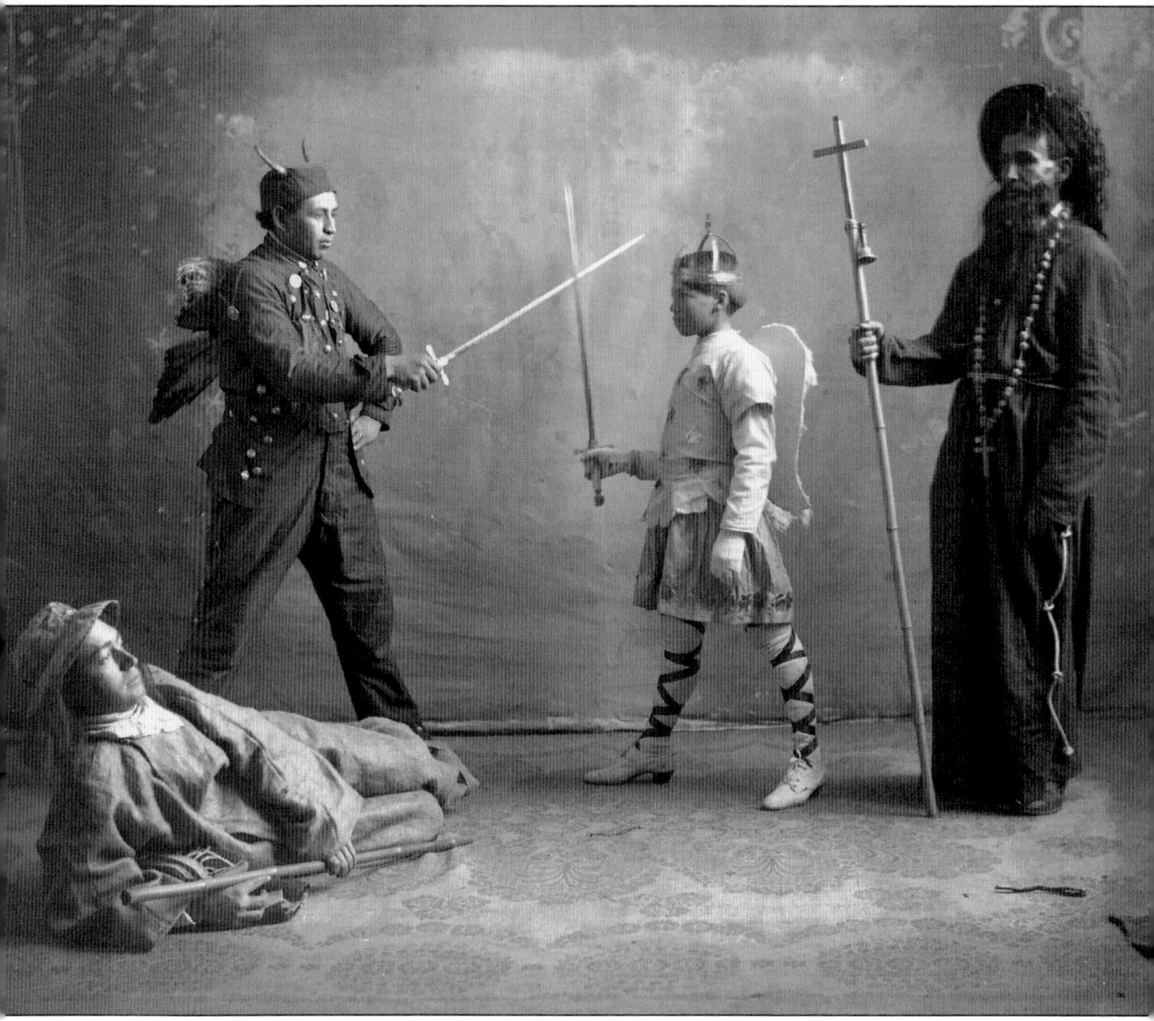

Los Pastores is a holiday drama that was introduced to the New World in the late 16th century by Spanish missionaries. It has been passed down primarily through oral tradition among families in Mexico and the American Southwest. In 1915, these actors paid tribute to the tale of the shepherds on their journey to pay homage to the Christ child. From left to right are Abrán Sena (Bartolo), Felipe Perea (Devil), Perfecto Baca (St. Michael), and Frank Montoya (Hermit). (Photograph by Aaron B. Craycraft, courtesy Palace of the Governors [NMHM/DCA], No. HP.2014.50.1.)

Six

Art Mecca

The genesis of Santa Fe as an art mecca begins with the Neolithic artifacts entombed beneath Santa Fe that provide a roadmap of the history of the nation's oldest capital city. Decorative shards of pottery from the 13th century, along with remnants of Native American baskets woven from twine, mark the passage of time. They remain under the protection of museum gatekeepers, allowing a glimpse into a world frozen in time.

Iconic idolatry followed in the 1600s with the arrival of the Spanish colonists. More than 300 years ago, Franciscan friars established their roots of devotion to the *santos*. These Catholic religious images, painted on deer or elk hide and adorned with straw appliqué, represent just one of the art forms that continue to enrich the region.

By the mid-19th century, the third wave of artists trickled in, some as military mapmakers who did their part to secure the region for the United States. Finally, it was tuberculosis, the leading cause of death in this country from 1880 through 1940, that solidified the foundation of Santa Fe as a major art center. The pristine arid climate brought hundreds of people to Sunmount Sanatorium in the foothills of the Sangre de Cristo Mountains. The solitude of convalescence awakened a core of creativity. The breathtaking landscape shaped by volcanic activity thousands of years ago, coupled with the shifting light cast by the sun in the high desert, formed a kaleidoscope of iridescent hues yearning to find artistic expression. The terrain provided a canvas for those indebted to the people and place that gave them a second chance at life.

And like the advent of penicillin that made the treatment of this dreadful disease possible, several individuals are credited for breathing life into the art community. The people whose vision helped to solidify Santa Fe's art community are included in this chapter in gratitude for their foresight.

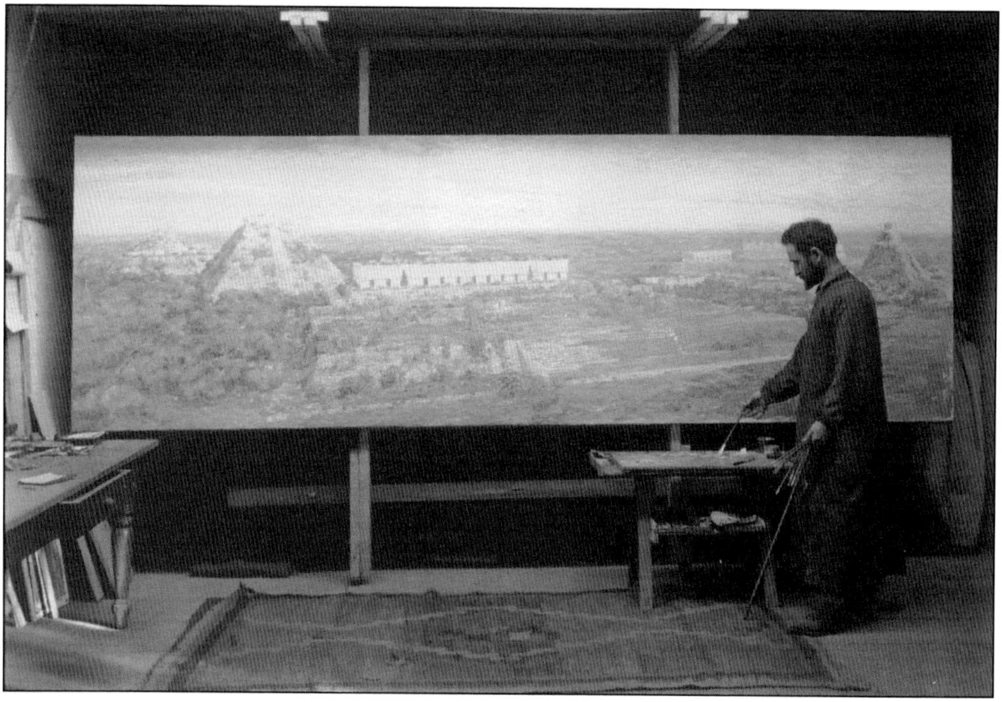

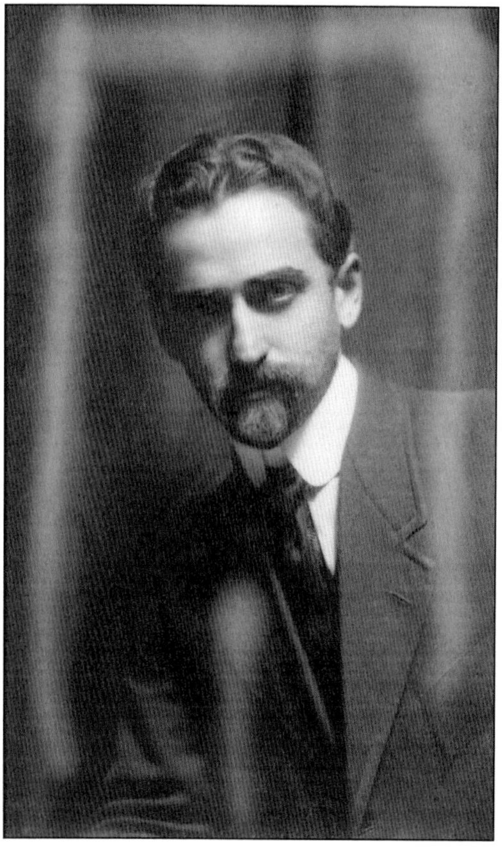

The first major commercial artist to arrive in Santa Fe was Portuguese artist and photographer Carlos Vierra. In the early part of the 20th century, he moved from New York to Santa Fe, seeking a cure for tuberculosis. At Sunmount Sanatorium, he met another patient, Brazilian architect John Gaw Meem. The Portuguese language created a bond between the two, which led them to spearhead the Pueblo Revival style of Santa Fe architecture. Vierra also helped to restore the Palace of the Governors, the oldest capitol building in the United States. Vierra created the painting seen here for the 1915 Panama-California Exposition in San Diego. (Photograph by Jesse Nusbaum, courtesy Palace of the Governors [NMHM/DCA], No. 16991.)

Carlos Vierra took aerial photographs of the ancient ruins at Chaco Canyon in 1928, a year prior to Charles Lindbergh's archaeological photographs of the area. (Courtesy Palace of the Governors [NMHM/DCA], No. 042621.)

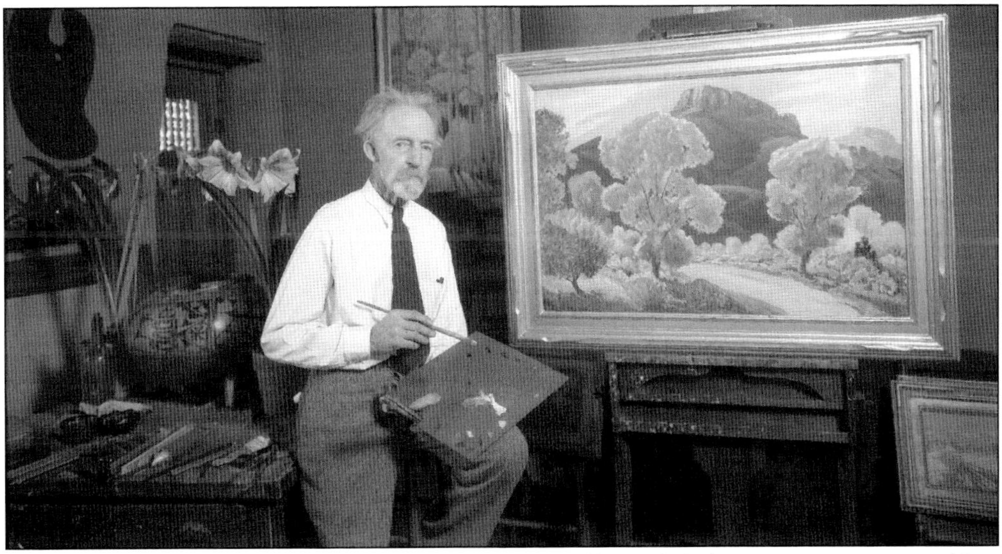

Sheldon Parsons was the second artist to arrive in Santa Fe in 1913. A prominent painter in New York, he completed commissions for Pres. William McKinley, Vice Pres. Garret Hobart, and other well-known politicians of that era. Like Vierra, he came to Santa Fe suffering from tuberculosis. In 1914, he moved into the historic house once owned by Padre Gallegos on Washington Avenue, which became a meeting place for the bourgeoning artist colony. Parsons became the first director of fine arts of the Museum of New Mexico. (Photograph by Harmon T. Parkhurst, courtesy Palace of the Governors [NMHM/DCA], No. 073941.)

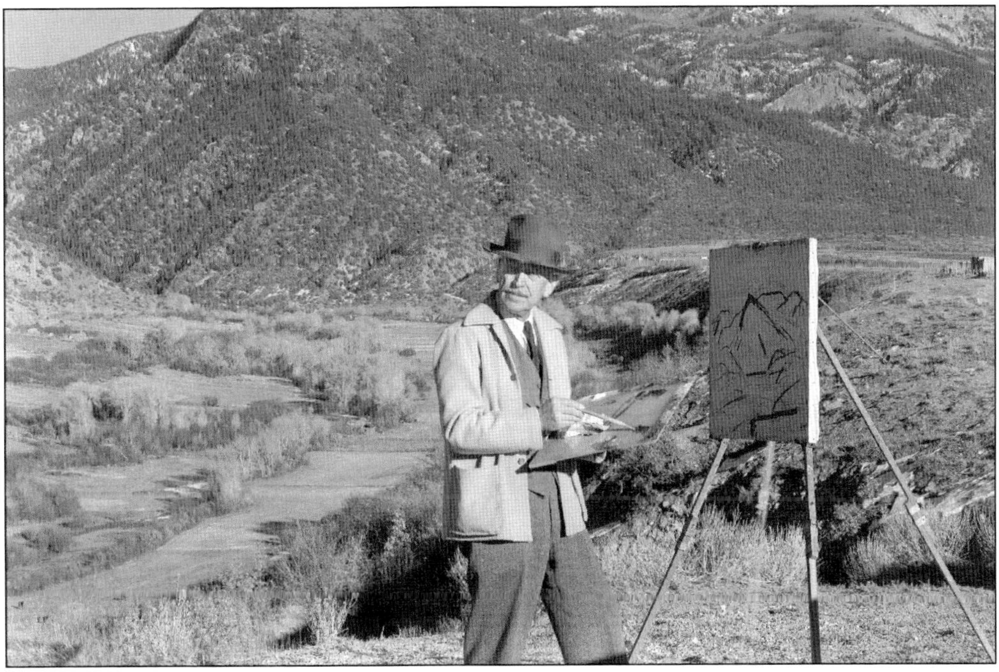

Victor Higgins was a member of the Taos Society of Artists and one of the modernistic 20th-century painters to participate in the opening exhibit of the Museum of Fine Arts of New Mexico in 1917. He was married to Sara Mack, the daughter of Santa Fe artist Sheldon Parsons. (Photograph by Laura Gilpin, courtesy Amon Carter Museum, No. P1979.230.1327.)

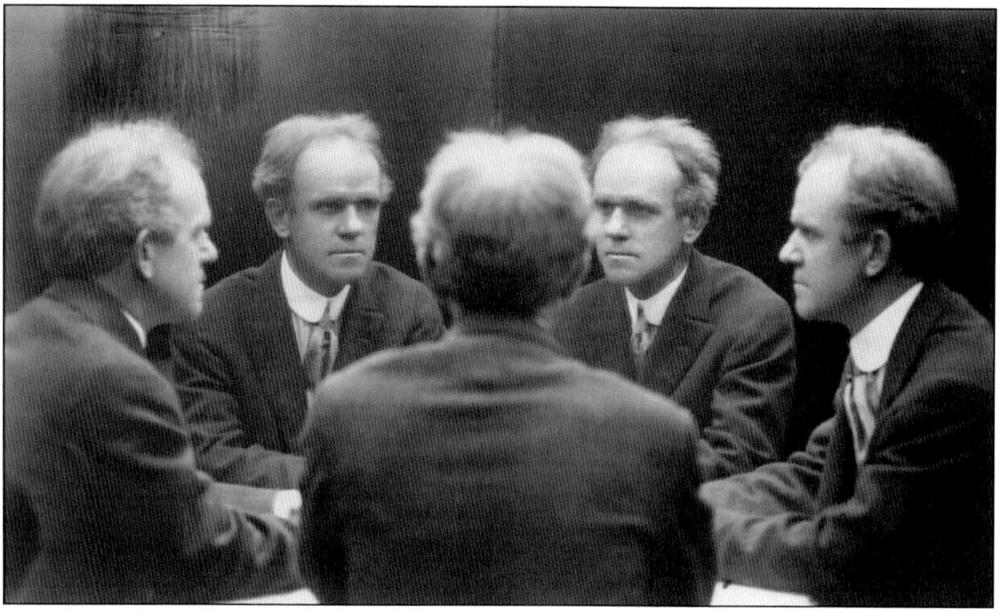

Gerald Cassidy was born in Covington, Kentucky, in 1869. He pursued an art career in New York, where he became a successful lithographer. Stricken with pneumonia in 1890, he was given six months to live. Cassidy headed west to convalesce at a sanatorium in Albuquerque, where he recovered. In 1912, the year of statehood for New Mexico, he moved to Santa Fe with his wife, journalist Ina Sizer. By 1915, the couple was living at the corner of Canyon Road and Acequia Madre Street. In a cruel twist of fate, he died tragically from the toxic fumes of turpentine and carbon monoxide emitted by a newly installed gas heater. That was in 1934, the year natural gas heating was introduced to Santa Fe. (Courtesy Palace of the Governors [NMHM/DCA], No. 037734.)

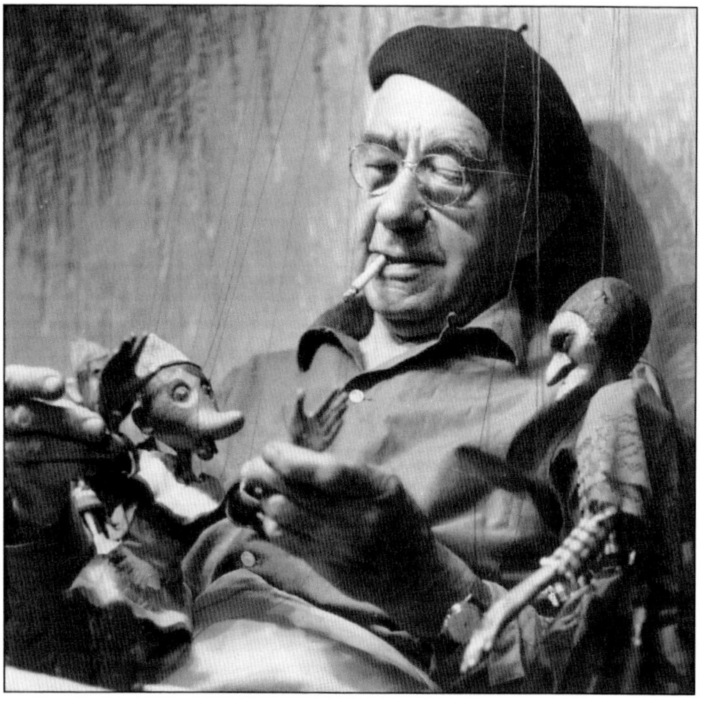

Gustave Baumann was born in Magdeburg, Germany, in 1881. He was raised in Chicago, where he had a successful career as a commercial artist prior to moving to Santa Fe in 1918. He worked at the Museum of New Mexico, and during the Great Depression he began making marionettes that he performed with in plays. During this time, he was part of the jury that awarded commissions to artists for the Works Progress Administration (WPA). (Courtesy Palace of the Governors [NMHM/DCA] No. HP.2011.07.001.)

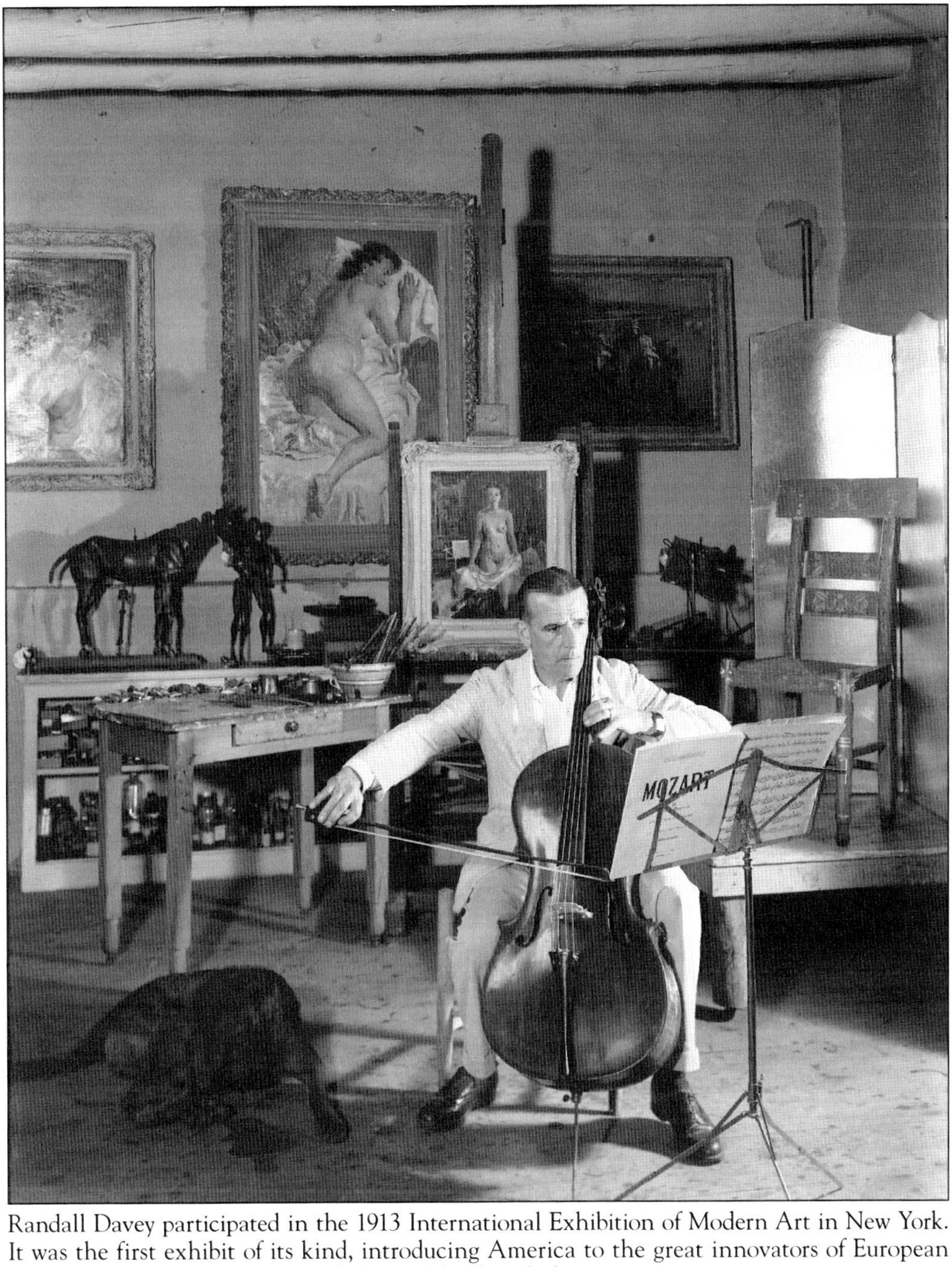

Randall Davey participated in the 1913 International Exhibition of Modern Art in New York. It was the first exhibit of its kind, introducing America to the great innovators of European art, from Cezanne to Picasso, and the worlds of symbolism, impressionism, post-impressionism, neo-impressionism, and cubism. He moved to Santa Fe in 1919 and became an integral part of the city's modern art movement. He died tragically in a car accident in 1964. In 1983, his home became part of the New Mexico Audubon Center and Sanctuary. (Photograph by Laura Gilpin, courtesy Amon Carter Museum, No. P1979.230.1309.)

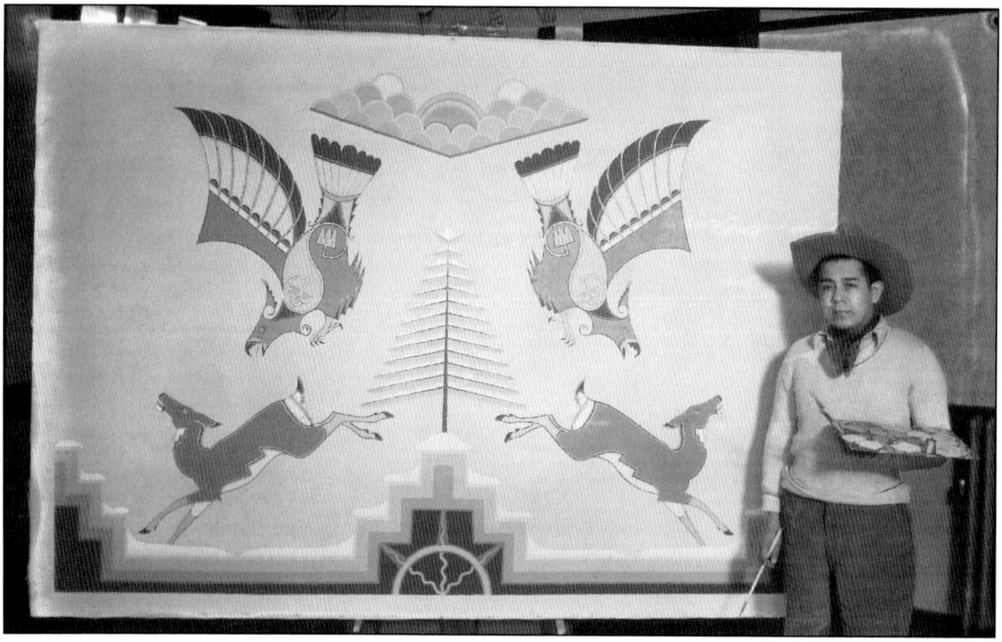

Velino Shije Herrera was born Ma Pe Wi in Zia Pueblo in 1902. In 1919, at the age of 17, he was part of a small group of Native American artists to have their work displayed at the Museum of New Mexico. As he grew to master his art, Herrera's work was widely exhibited in the United States and Europe and was included in the 1931 Exposition of Tribal Indian Arts. (Photograph by Harmon T. Parkhurst, courtesy Palace of the Governors [NMHM/DCA], No. 073995.)

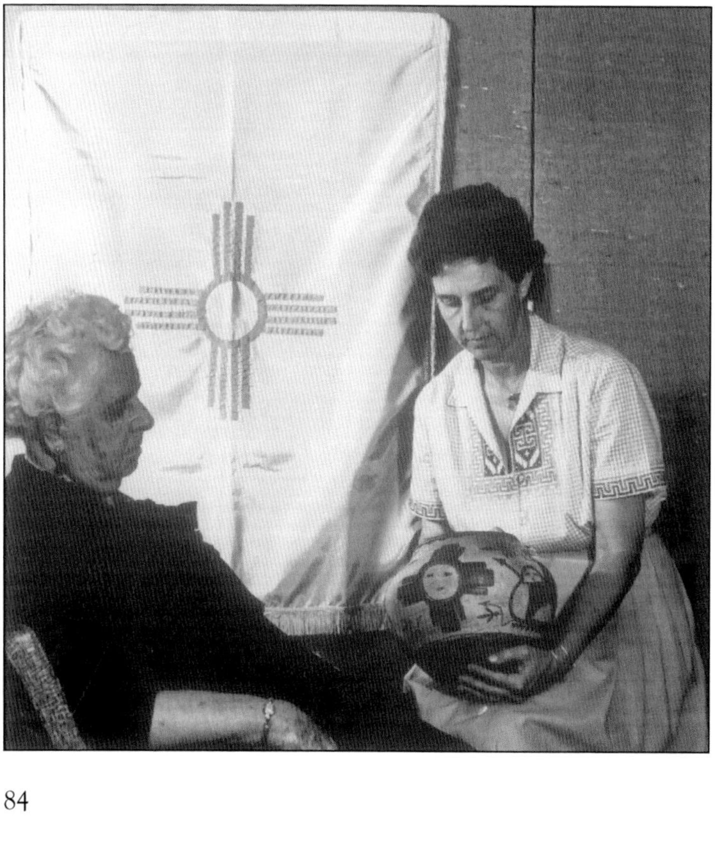

Velino Shije Herrera's abstract work was often based on sacred Pueblo symbolism. That artistic choice, and the fact that he allowed the State of New Mexico to use his design of the Zia symbol in the state flag, led to his ostracism by Zia Pueblo. His design for the New Mexico state flag is shown here, with Mrs. Harry P. Mera (left) and Betty Toulouse holding a Zia pot. (Courtesy Palace of the Governors [NMHM/DCA], No. 050131.)

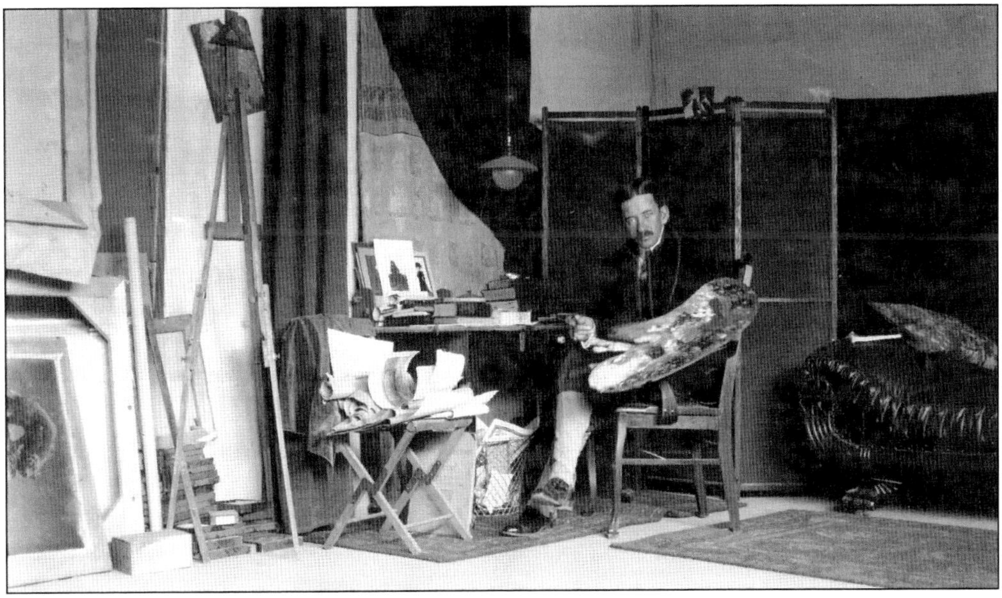

Best known for his paintings of the American Indian, the work of the Swedish artist Carl Lotave is featured at the Smithsonian Institution in Washington, DC. He traveled frequently to Santa Fe from his home in Colorado Springs, Colorado, where he maintained an art studio in 1909. (Courtesy Palace of the Governors [NMHM/DCA], No. 117384.)

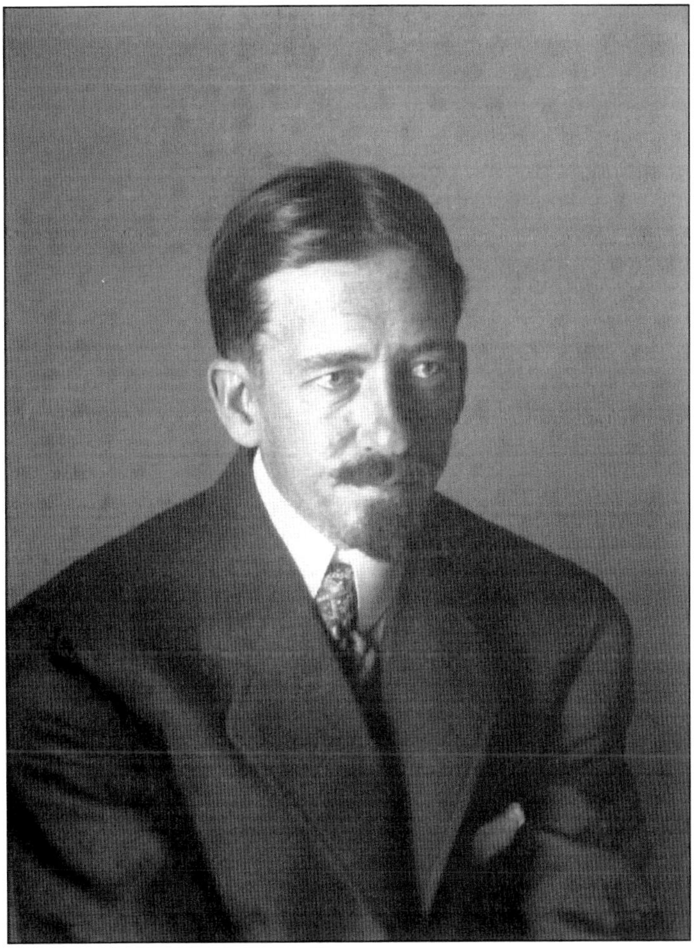

After undergoing an operation for cancer in July 1924, Carl Lotave committed suicide in his apartment in New York City. An article on his death and suicide appeared on the front page of the *New York Times* on December 28, 1924. (Photograph by Jesse Nusbaum, courtesy Palace of the Governors [NMHM/DCA], No. 158216.)

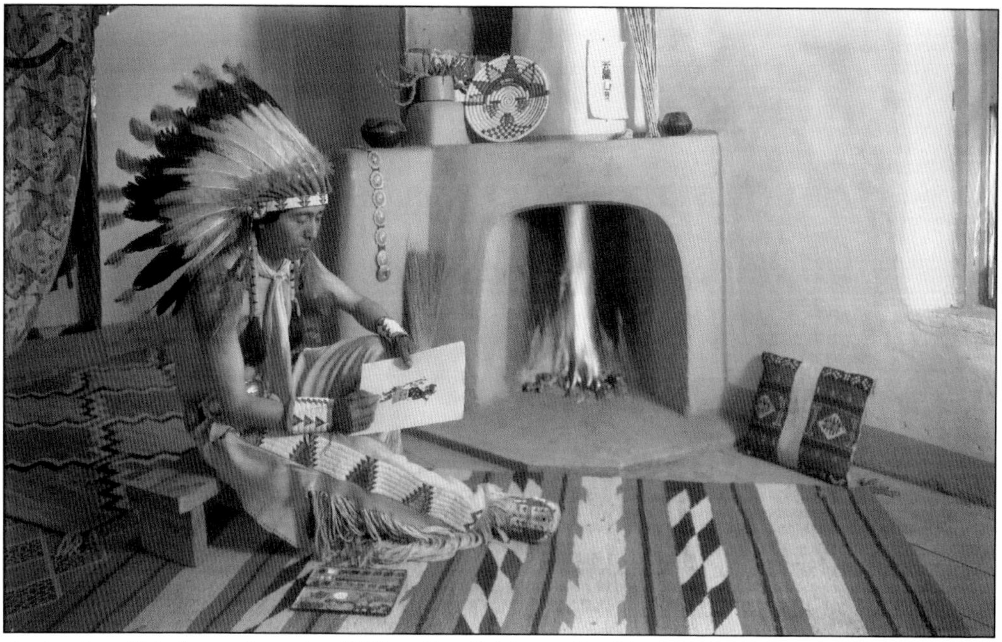

Artist Awa Tsireh was born in 1898 at San Ildefonso Pueblo. His Spanish name was Alfonso Roybal. As a young man, he befriended fellow artist William P. Henderson, who served as his mentor. Henderson's 1917 painting of Tsireh is part of the Museum of New Mexico's permanent collection. He was a self-taught painter and muralist who conveyed his native roots through symbolism and realism. Tsireh's artwork is featured in many museums, including the Smithsonian American Art Museum. (Photograph by Harmon T. Parkhurst, courtesy Palace of the Governors [NMHM/DCA], No. 066674.)

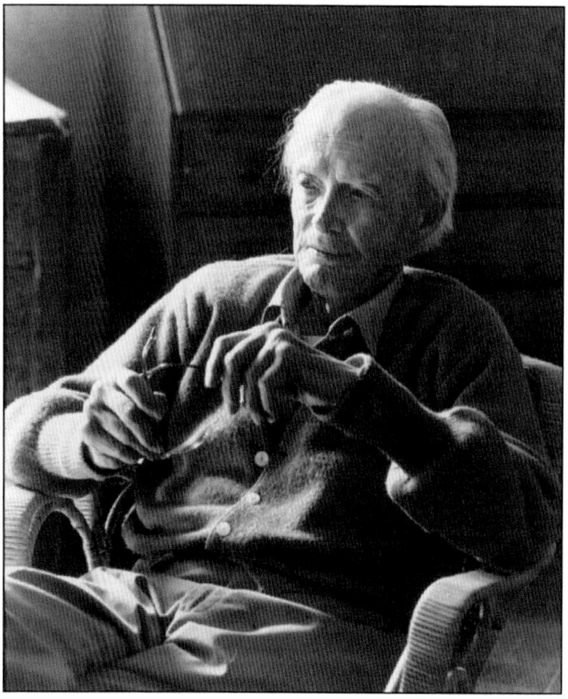

Andrew Dasburg was born in Paris in 1887. The artist participated in the inaugural year of the International Exhibition of Modern Art in New York City, also known as the 1913 Armory Show because it was held at the 69th Regiment armory building. The artist moved to Taos in 1918 and became part of the Taos modernists, a group that helped to define abstract art in this country. In 1921, he moved to Santa Fe and became world-renowned for his work in cubism. Dasburg returned to Taos in 1960, where he died on August 13, 1979, at the age of 92. Dasburg was the last surviving artist from the 1913 International Exhibition of Modern Art. (Photograph by Laura Gilpin, courtesy Amon Carter Museum, No. P1979.48.1.)

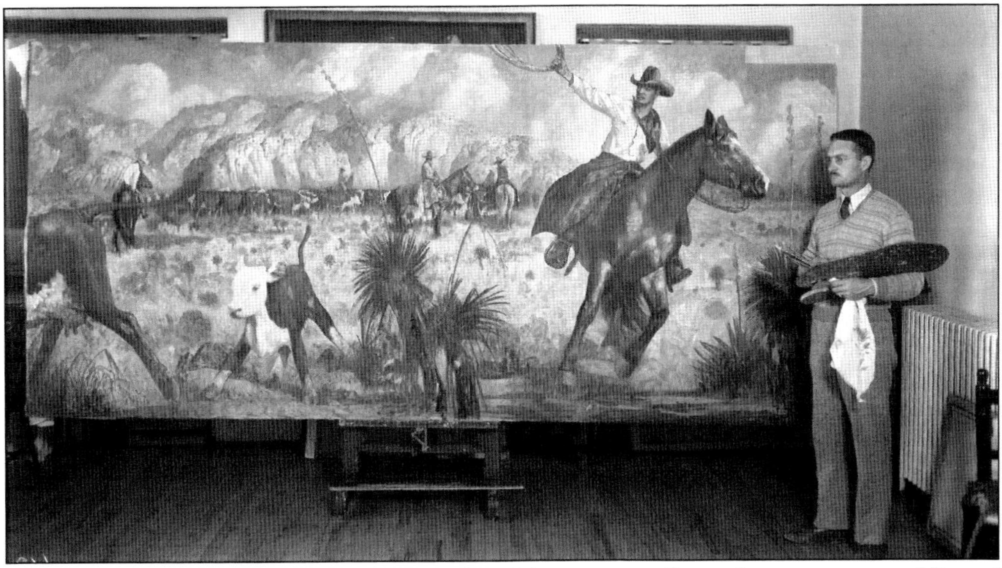

Theodore van Soelen came to New Mexico from Minnesota, suffering from pneumonia followed by tuberculosis. He met his wife, Virginia Carr, in Albuquerque in 1921. She was the daughter of a prominent cattle baron. The couple built a house in the village of Tesuque, six miles north of Santa Fe, in 1926. During the Great Depression, he was one of the artists chosen to paint a fresco at the Grant County Courthouse in Silver City, in southern New Mexico, for the WPA. (Photograph by Harmon T. Parkhurst, courtesy Palace of the Governors [NMHM/DCA], No. 073985.)

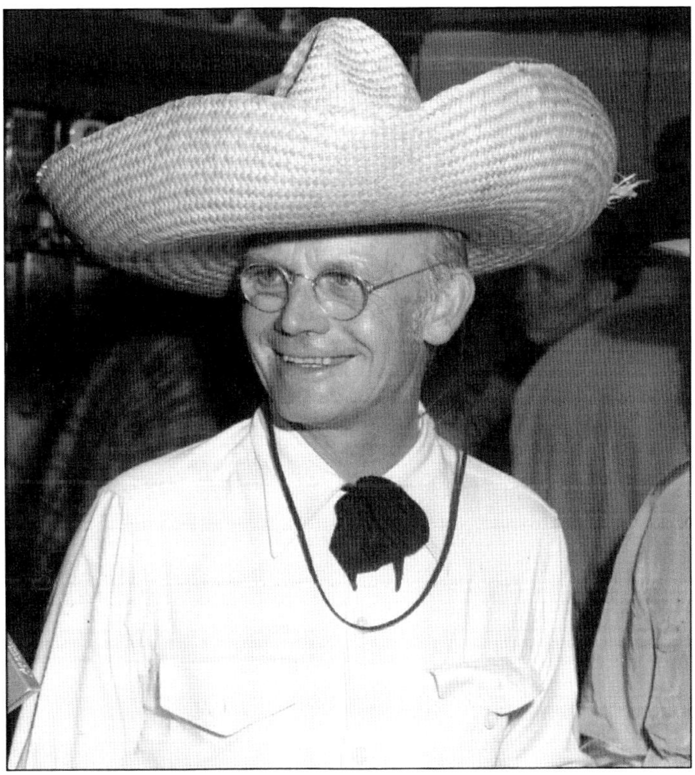

William Shuster moved to Santa Fe to recover from the mustard gas poisoning he suffered as a soldier during World War I. He became a prolific artist and member of Los Cinco Pintores, a group of five artists who had the first modern art exhibit at the Museum of New Mexico in 1917. In 1926, Shuster created Zozobra, an effigy of "Old Man Gloom" that is burned each year at the start of the Fiesta de Santa Fe. In 2007, Zozobra was certified as the largest marionette in the world by the *Guinness Book of World Records*. (Photograph by Robert H. Martin, courtesy Palace of the Governors [NMHM/DCA], No. 040201.)

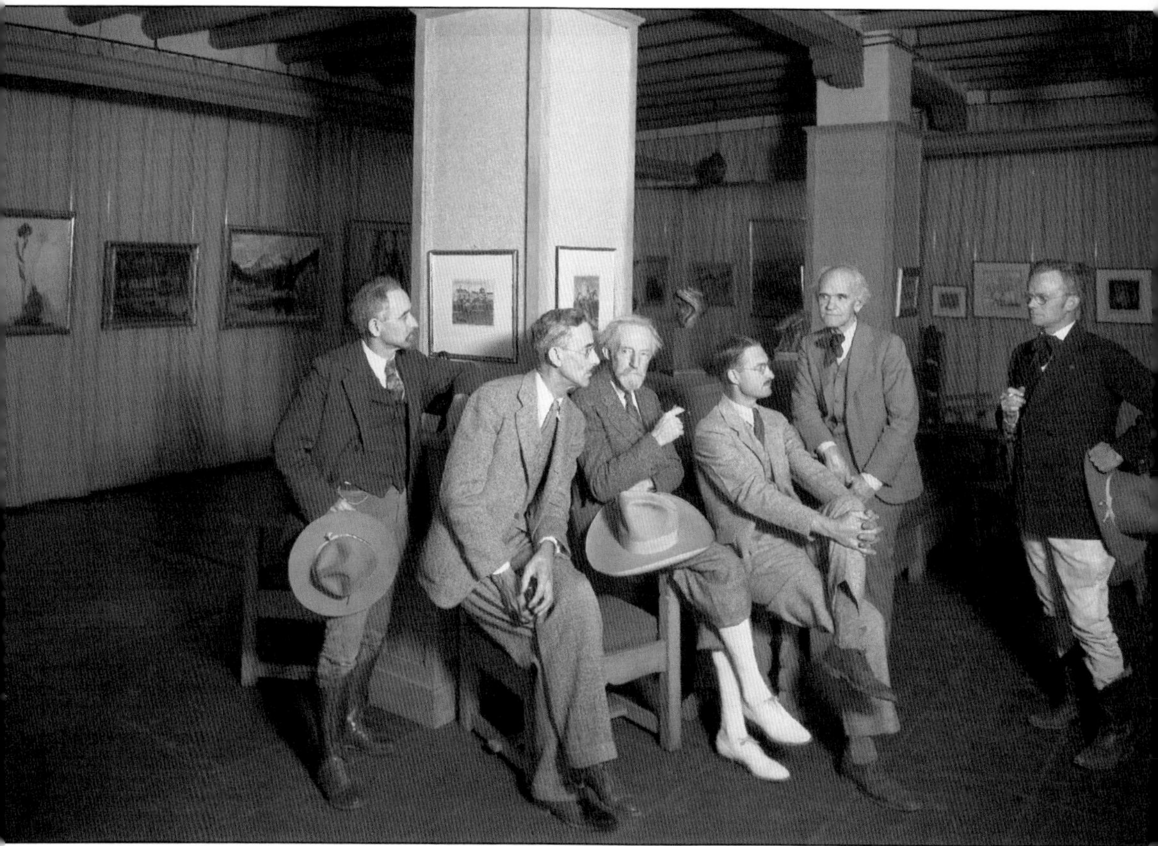

During the early part of the 20th century, many artists came to Santa Fe seeking a cure from tuberculosis. With the exception of Datus Myers, all the artists in this 1925 photograph at La Fonda Hotel had a connection to the deadly disease. From left to right are Carlos Vierra, Datus Myers, Sheldon Parsons, Theodore Van Soelen, Gerald Cassidy, and Will Shuster. (Photograph by Harmon T. Parkhurst, courtesy Palace of the Governors [NMHM/DCA], No. 020787.)

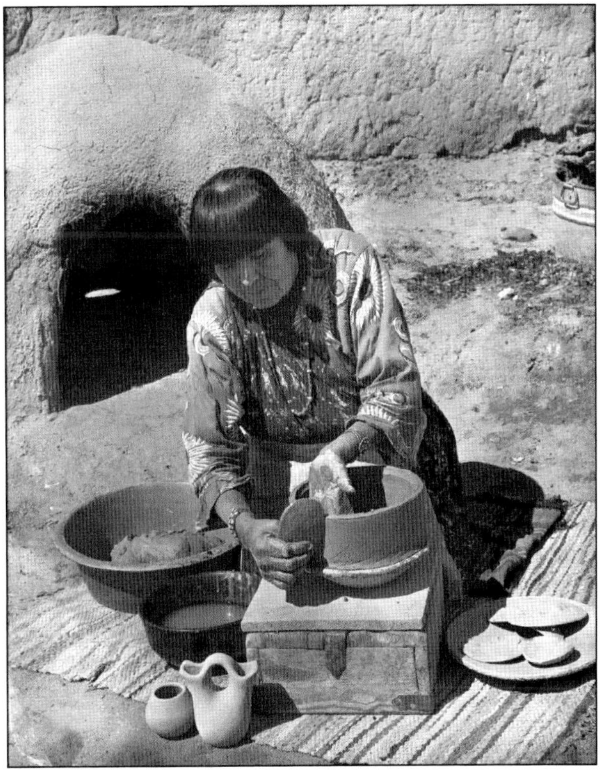

New Mexico's world-renowned potter Maria Martinez was born in 1887 at San Ildefonso Pueblo. She was instrumental in reviving the ancient technique of black-on-black pottery from the Neolithic era in the Southwest, along with her husband, Julian Martinez, and other family members. This ancient craft has become synonymous with the Pueblo people of northern New Mexico. Through her work, Maria became internationally known and continued to work on her pottery into her 90s. She died in 1980 at the age of 93. (Photograph by Tyler Dingee, courtesy Palace of the Governors [NMHM/DCA], No. 65116.)

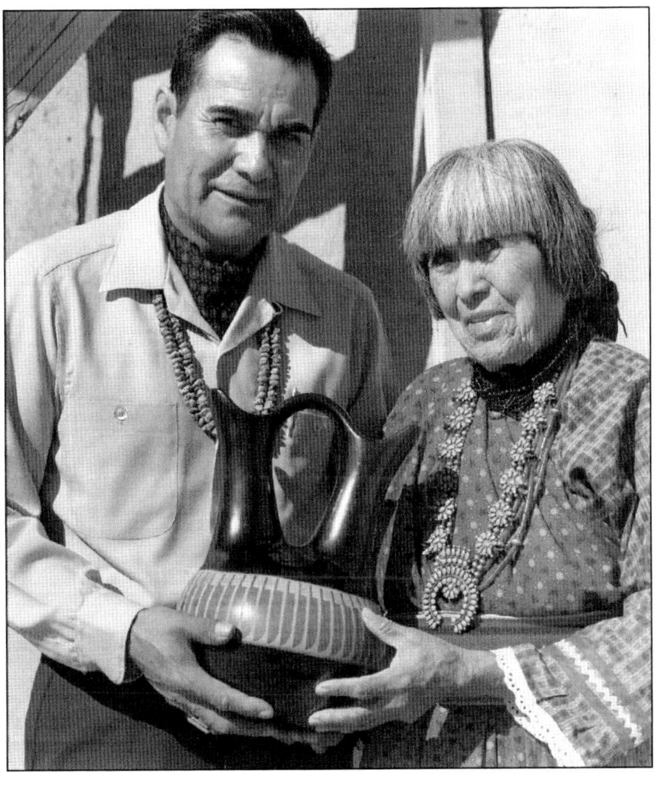

Popovi Da (Red Fox), the son Maria and Julian Martinez, was born at San Ildefonso Pueblo in 1923. As a child, he learned to make pottery from his parents, and he became a famous artist in his own right. A World War II veteran, Da assisted his mother with her clay pottery, incorporating his geometric designs. He became a governor of San Ildefonso Pueblo and chairman of the All-Indian Pueblo Council. His artwork can be found in collections around the country, including the Smithsonian American Art Museum. He died in 1971. (Photograph by Laura Gilpin, courtesy Amon Carter Museum, No. P1979.149.13.)

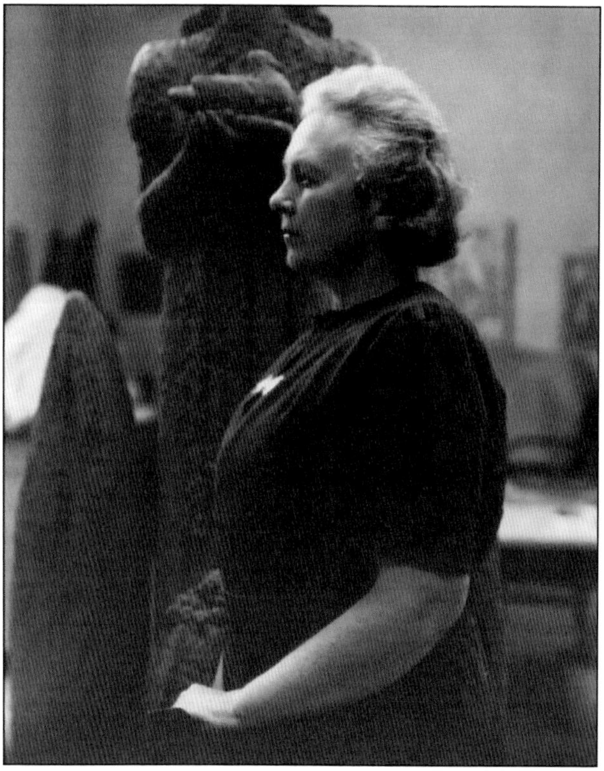

Sculptor Eugenie Shonnard was born in 1886 in Yonkers, New York. By the time she was 27, she had gone completely deaf. Because of this disability, her senses of sight and touch became more pronounced, which enabled her to pursue a successful career as a sculptor. Her work was exhibited at the Museum of Modern Art and the 1939 World's Fair in New York City. Shonnard came to Santa Fe in 1927 at the invitation of Edgar Lee Hewett, the founder of the Museum of New Mexico. Hewett felt that her previous work showed she was ideally suited to sculpt Native Americans. Shonnard felt an immediate connection to the land and its people. She befriended many Native Americans, including Maria Martinez. She was present at the birth of Maria's son, Popovi Da. (Photograph by Laura Gilpin, courtesy Amon Carter Museum, No. P1979.92.28.)

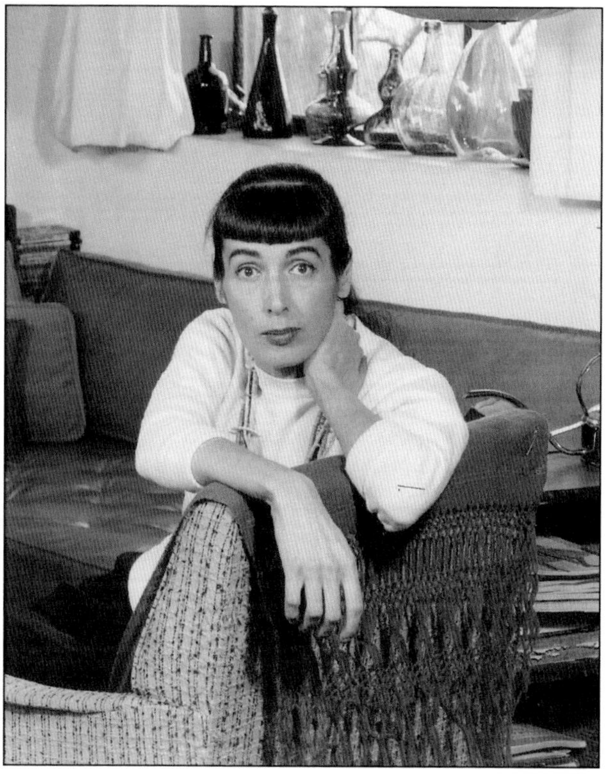

Bernique Longley was an art student at the Chicago Institute of Art in 1946 when she made a life-changing move. During a refueling stop at the Santa Fe airport, the artist fell head over heels in love with Santa Fe and moved to town. Longley spent the rest of her life capturing the essence of the native people in her color portraits. Her paintings have been exhibited at the Museum of New Mexico, the Colorado Springs Fine Arts Center, and the Dallas Museum of Art. The prolific artist continued to paint until her death in 1999. (Photograph by Laura Gilpin, courtesy Amon Carter Museum, No. P1978.48.1.)

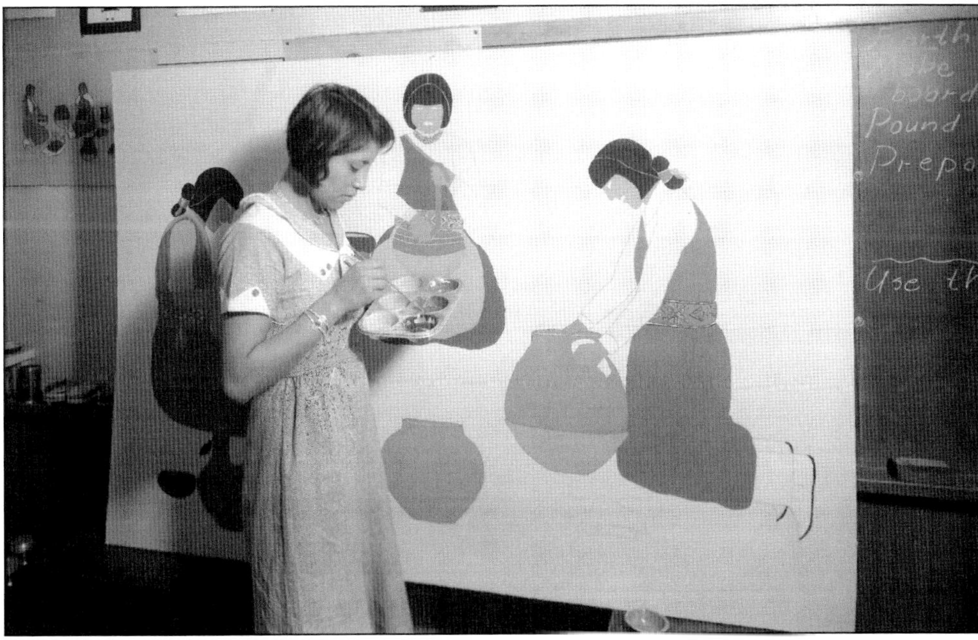

Pablita Velarde was born in 1918 at Santa Clara Pueblo in northern New Mexico. When she was 14, she attended the Dorothy Dunn Studio, the fine arts program at the Santa Fe Indian School. Velarde was one of the first female Native American artists of the 20th century. Early in her career as an artist, she transitioned from watercolor paintings to creating her own natural pigment paints. She sought these materials from the rich mineral and rock deposits in the mountains surrounding her pueblo. (Photograph by Harmon T. Parkhurst, courtesy Palace of the Governors [NMHM/DCA], No. 073942.)

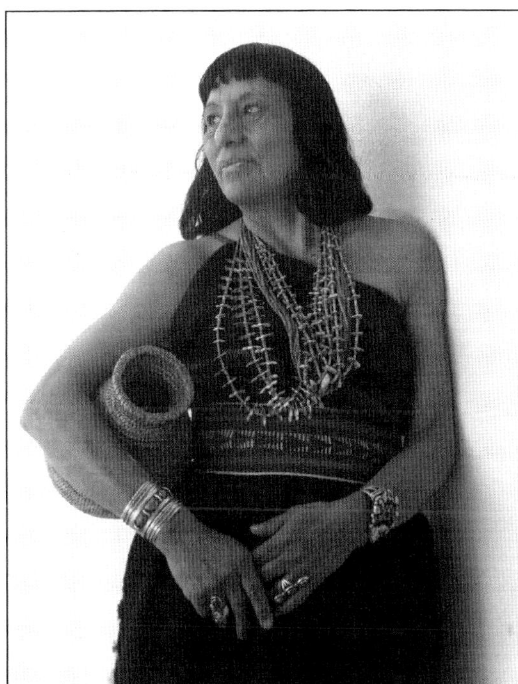

The depictions of Pueblo life by Pablita Velarde can be found at the museum at Bandelier National Monument in northern New Mexico. Her work has been exhibited at the Smithsonian Institution and throughout the United States. Velarde has been honored in the United States and in France, where she received the Palmes Académiques award for excellence in art in 1954. She died in 2006 at the age of 88. (Photograph by Laura Gilpin, courtesy Amon Carter Museum, No. P1979.133.87.)

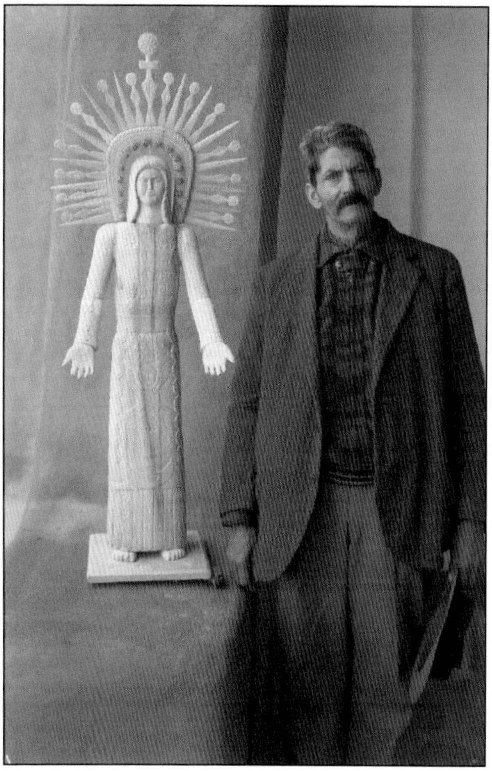

José Dolores López, a native of the village of Córdova in northern New Mexico, was one of the early Hispanic sculptors. *Our Lady of Light*, featured in this picture with the artist, was created during the Great Depression for the WPA. That piece, along with his sculpture *Adam and Eve*, was exhibited at the Corcoran Gallery of Art in 1934 in Washington, DC. Pres. Franklin D. Roosevelt and his wife, Eleanor, made a special visit to the gallery to see the work, which was made possible through one of Roosevelt's New Deal projects. (Photograph by Harmon T. Parkhurst, courtesy Palace of the Governors [NMHM/DCA], No. 094470.)

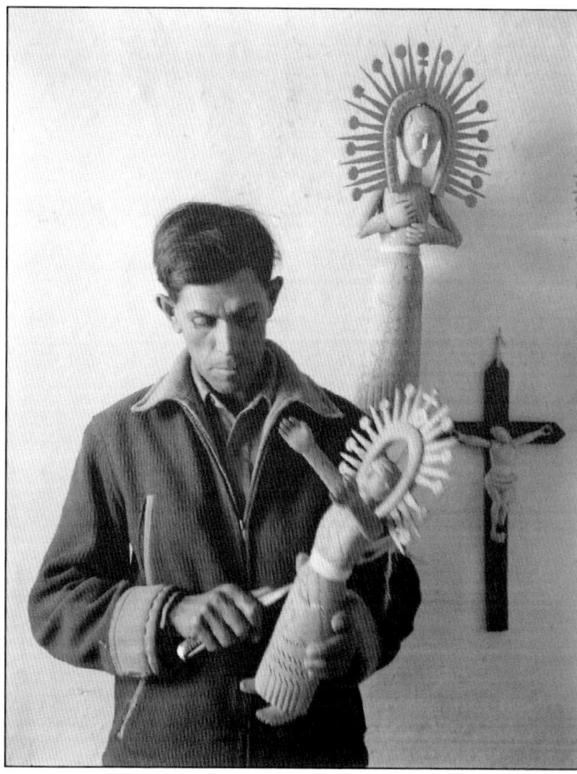

George López, the son of José Dolores López, was a sixth-generation woodcarver. In 1982, he received the National Endowment for the Arts National Heritage Award for his work as a sculptor and wood carver of religious santos. During World War II, he worked at Los Alamos National Laboratory. In 1952, he left that job and devoted his life to woodcarving and mentoring the younger generations in his village of Córdova. (Photograph by Laura Gilpin, courtesy Amon Carter Museum, No. P1979.202.222.)

Alfred Morang (far right) contracted tuberculosis and moved to Santa Fe in 1937 to take advantage of the arid climate. When he recovered, he became a member of the Transcendental Painting Group, along with artists Raymond Jonson, William Lumpkins, and Emil Bisttram. Together these young artists began a movement that embodied the world of abstract art and attracted national attention. Morang died tragically in 1958 in a fire in his art studio on Canyon Road. (Photograph by Robert H. Martin, courtesy Palace of the Governors [NMHM/DCA], No. 041228.)

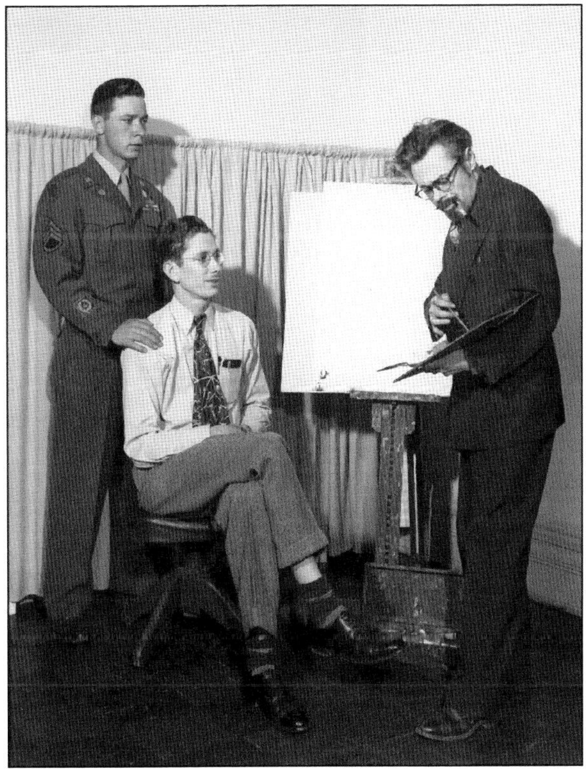

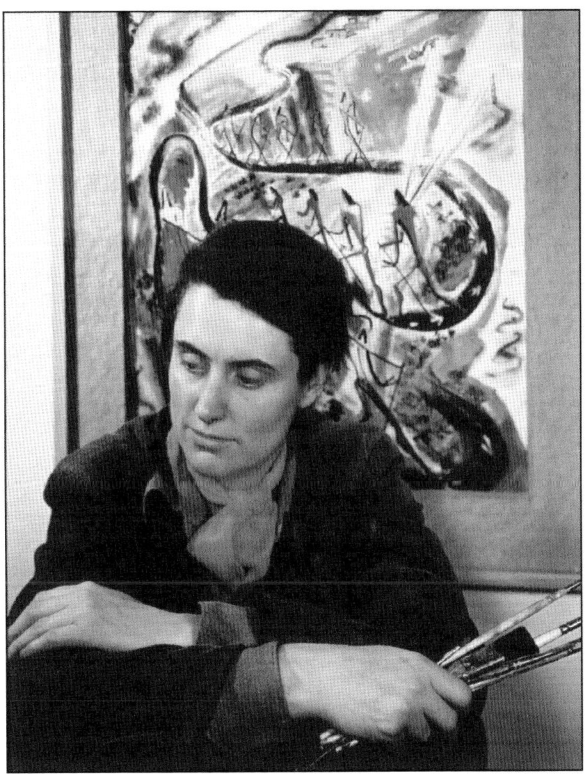

Agnes Sims was born in Devon, Pennsylvania, where she attended the Academy of Fine Art and the Philadelphia School of Design for Women. Her art has been featured at the Brooklyn Museum and the US embassy in London. After a visit to Santa Fe in 1938, she went back to Philadelphia for her things and devoted the rest of her life to capturing the prehistoric rock art of New Mexico and indigenous life through her mixed-media art and sculptures. Her work depicting the petroglyphs of the Galisteo Basin was published as the book *San Cristobal Petroglyphs* in 1950. Sims died in 1990 at the age of 80. (Photograph by Laura Gilpin, courtesy Amon Carter Museum, No. P1979.149.40.)

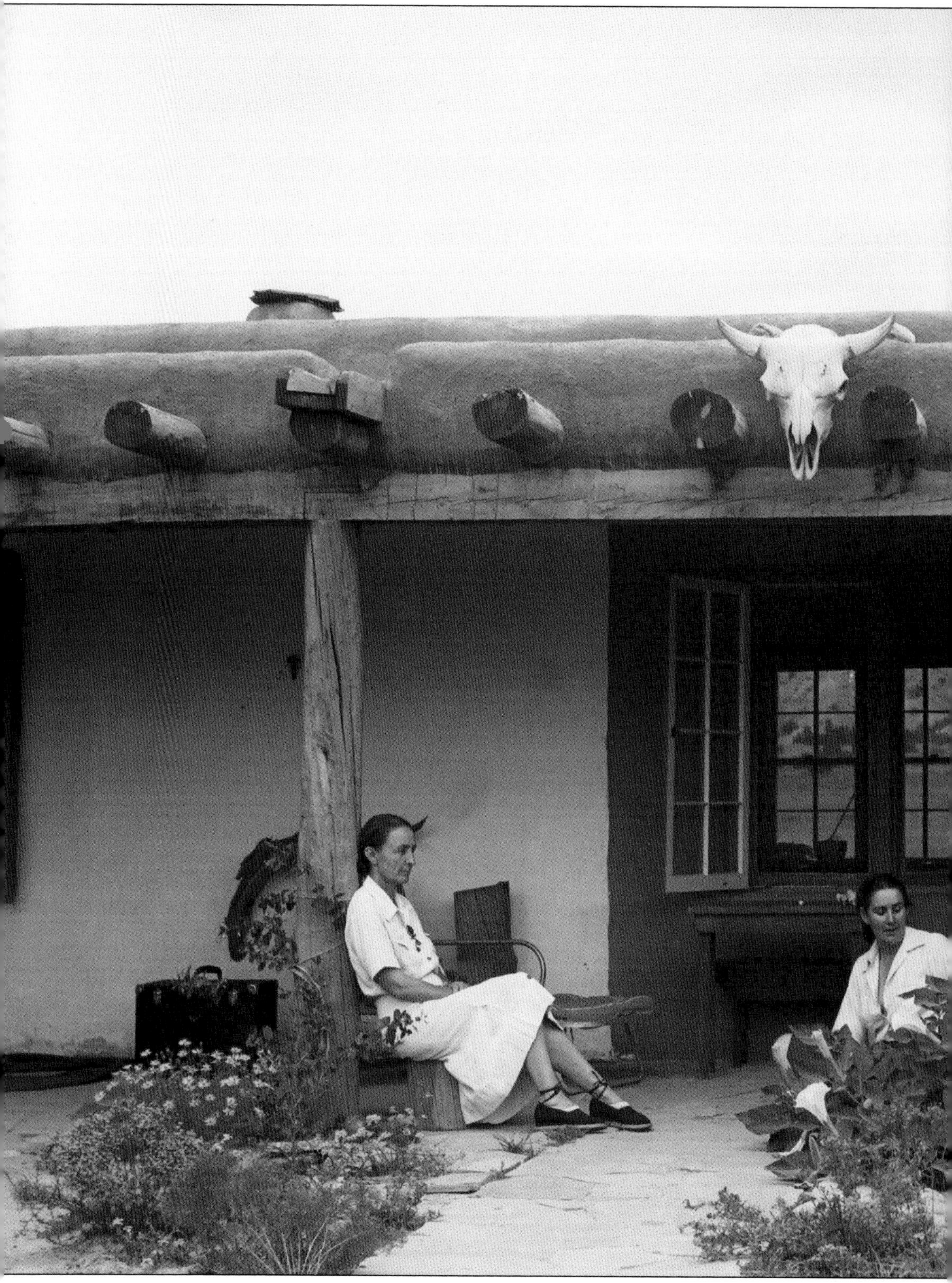

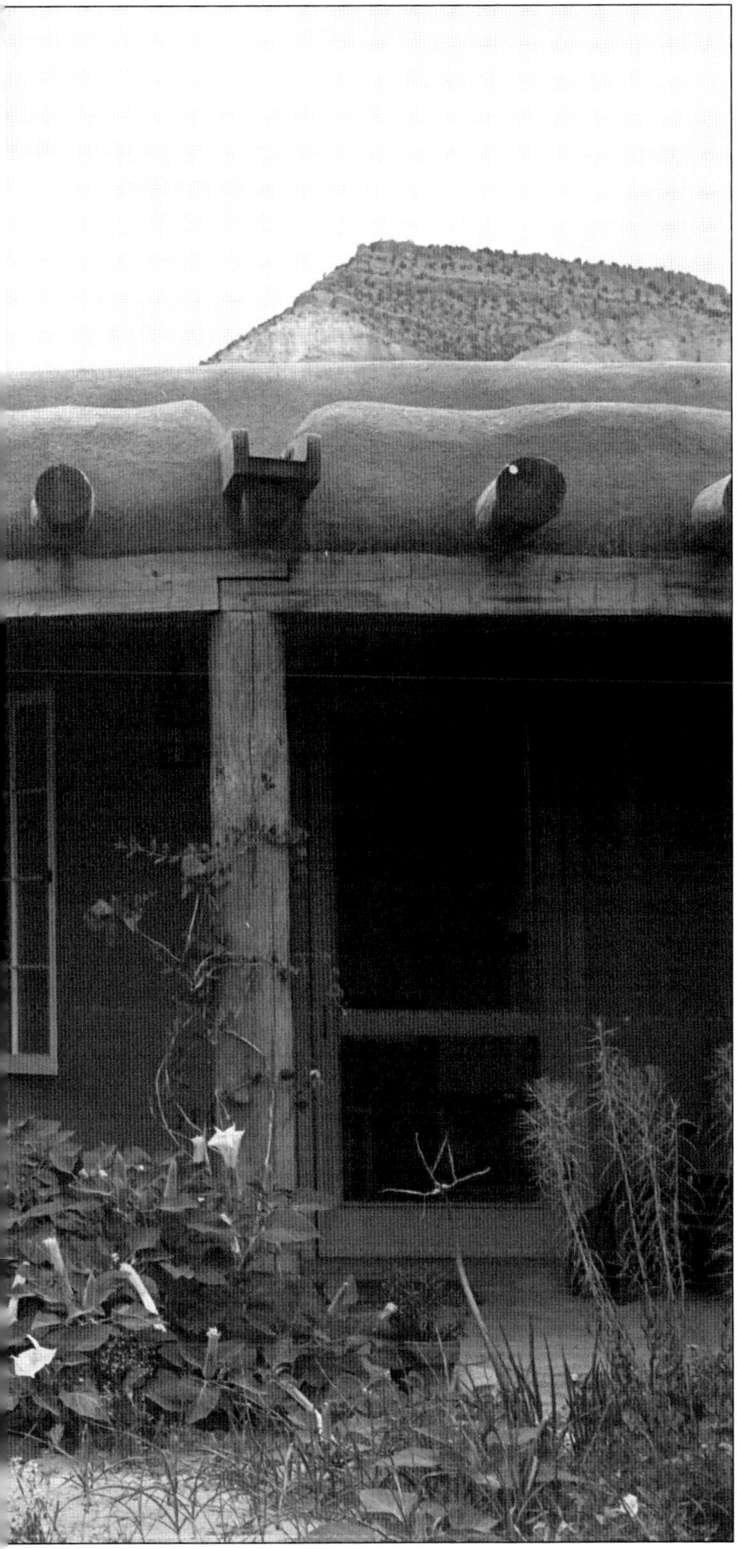

Georgia O'Keeffe (left) is pictured with her friend Maria Chabot on her porch in 1942. The bovine skull decorating the top of her portal was one of many skulls she painted throughout her career, which has become synonymous with the landscape of New Mexico. Her paintings of skulls and flowers are recognized throughout the world. From 1940 until her death in 1986, she lived at her home in the village of Abiquiu in northern New Mexico. Her home was located on a 21,000-acre property known as Ghost Ranch, which is now owned by the Presbyterian Church. Seen in the background is Pedernal Mountain, where O'Keeffe's ashes were scattered after her death. Her home and studio became a national historic landmark in 1998. (Photograph by John Candelario, courtesy Palace of the Governors [NMHM/DCA], No. 165668.)

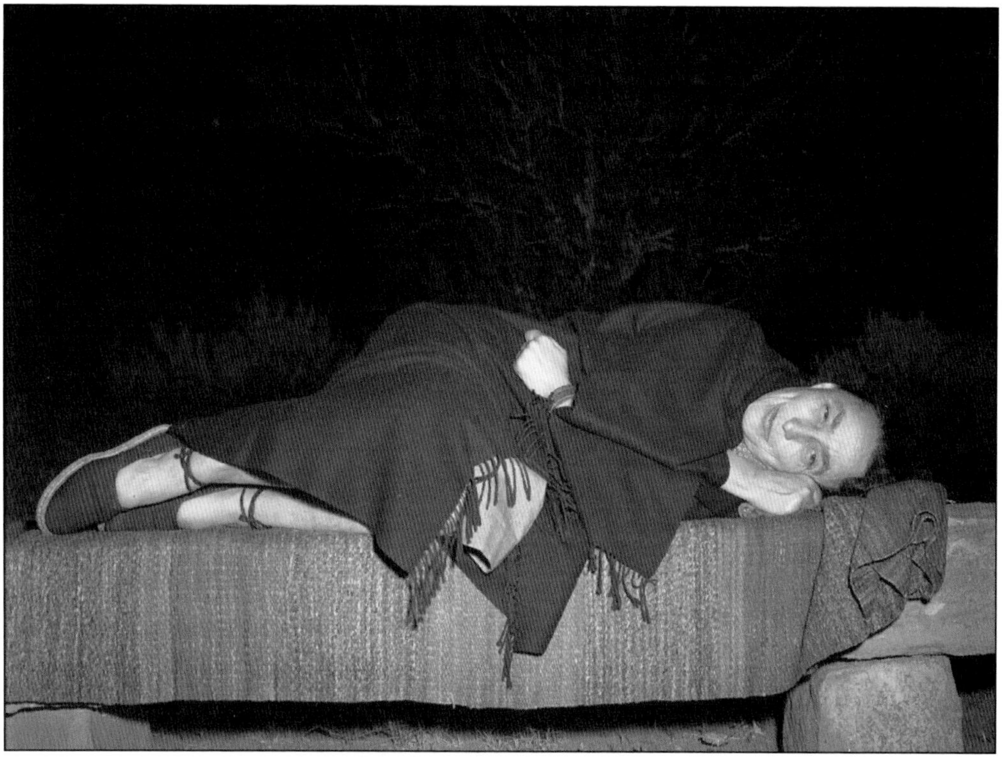

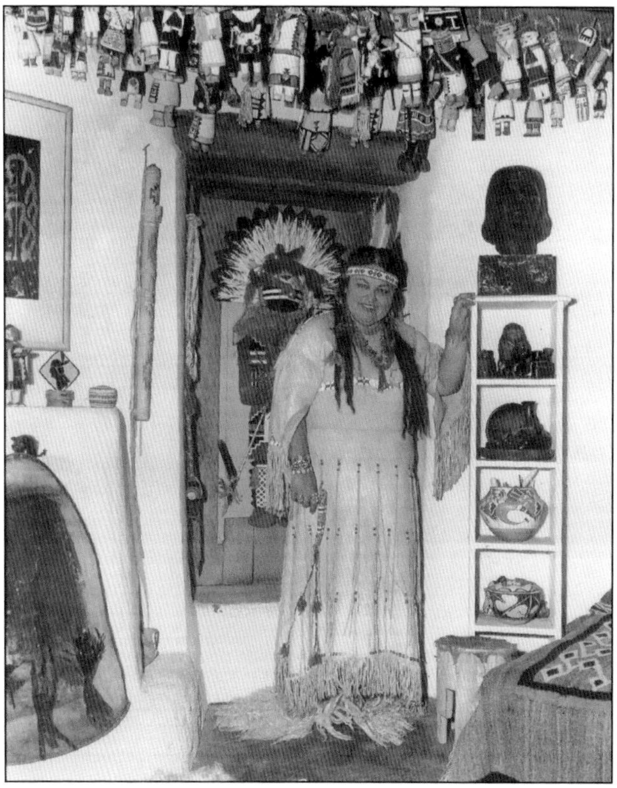

Georgia O'Keeffe reclines on a bench during a camping trip at Ghost Ranch. In 1997, the Georgia O'Keeffe Museum opened in Santa Fe. It is one of the only major museums in the world named for a female artist. (Photograph by John Candelario, courtesy Palace of the Governors [NMHM/DCA], No. 165656.)

Pansy Stockton moved to Santa Fe in 1942 and became active in the local art scene. Her work included the use of hundreds of plant fragments. An advocate for Native Americans, she was formally adopted by the Ogallala Sioux tribe in 1936 for her work on the tribe's land rights. (Photograph by Robert H. Martin, author's collection.)

Seven

War and Remembrance

Remnants of war have defined the history of Santa Fe since its founding. In 1610, the Presidio de la Santa Cruz, the large military barracks and horse corrals adjacent to the Palace of the Governors, was built. Directly across the street, *la castrense*, the military chapel, was added for the soldiers. In 1846, the US Army built Fort Marcy at the western end of the Santa Fe Trail. Named after Secretary of War William Marcy, it was the first US Army fort in New Mexico. The Mormon Battalion Monument, 25 miles from Santa Fe, is a memorial to the only religion-based squadron in the history of the United States, which entered Santa Fe in 1846 with Brig. Gen. Stephen Watts Kearny. A battle of the American Civil War was fought 20 miles from Santa Fe at Glorieta on March 26, 1862. In 1898, volunteers were recruited from the area for Roosevelt's Rough Riders for the Spanish-American War.

In all of Santa Fe's history, one defining event during World War II reverberates even today. The Manhattan Project military checkpoint was located just off the plaza at 109 East Palace Avenue. Military personnel, scientists, contractors, janitors, and everyone involved with the creation of the world's first atomic bomb had to register there. The only address for the Manhattan Project was PO Box 1663, Santa Fe, New Mexico.

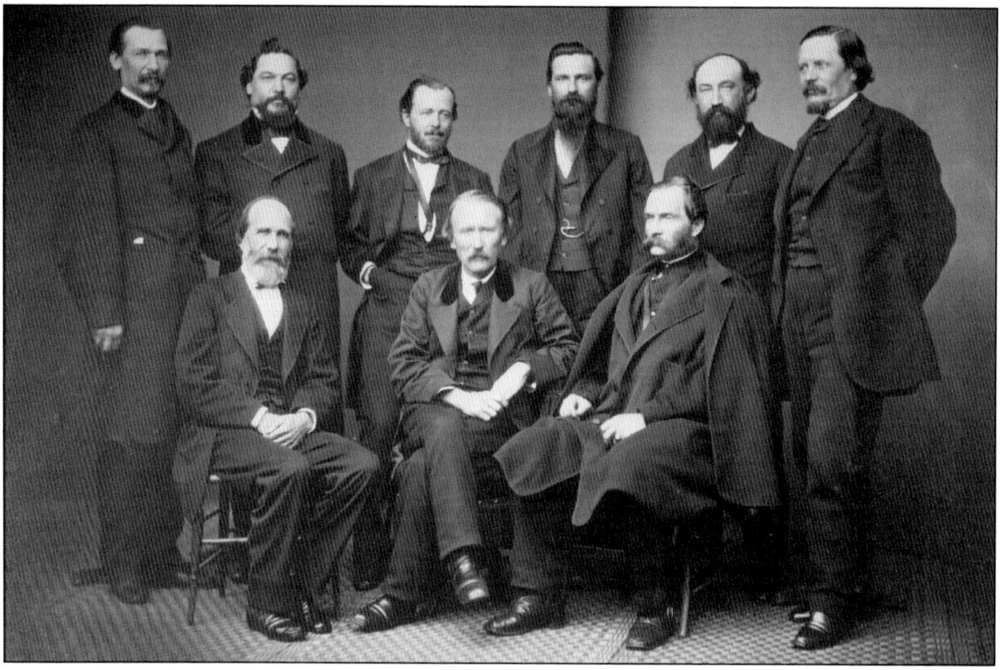

This 1866 photograph shows military personnel in a group portrait at the Masonic temple in Santa Fe. All of these officers were veterans of both the Mexican-American War and the Civil War. From left to right are (seated) Col. D.H. Rucker, Kit Carson, and Bvt. Brig. Gen. James Carleton; (standing) Col. E.H. Bergmann, delegate Charles P. Clever, Col. Nelson H. Davis, Col. Herbert M. Enos, surgeon Basil K. Norris, and Col. J.C. McFerran. (Photograph by Nicholas Brown, courtesy Palace of the Governors [NMHM/DCA], No. 009826.)

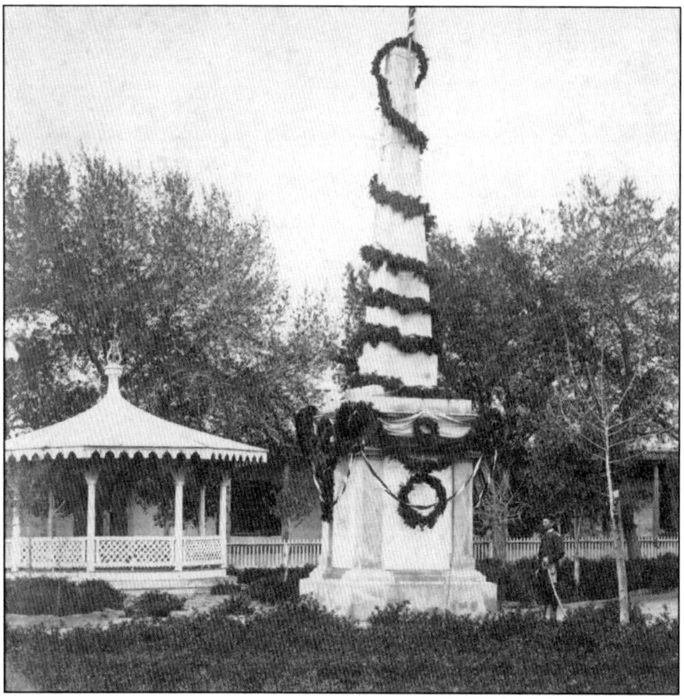

The Soldiers Monument on the Santa Fe Plaza was dedicated in 1868. It is the oldest monument commemorating the Civil War in New Mexico. Often referred to as the Gettysburg of the West, New Mexico saw Civil War fighting in February and March 1862. (Photograph by Nicholas Brown, courtesy Palace of the Governors [NMHM/DCA], No. HP.1974.25.21.)

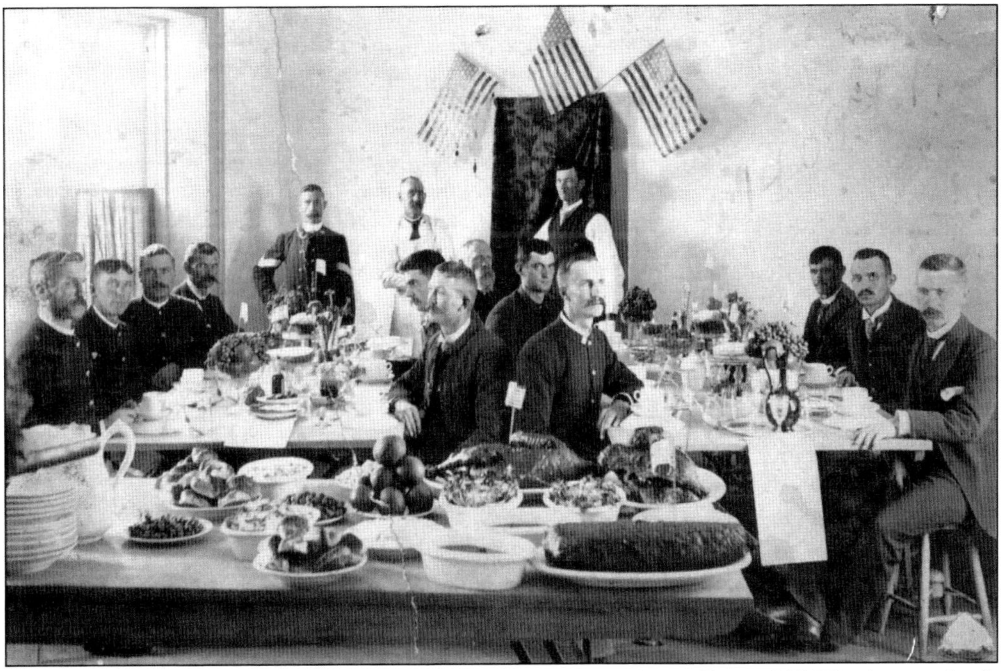

Officers gather at the banquet headquarters at Fort Marcy in Santa Fe in 1887. The fort was built in 1846 for Brig. Gen. Stephen Watts Kearny, who brought 2,500 soldiers to claim New Mexico for the United States. Part of Kearny's contingent included the Mormon Battalion, the only religious-based unit in US history. Fort Marcy served as a military outpost through the end of the 19th century. (Courtesy Palace of the Governors [NMHM/DCA], No. 01706.)

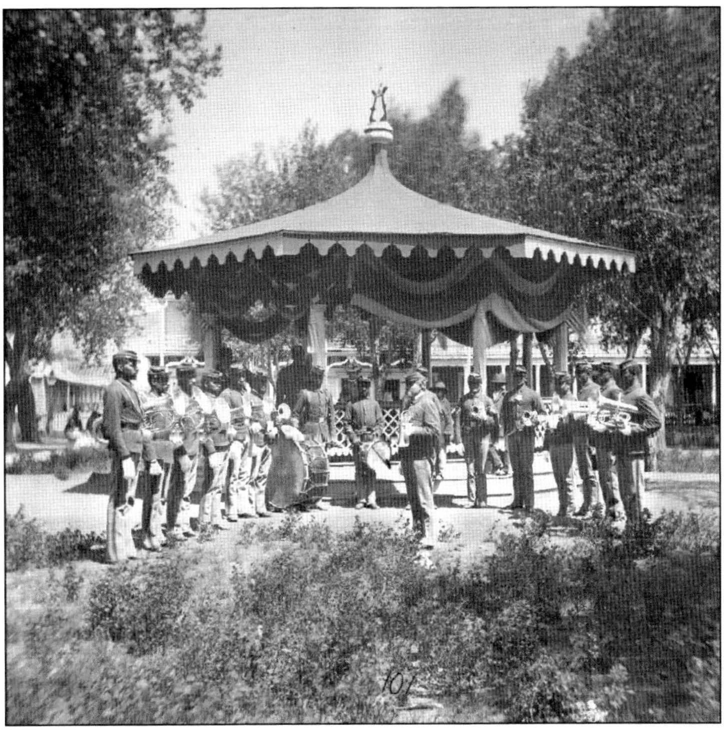

The 9th Cavalry Band plays on the Santa Fe Plaza in 1880. This division of the US Army was one of the few African American contingents that served during the Indian and Spanish-American Wars. Also referred to as Buffalo Soldiers, they provided protection to settlers from marauding Indians and Mexican bandits in their expansion westward. (Photograph by Ben Wittick, courtesy Palace of the Governors [NMHM/DCA], No. 050887.)

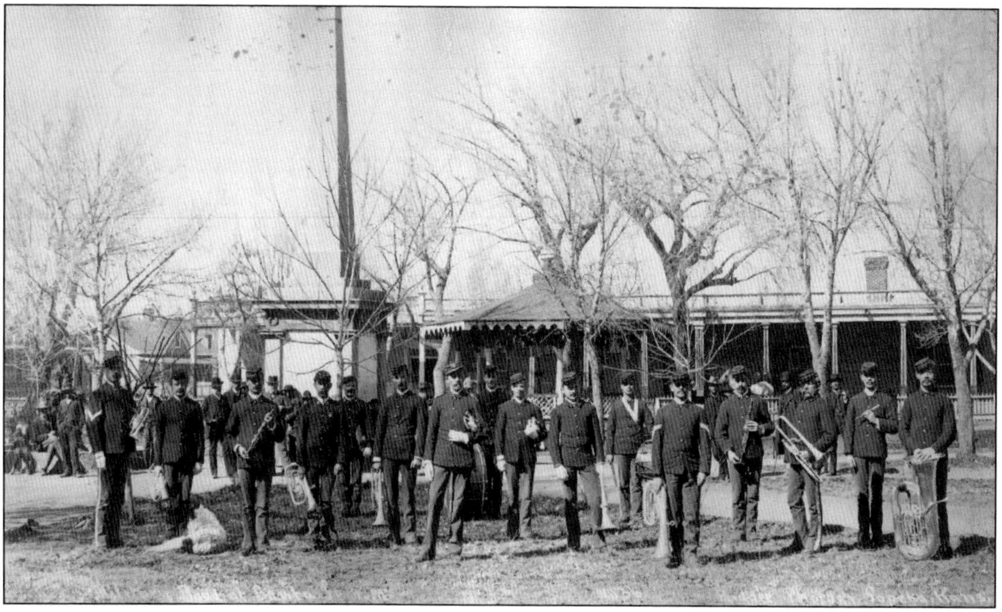

Herman Trutner leads the 13th US Infantry Band in its performance on the plaza in front of the Palace of the Governors. Formed in 1901, the regiment protected the border with Mexico through 1921. (Photograph by James R. Riddle, courtesy Palace of the Governors [NMHM/DCA], No. 001705.)

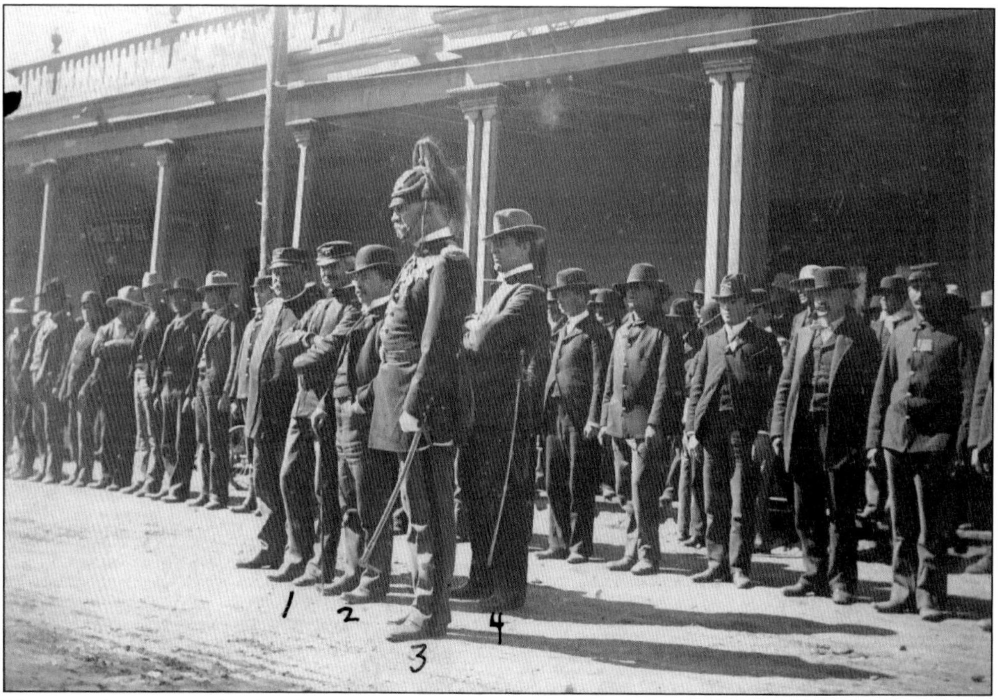

The 1st Volunteer US Cavalry is sworn in by Capt. Charles L. Cooper in front of the Palace of the Governors in 1898. Later called Roosevelt's Rough Riders, it fought during the Spanish-American War. (Photograph by C.G. Kaadt, courtesy Palace of the Governors [NMHM/DCA], No. 006051.)

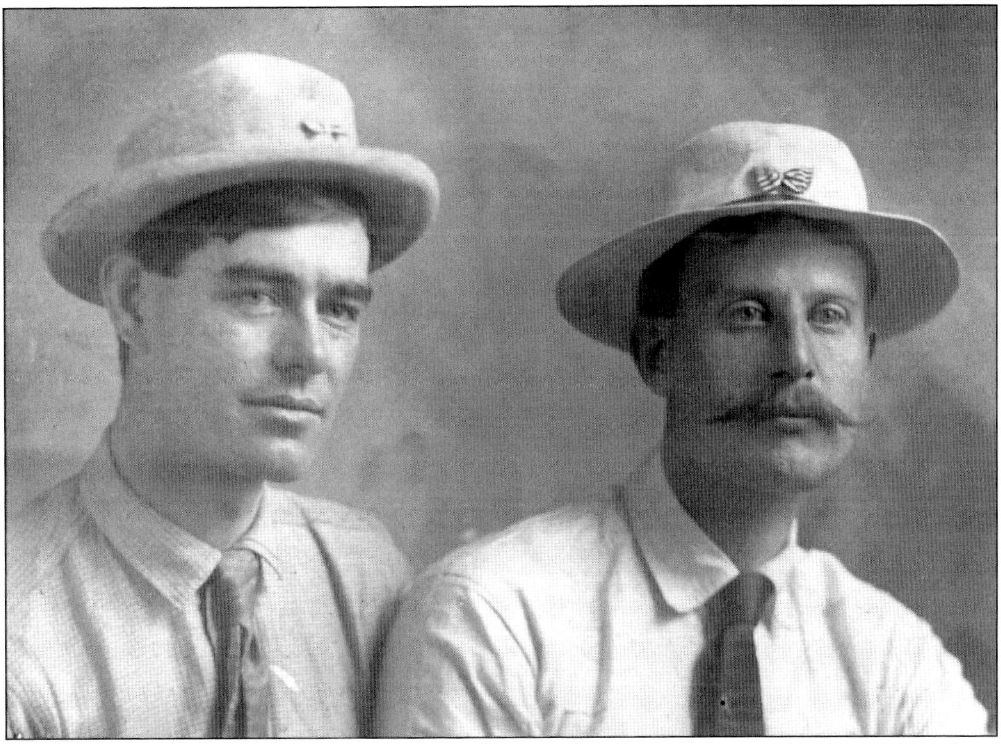

Dunkle (left) and Barber, members of Roosevelt's Rough Riders, are pictured in Santa Fe on June 24, 1898. Part of this regiment was comprised of volunteers from New Mexico, Arizona, Texas, and Oklahoma. (Courtesy Palace of the Governors [NMHM/DCA], No. 008259.)

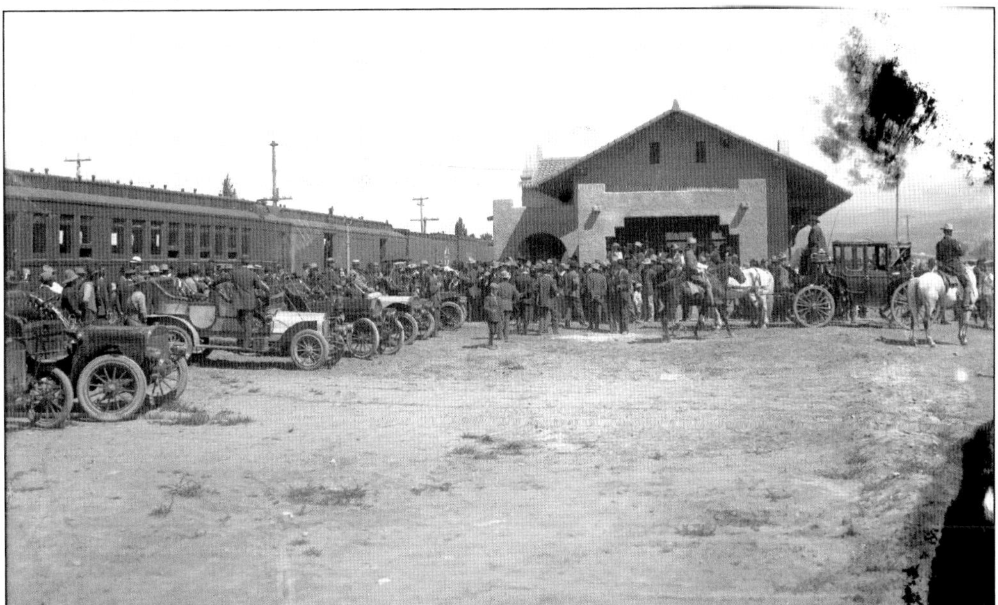

Military personnel gather at the Santa Fe railroad depot in 1913, one year after statehood and the beginning of the Mexican Revolution. (Photograph by Jesse Nusbaum, courtesy Palace of the Governors [NMHM/DCA], No. 06143.)

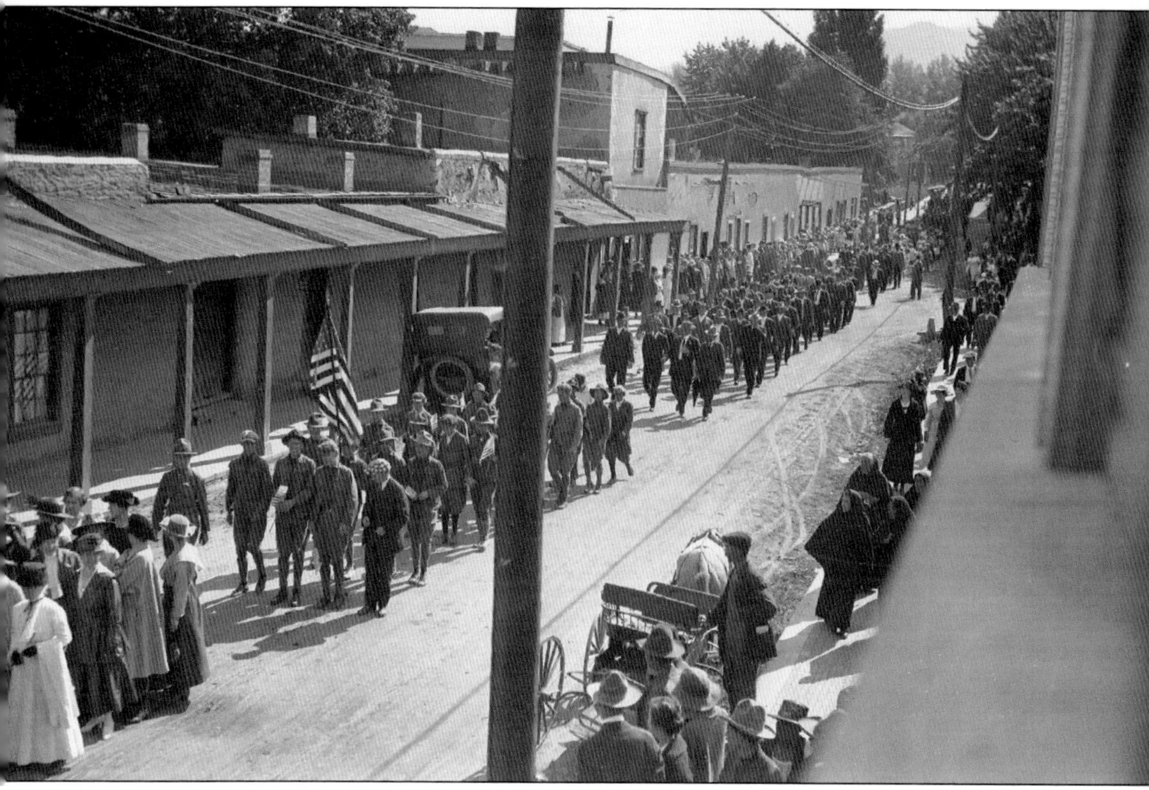

The community of Santa Fe bids farewell to its sons in this 1917 photograph on Palace Avenue. They were being sent to Europe to fight in World War I, while others would be heading to protect the border during the Mexican Revolution. (Photograph by William H. Roberts, courtesy Palace of the Governors [NMHM/DCA], No. 149995.)

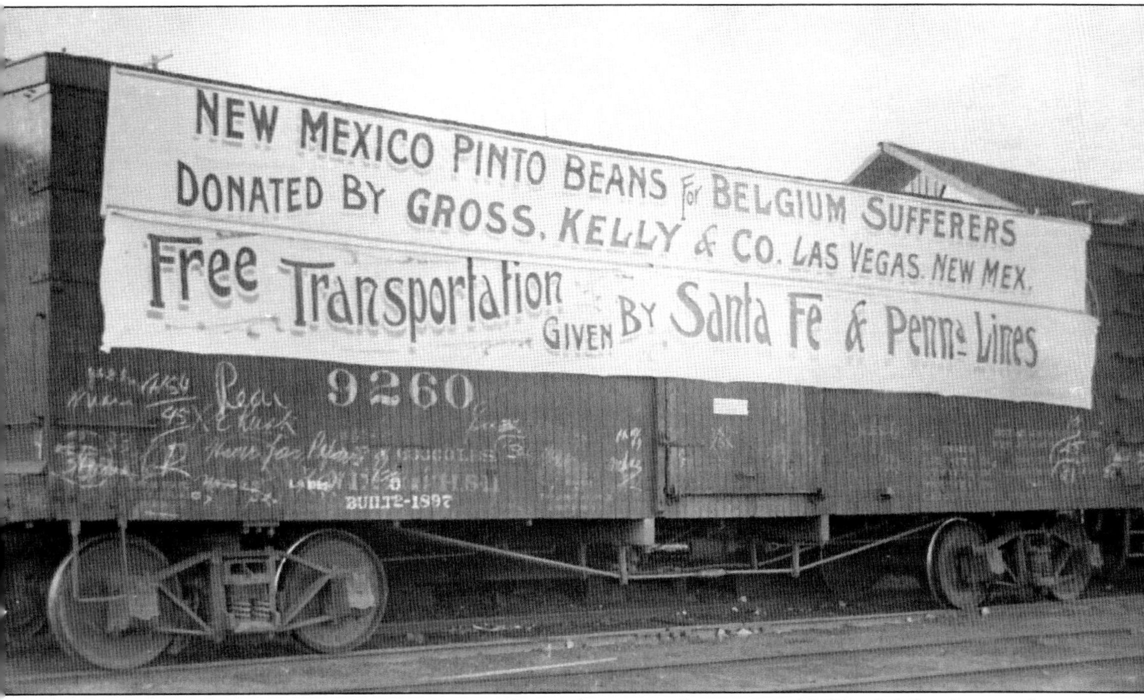

Throughout New Mexico, merchants were doing their part during World War I. The dry goods merchants Gross-Kelly shipped pinto beans to support the troops in 1917. The Gross-Kelly mercantile business was started in 1895 by Jacob Gross and Harry Kelly. The two men met while working in Kansas for Miguel Otero of the Otero Seller Company, which distributed products along the Atchison, Topeka & Santa Fe Railway. They bought the business and opened stores in railroad towns throughout New Mexico that operated until 1954. (Courtesy Palace of the Governors [NMHM/DCA], No. 04196.)

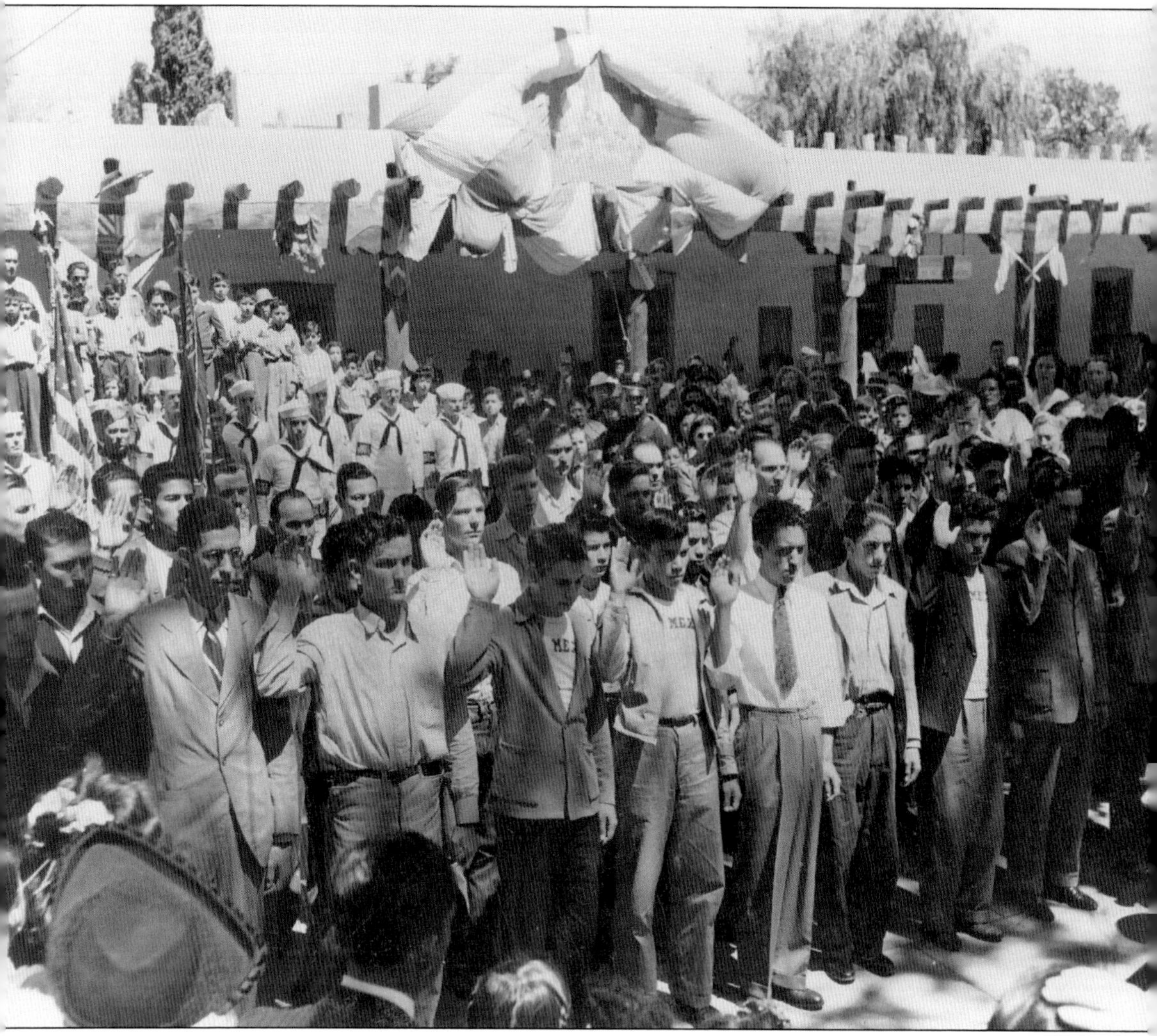

After the December 7, 1941, bombing at Pearl Harbor, the nation's young men and women were beckoned to protect the country. This photograph was taken during the Fiesta de Santa Fe in 1942 as young men were being inducted into the Navy in front of the Palace of the Governors. (Courtesy Palace of the Governors [NMHM/DCA], No. HP.2007.20.410.)

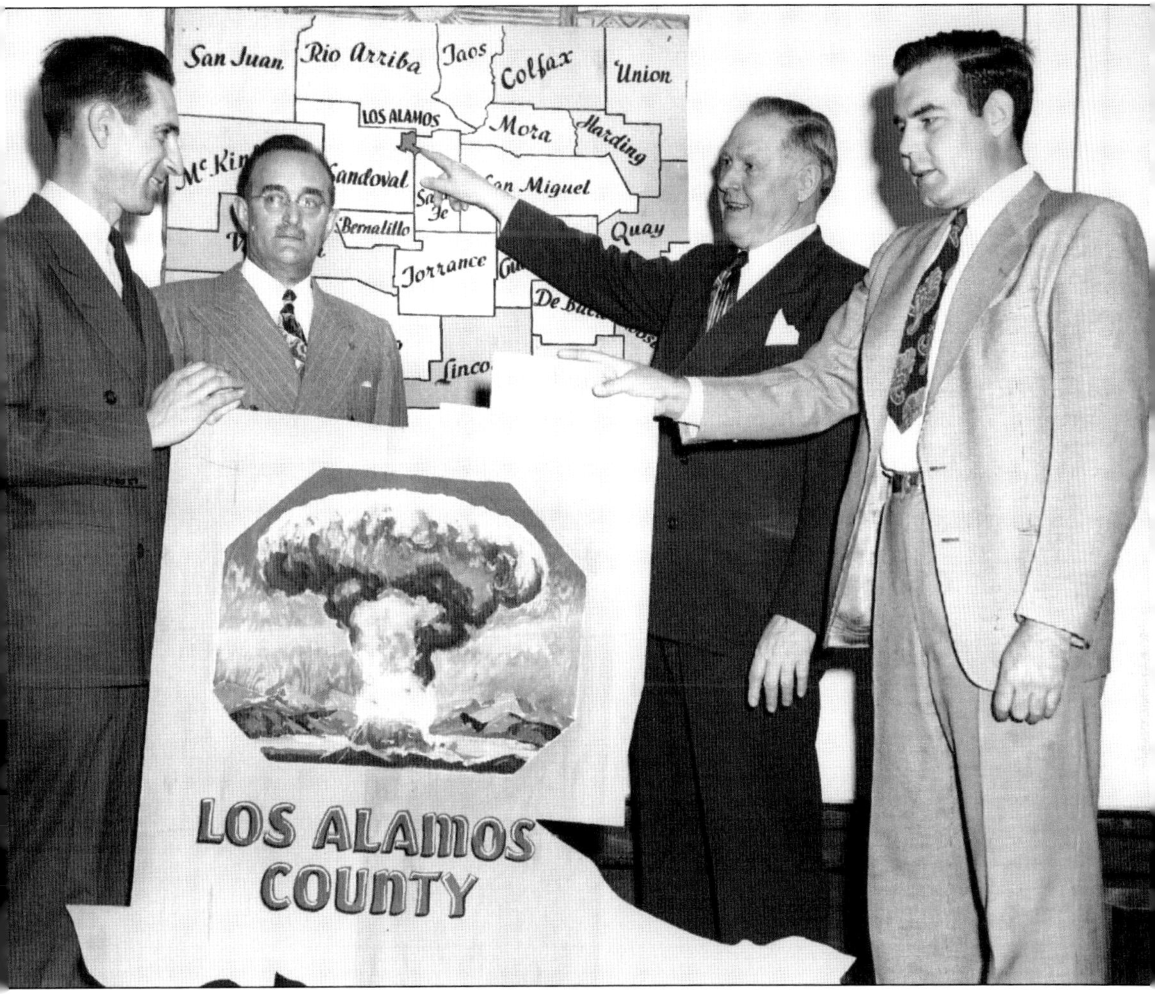

New Mexico governor Thomas J. Mabry (second from right) enthusiastically promoted Los Alamos County, where the first atomic bomb was assembled 30 miles from Santa Fe. Situated on the Pajarito Plateau and surrounded by four mesas, Los Alamos was the ideal clandestine location for the Manhattan Project during World War II. (Photograph by Harold D. Walter, courtesy Palace of the Governors [NMHM/DCA], No. 053108.)

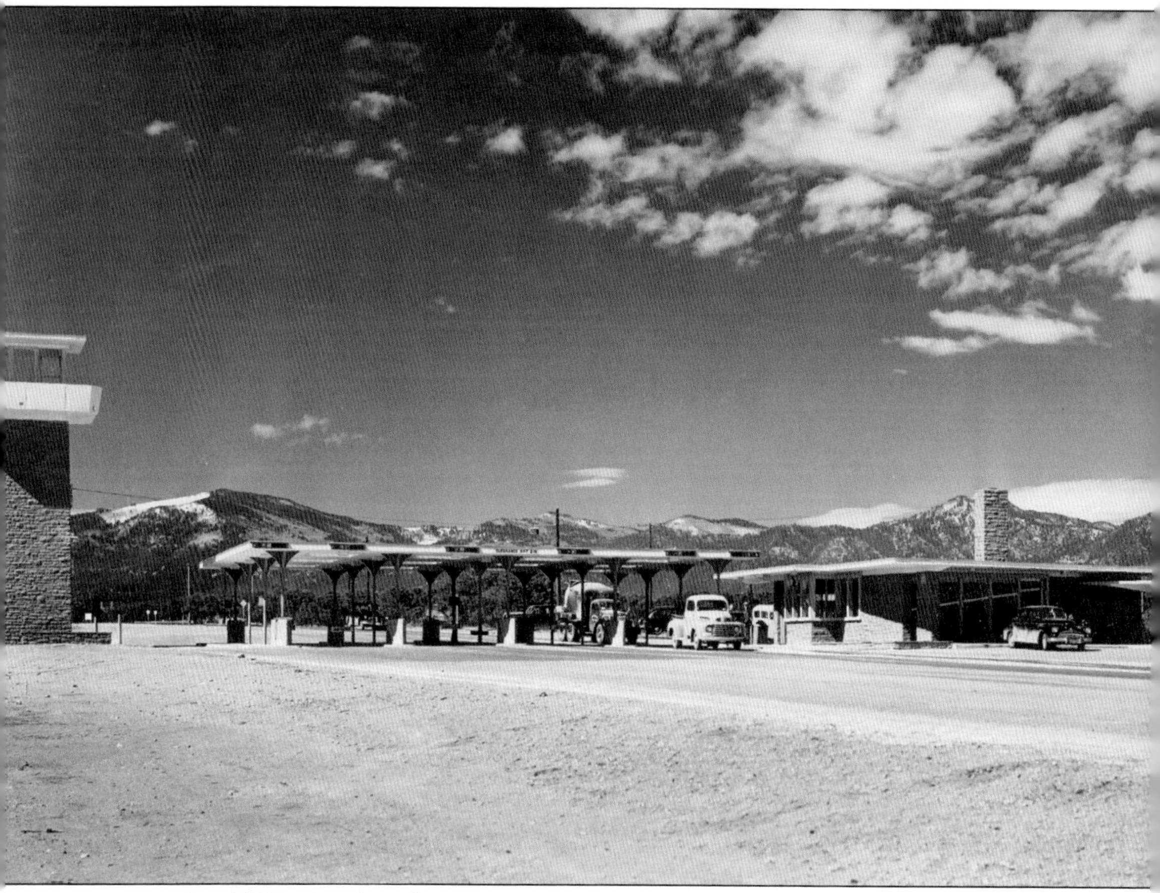

During World War II, only authorized personnel could enter the Los Alamos National Laboratory, so a military checkpoint was erected at the entrance. Family members who wanted to visit loved ones working at the lab needed government approval. (Photograph by Matthew J. O'Keefe, courtesy Palace of the Governors [NMHM/DCA], No. 059323.)

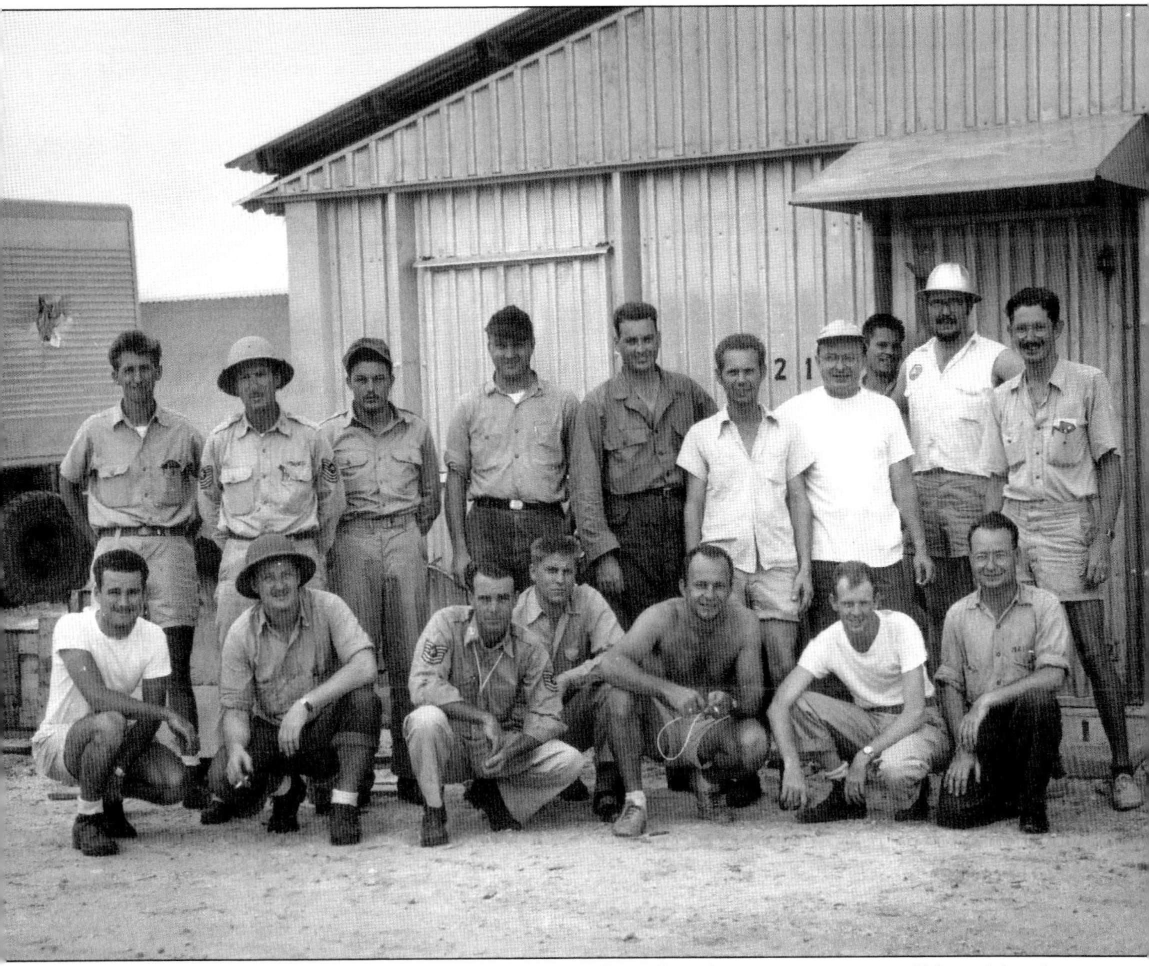

Scientists from Los Alamos National Laboratory conducted nuclear weapon tests at Bikini Island in 1949. The photographer Robert H. Martin is standing on the far right. (Author's collection.)

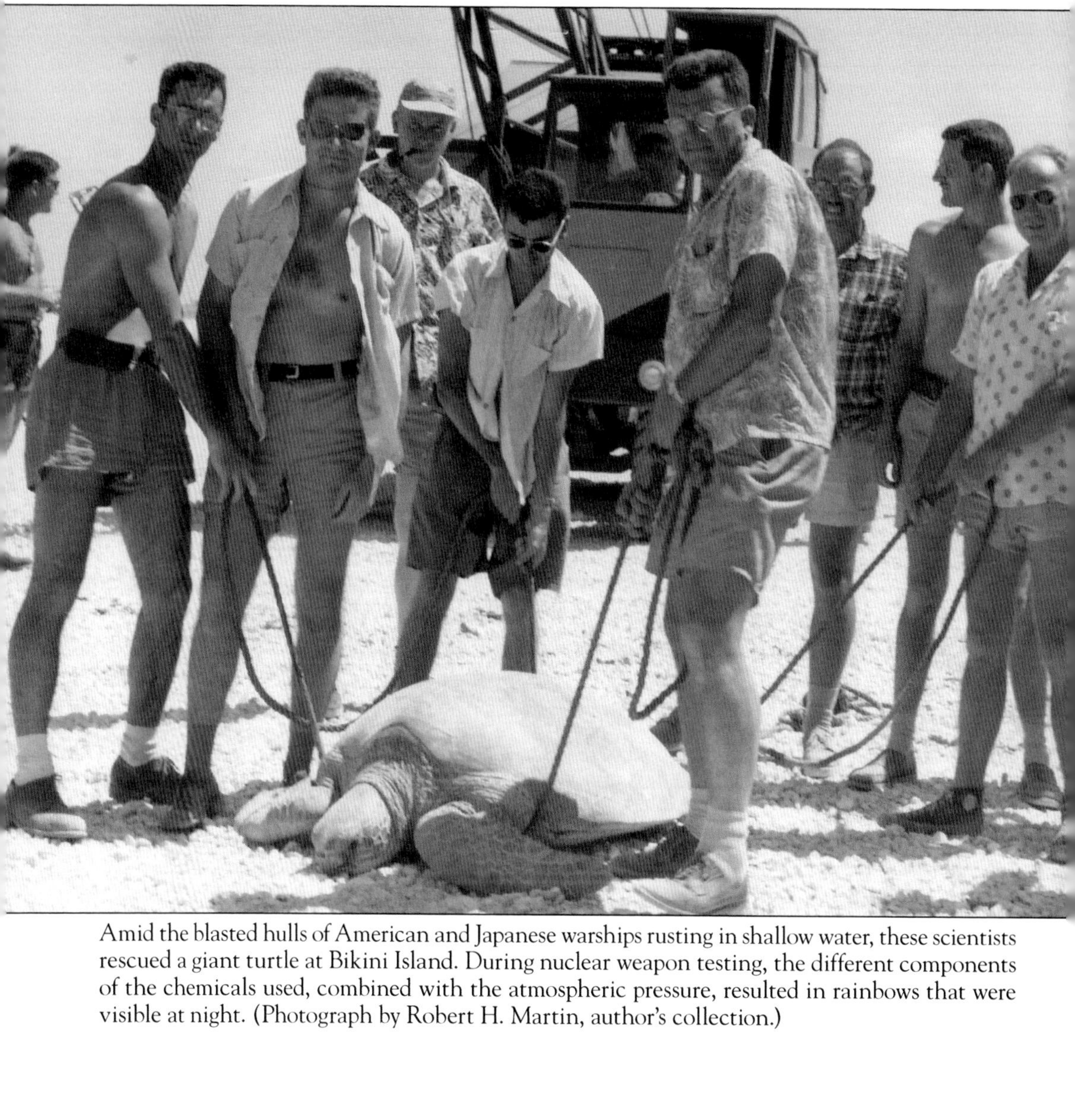

Amid the blasted hulls of American and Japanese warships rusting in shallow water, these scientists rescued a giant turtle at Bikini Island. During nuclear weapon testing, the different components of the chemicals used, combined with the atmospheric pressure, resulted in rainbows that were visible at night. (Photograph by Robert H. Martin, author's collection.)

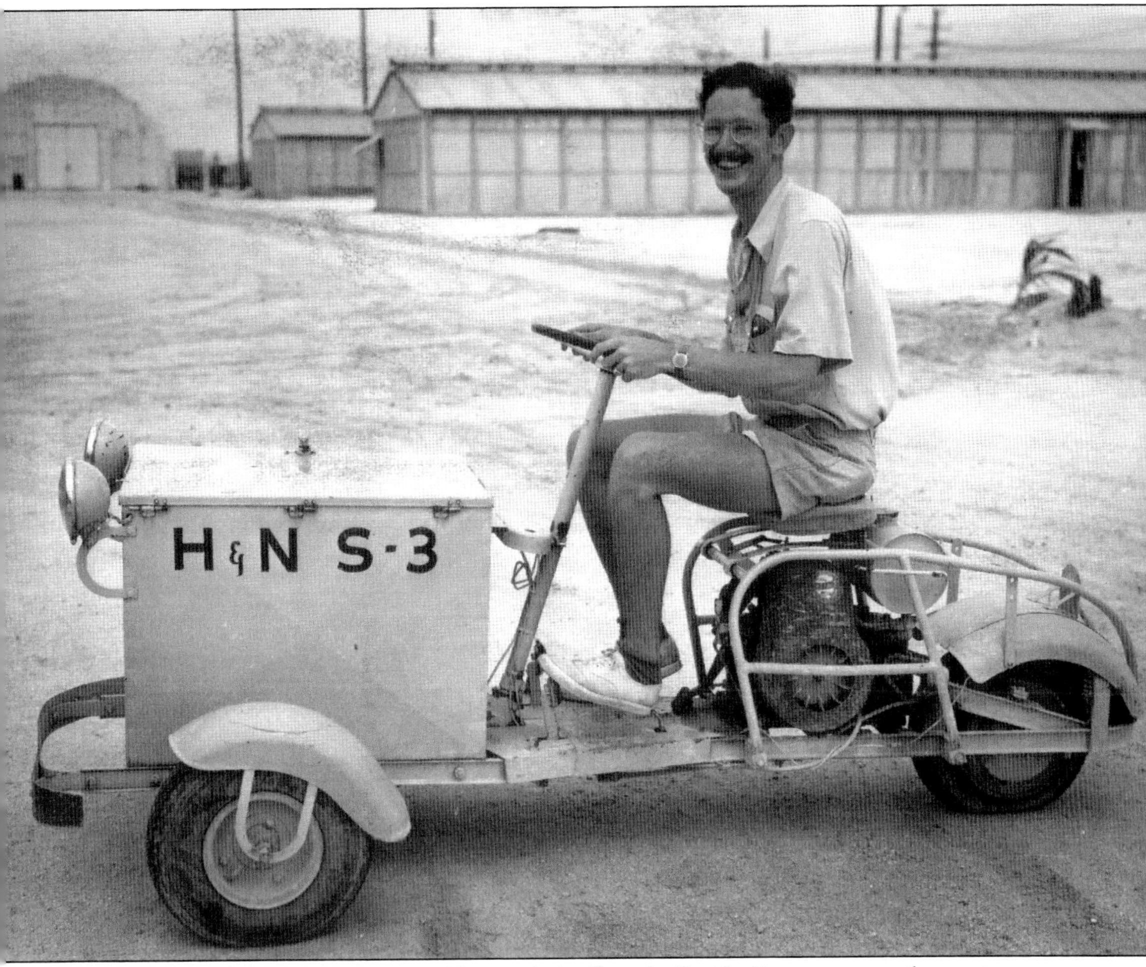

Photographer Robert H. Martin was at Eniwetok Atoll in the Pacific Ocean as part of a contingent of scientists from Los Alamos National Laboratory doing nuclear testing. Scientists from around the world were chosen to work on these bombs. (Author's collection.)

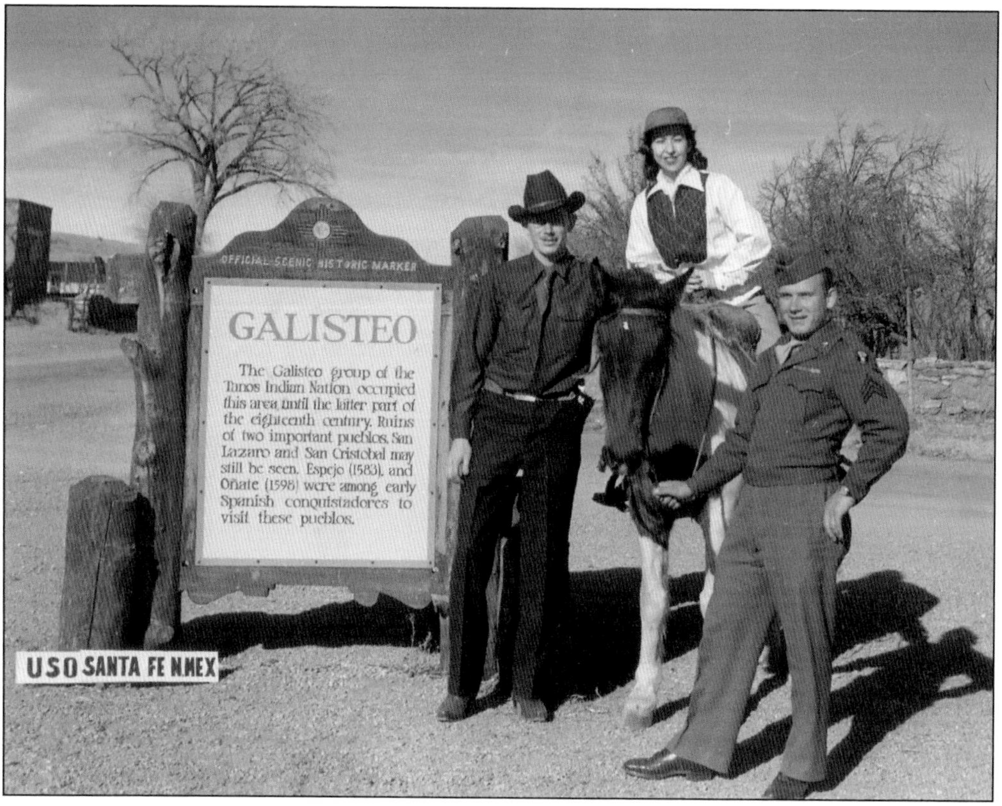

During World War II, the USO sponsored community outreach programs throughout New Mexico to help the family members of soldiers fighting the war. Robert H. Martin is wearing a cowboy hat in this publicity photograph taken in the community of Galisteo, 23 miles from Santa Fe. (Photograph by Robert H. Martin, author's collection.)

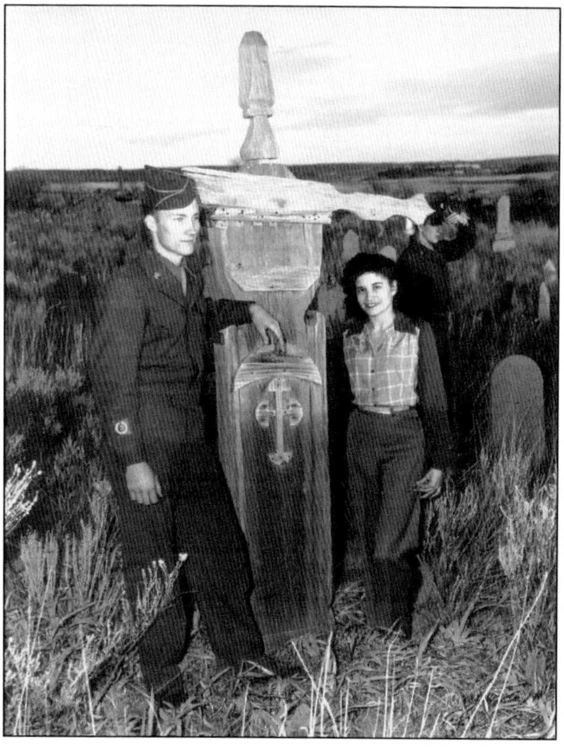

A soldier and woman pose for a USO publicity photograph at Galisteo during World War II. (Photograph by Robert H. Martin, author's collection.)

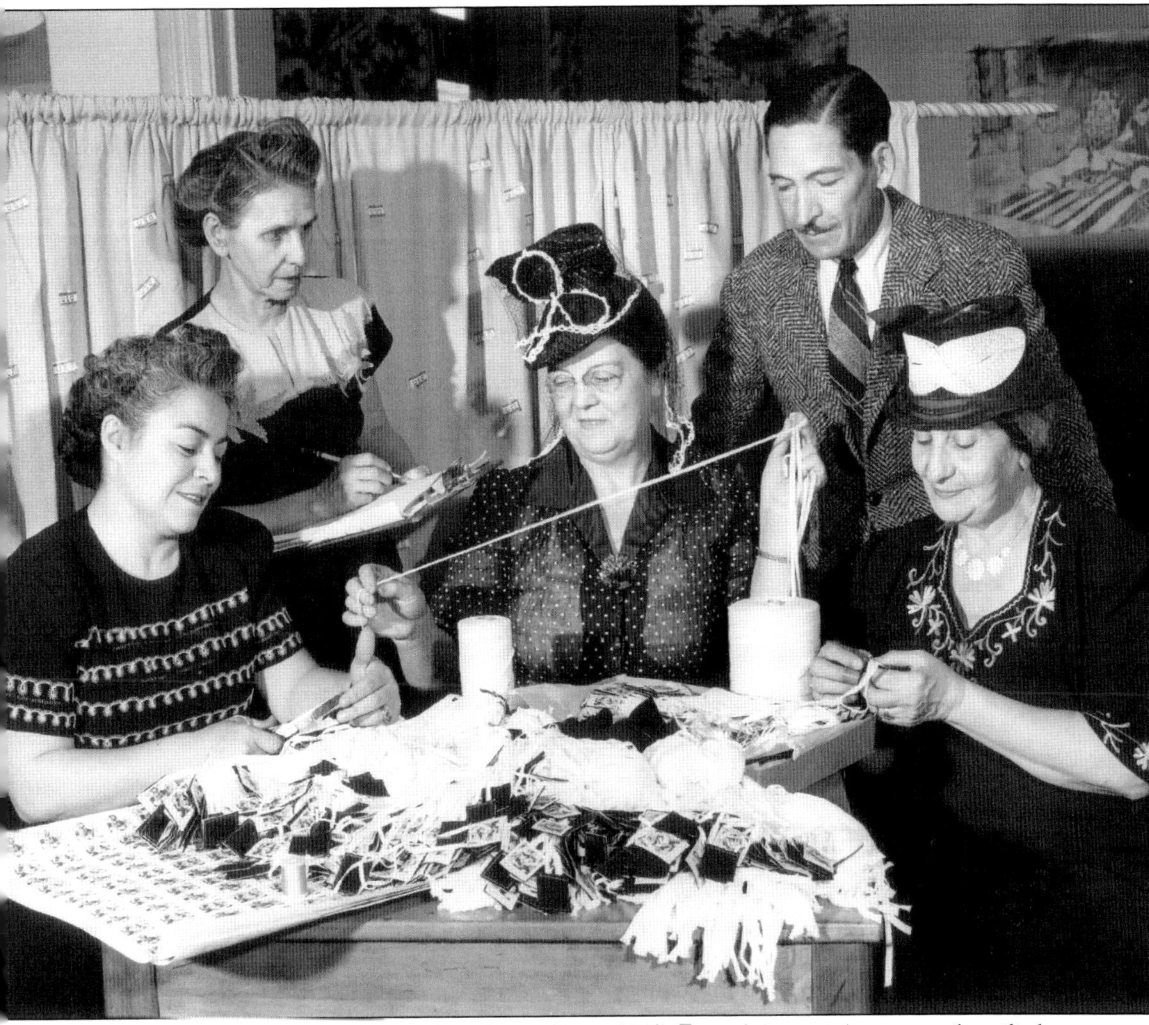

Women make scapulars at the USO in Santa Fe in 1947. From left to right are unidentified, Lorencita Lujan (standing), unidentified, John Moody, and Victoria Roybal. (Photograph by Robert H. Martin, author's collection.)

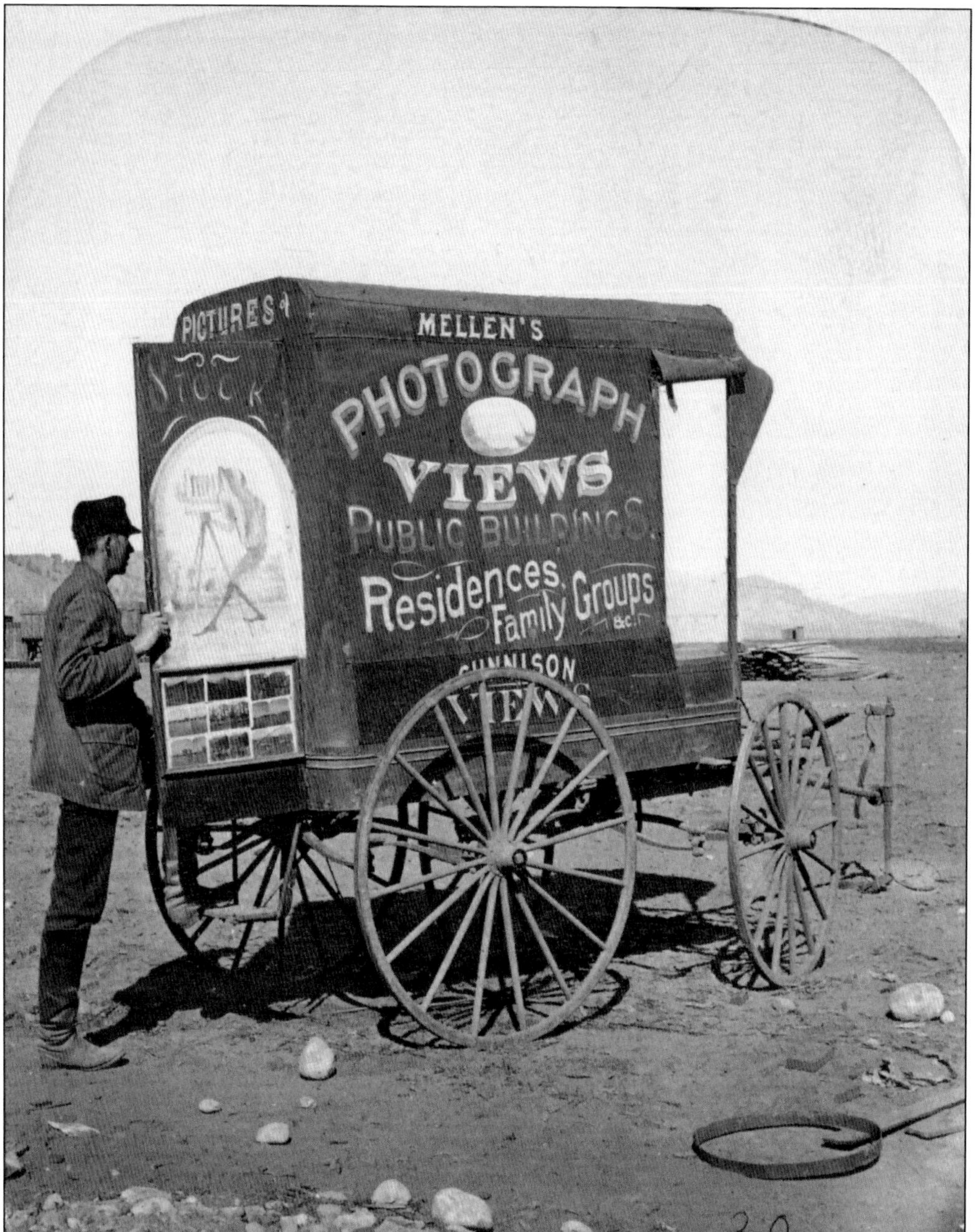

George E. Mellen was one of the early photographers who traveled the West in the 1880s. This wagon was used to transport his equipment and doubled as a studio and photograph processing center. This photograph was taken around 1881. (Photograph by George E. Mellen, courtesy Palace of the Governors [NMHM/DCA], No. 1600551.)

Eight

Eye on Santa Fe

Since the mid-19th century, images of Santa Fe's people and timeless terrain have been captured by photographers near and far. Some of the early photographers were just passing through, while others came to work in Santa Fe. Many had professions in the arts, archaeology, and anthropology; others were soldiers. The lives of these people were as diverse as the subjects they photographed. What they all had in common was bravado and a zest for adventure. It was an exciting time out West, far from the center of this relatively new industry in New York and Europe. These photographers were learning as they went along. They faced seemingly insurmountable obstacles: the lack of readily available equipment and supplies, the length of time it took to get supplies over the Santa Fe Trail, and the occasions that supplies were lost to marauding Indians and bandits en route to Santa Fe. It was difficult to develop glass negatives in tents on the open range. They encountered resistance from the Native Americans, whom they desperately wanted to capture on film. But despite all of these hardships, the breathtaking mountain vistas and the natural light that changed by the hour were well worth all they endured. They somehow knew that they were in the right place at the right time, documenting the frontier of civilization.

Later, with the arrival of the railroad in 1880, followed by two world wars, a hodgepodge of diversity came to the town. By 1950, Santa Fe's reputation as an art colony, cultural haven, and military checkpoint for the atomic age grew exponentially. Each decade of film, when taken as a whole, created a cyclorama of history that defines the world renowned community in the high-desert mountains of the Southwest. Today, in the digital age, the faces and places continue to captivate the imagination and the photographic eye. This chapter pays tribute to the photographers whose vision documented the rich history of early Santa Fe.

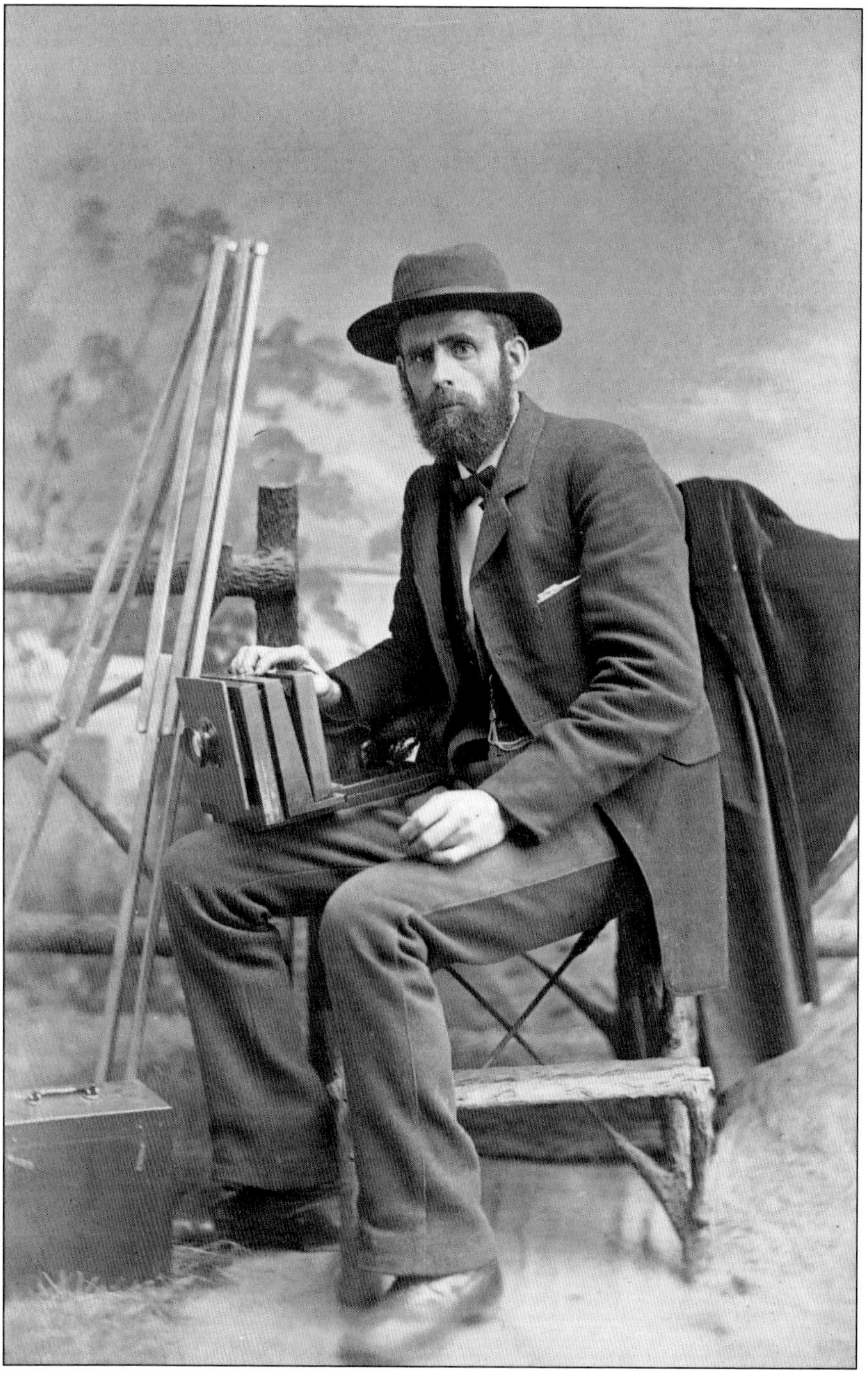

Unfortunately, there are no photographs of Nicholas Brown, who was the owner of N. Brown of the Great West Photograph Gallery in St. Louis in 1859. He came to Santa Fe some time thereafter and specialized in ambrotype, daguerreotype, and glass-plate negative photography. Many of the earliest photographs at the Palace of the Governors Photograph Archives are attributed to Brown. Seen here is the photographer Henry T. Hiester, who came to Santa Fe in 1870 from Chariton, Iowa. (Photograph by Henry T. Hiester [NMHM/DCA] No.HP.1975.25.2)

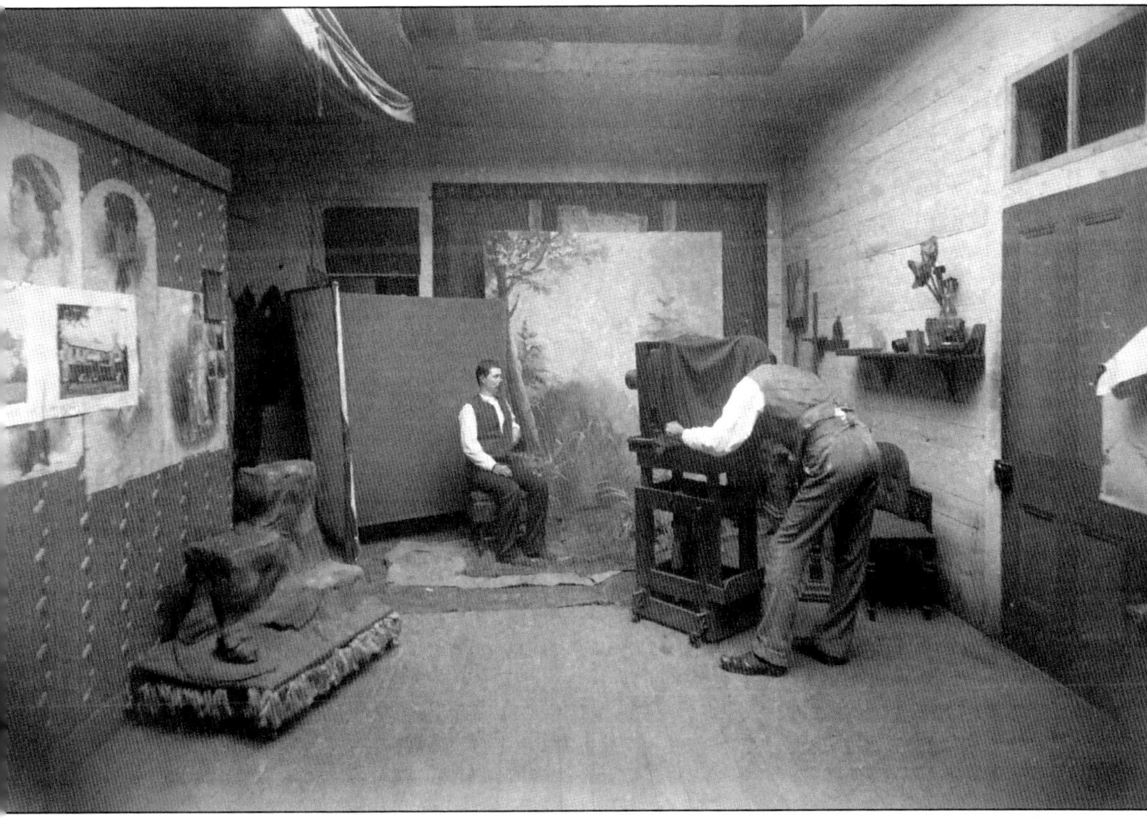

Although no other information on Henry T. Hiester exists in New Mexico, this photograph of his studio is indicative of the way photography studios looked in the latter part of the 19th century. (Photograph by Henry T. Hiester, courtesy Palace of the Governors [NMHM/DCA], No. HP.1974.25.2.)

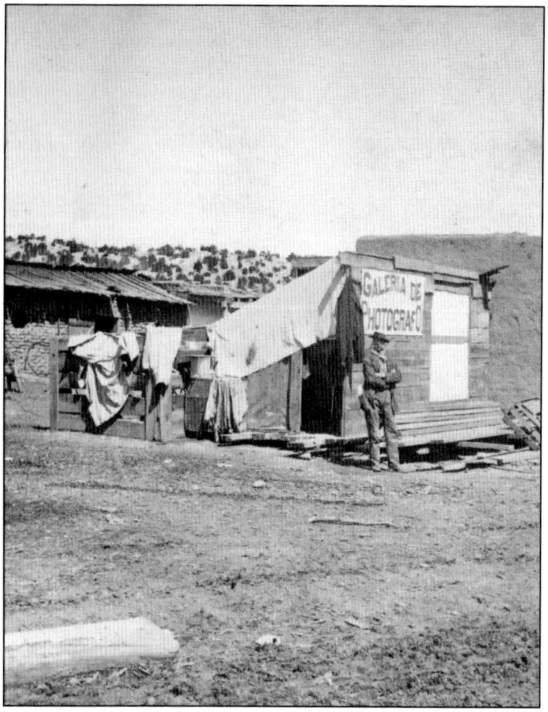

Ben Wittick operated this makeshift photograph gallery in New Mexico between 1880 and 1890. He set up photograph galleries in Gallup, Albuquerque, Santa Fe, and Fort Wingate, where the Navajo, Apache, and Zuni tribes resided. (Photograph by Ben Wittick, courtesy Palace of the Governors [NMHM/DCA], No. 149378.)

Ben Wittick had a special knack for befriending different Indian tribes. He became known for capturing the essence of Native life better than any other photographer of that time. He was also the first outsider allowed to photograph ceremonies. Wittick befriended the Pueblo people along the Rio Grande and had a special kinship with the Hopi, who allowed him to photograph their religious ceremonies. (Photograph by Ben Wittick, courtesy Palace of the Governors [NMHM/DCA], No. PU-Mu-179.)

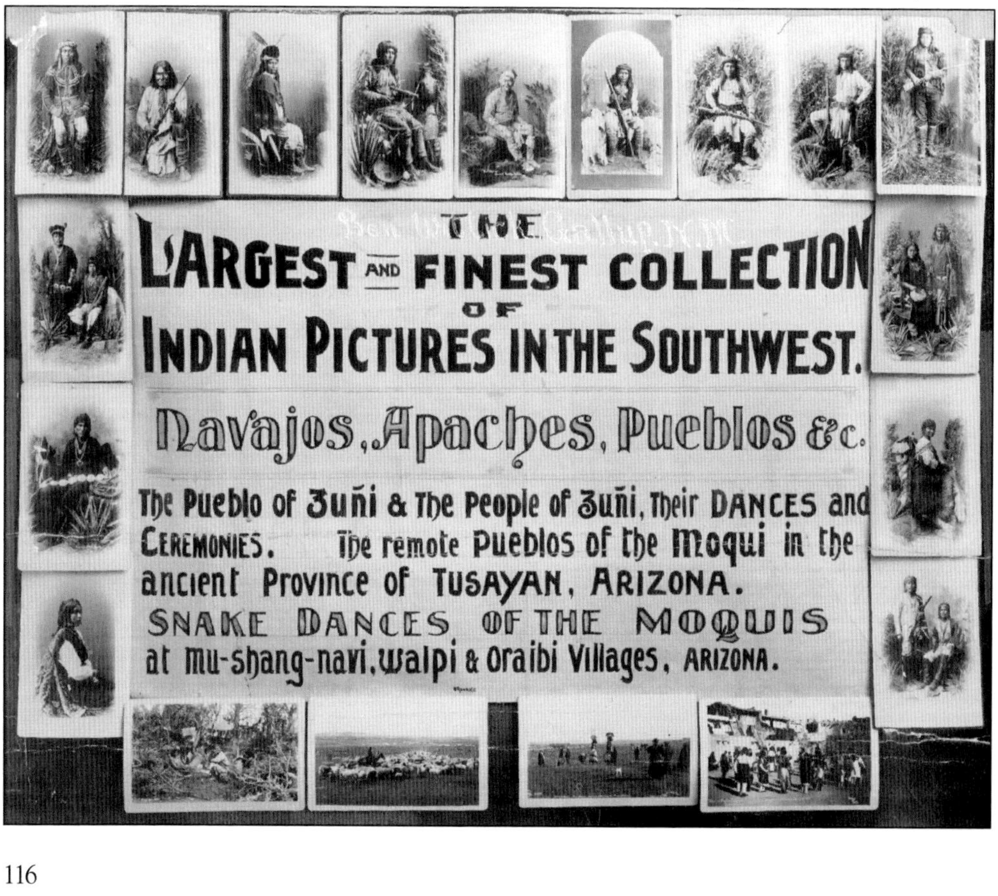

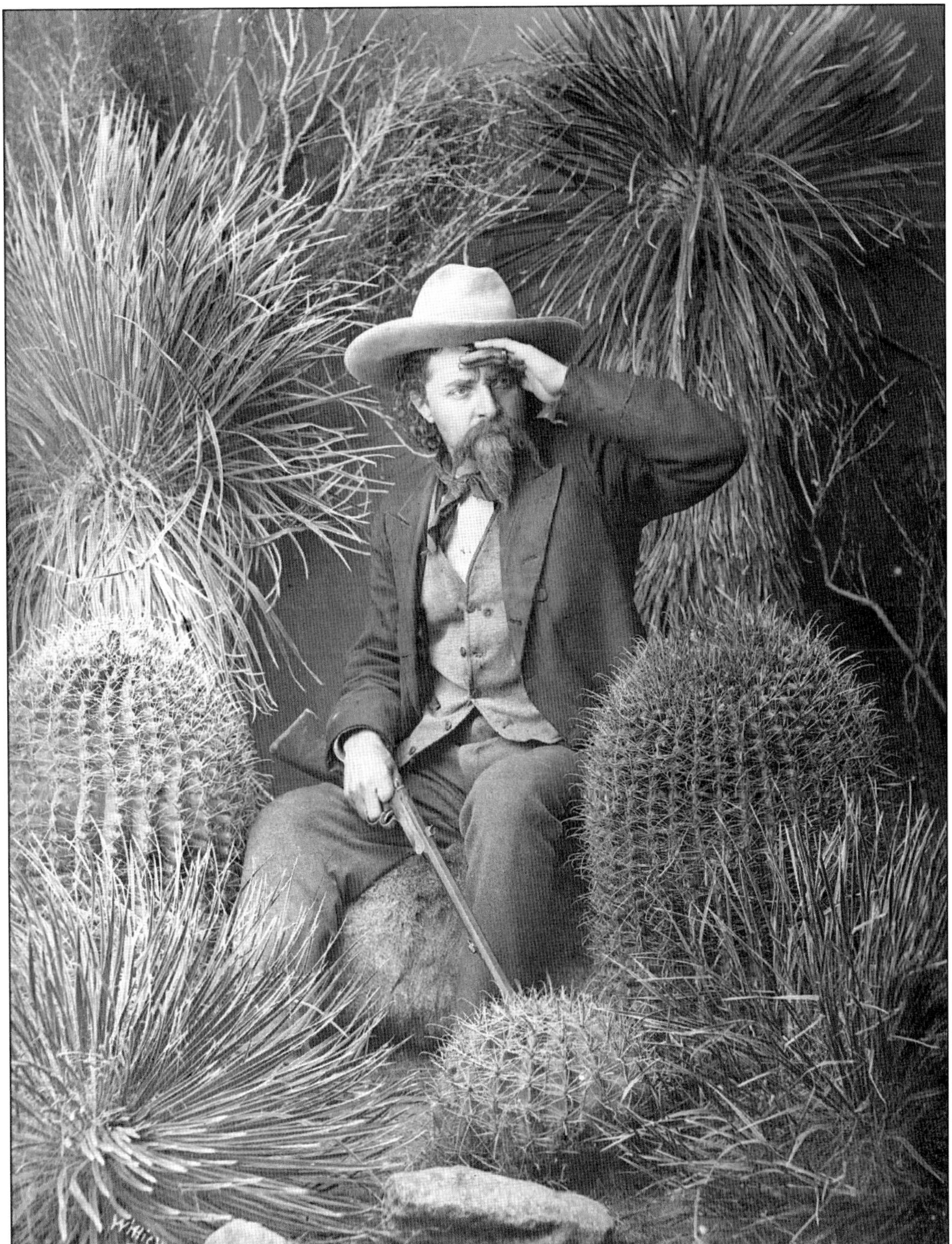

Ben Wittick was born in Pennsylvania in 1845. After the Civil War, he operated a photography studio in Moline, Illinois. Restless and inquisitive by nature, he left his wife and six children to pursue an opportunity to work for the railroad, where he worked until 1883 before setting off on his own. Wittick set up photographic studios using props and backdrops that delighted his many Native American subjects. In 1903, just outside of Gallup at Fort Wingate, a Hopi medicine man foretold his demise. Shortly after that prediction, Wittick died at Fort Wingate from a rattlesnake bite. (Photograph by Ben Wittick, courtesy Palace of the Governors [NMHM/DCA], No. 039391.)

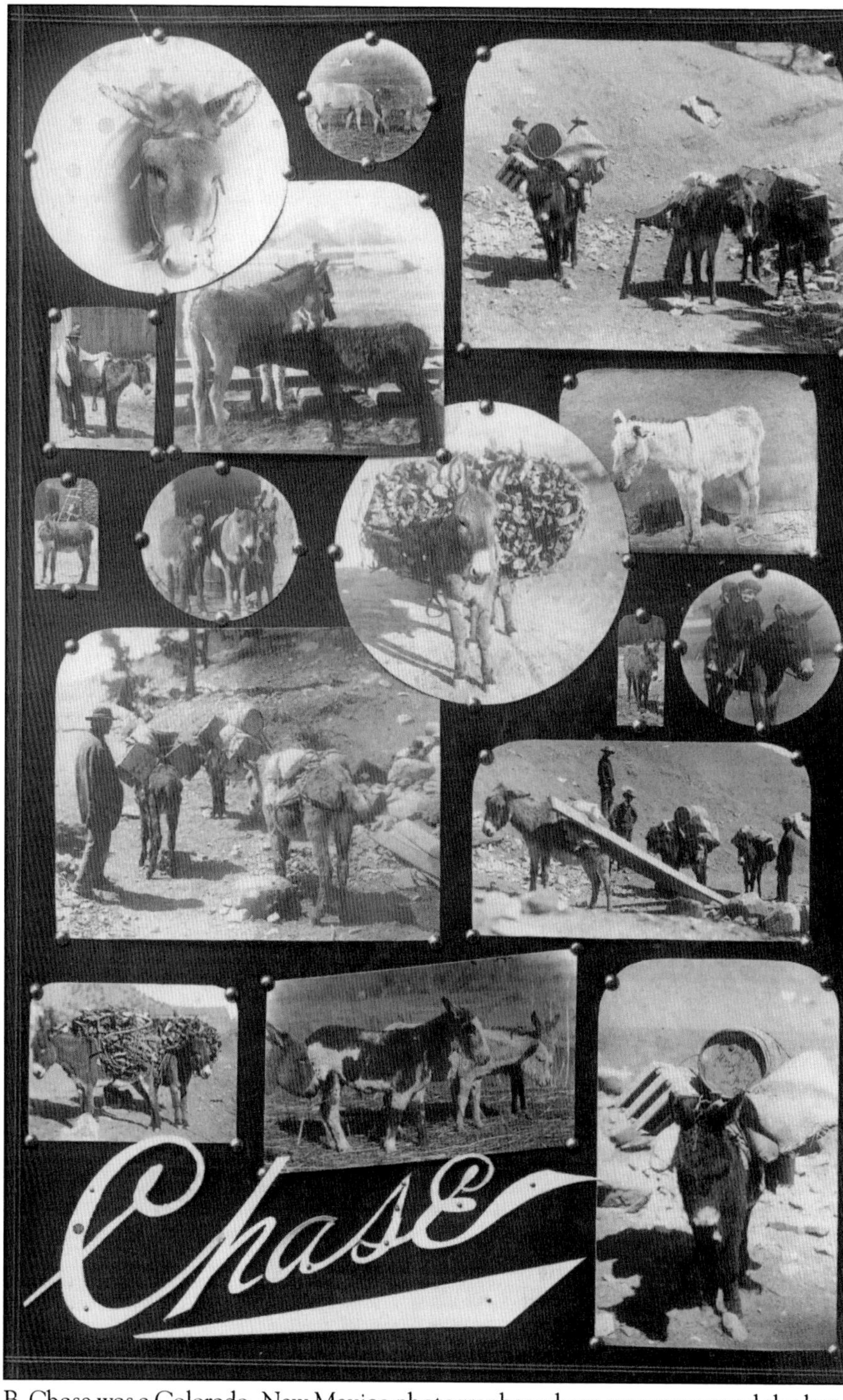

Dana B. Chase was a Colorado–New Mexico photographer whose career spanned the last third of the 19th century. His work featured both urban and rural subjects from Denver to Santa Fe and as far south as Mesilla in southern New Mexico. He photographed Indian ceremonies, landmarks, ranching, towns, and events. He was one of the leading photographers of his era detailing frontier life. (Courtesy Palace of Governors [NMHM/DCA], No. 011774.)

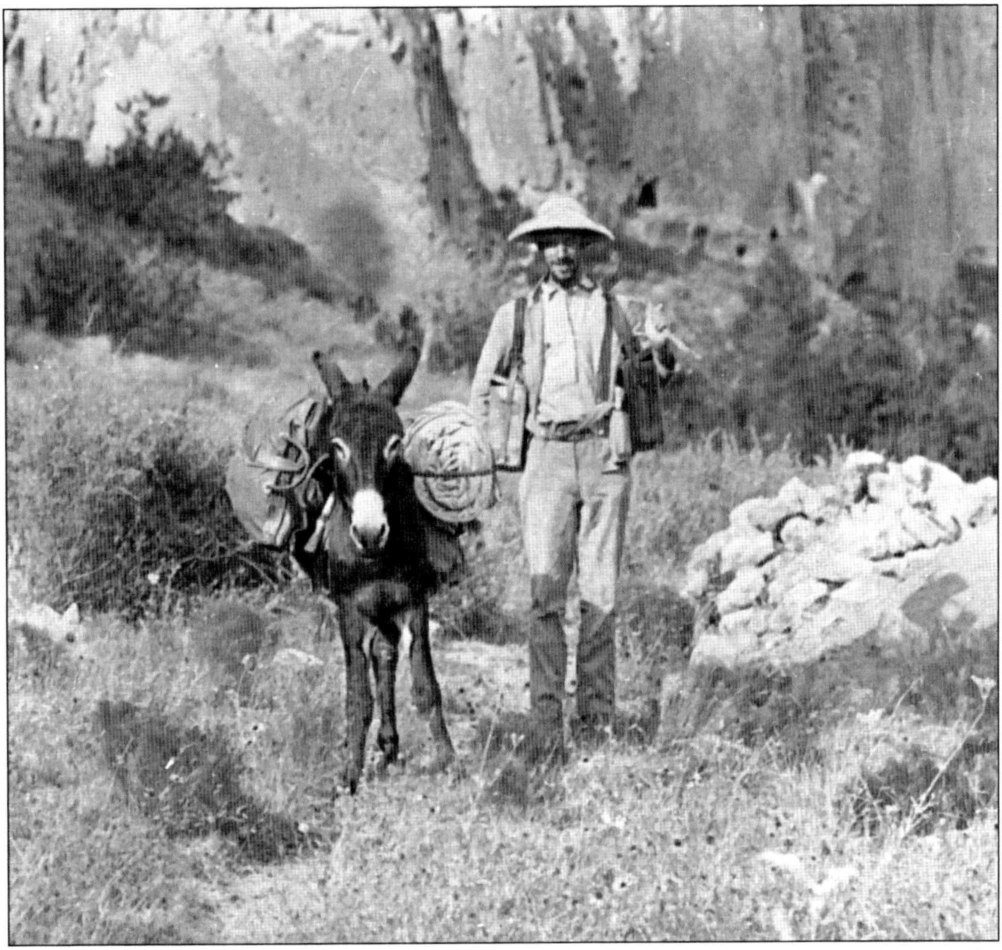

Jesse Nusbaum was born in Greely, Colorado, in 1887. He came to New Mexico in 1907 as the youngest professor at the New Mexico Normal School in Las Vegas. Shortly thereafter, he assisted A.V. Kidder as an assistant at Mesa Verde as a photographer and archaeologist. Nusbaum became the first archaeologist employed by the National Park Service in New Mexico. In 1909, he was hired by Edgar E. Hewett at the School of American Archaeology and the Museum of New Mexico. In 1915, he constructed a replica of the Museum of New Mexico for the Panama-California Exposition in San Diego. In 1917, he oversaw the construction of Santa Fe's Fine Arts Museum. From 1938 to 1958, while working for the National Park Service as its senior archaeologist, Nusbaum was also a consulting archaeologist to the Department of the Interior. In 1931, he returned to Santa Fe and helped build the Laboratory of Anthropology, becoming its first director. Throughout his prolific career, he captured the essence of the people of Santa Fe. The indelible footprint left by Jesse L. Nusbaum's photography is but a tiny part of his contributions to the Southwest. He died in Santa Fe in 1975. Nusbaum is pictured here with his burro at Mesa Verde National Park in 1907. (Courtesy Palace of the Governors [NMHM/DCA], No. LS.0962.)

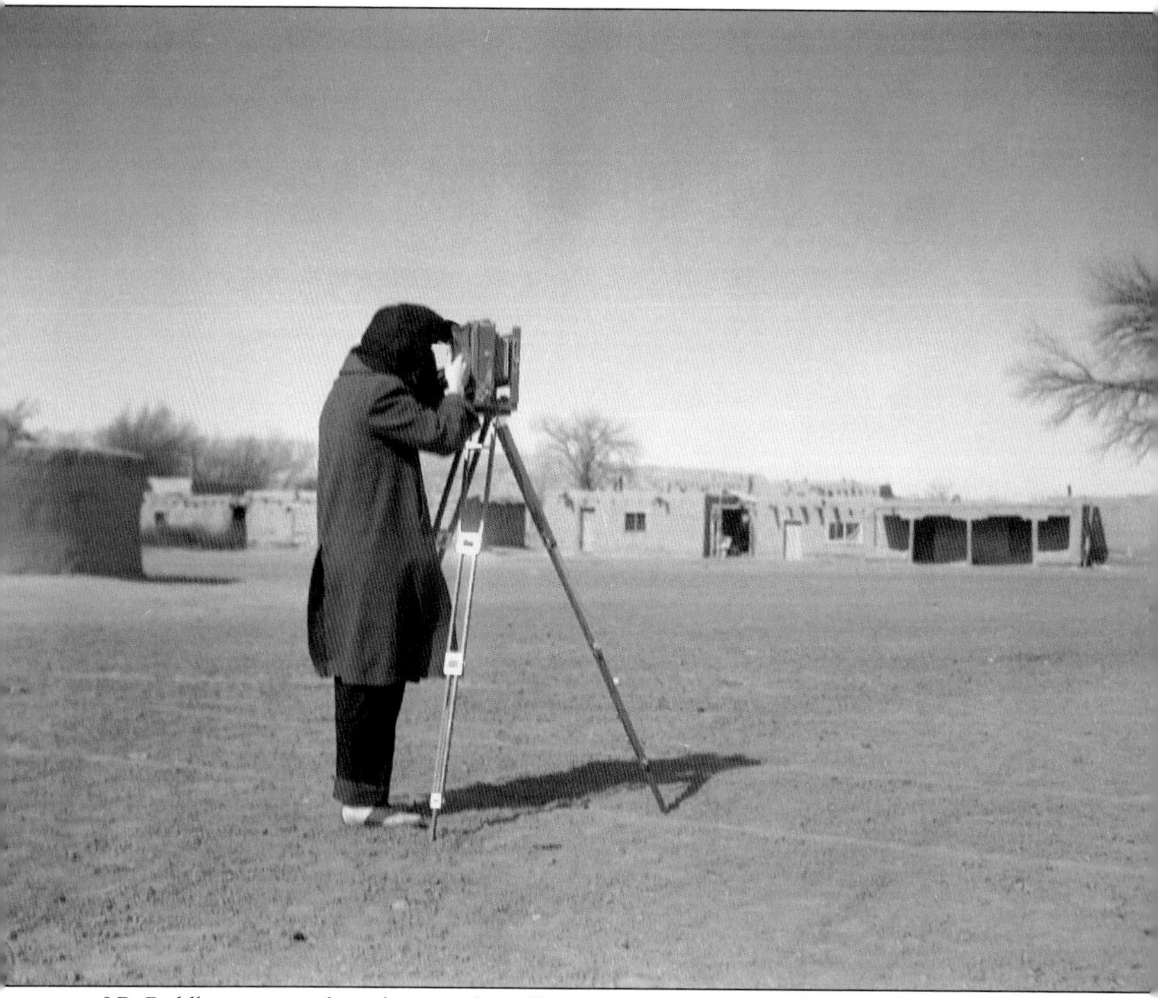

J.R. Riddle was a traveling photographer affiliated in the 1880s with the firm of Leonard & Martin in Topeka, Kansas. He followed a regular itinerary along the route of the Atchison, Topeka & Santa Fe Railway system. Every two years, he would stop in New Mexico to take portrait photographs in a tent studio that he would set up. He came to Santa Fe in 1880, 1882, 1886, and 1888. (Photograph by Harmon T. Parkhurst, courtesy Palace of the Governors [NMHM/DCA], No. 003818.)

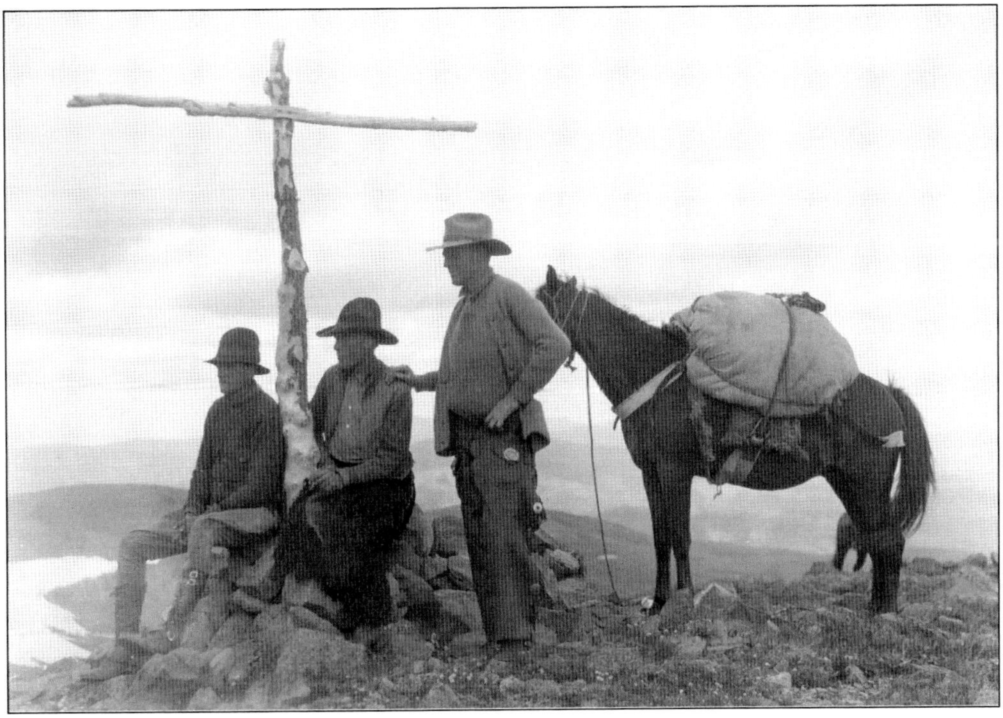

Talcott Harmon Parkhurst was born in 1883 in Middletown, New York. Seen in this photograph standing next to the horse, he came to New Mexico in 1910. He was a part of the Smithsonian Institution's expedition to study the ruins at Santa Rita de los Frijoles, which is now Bandelier National Monument. The self-taught photographer was then hired by Jesse Nusbaum at the Museum of New Mexico, where he worked from 1910 to 1915. Parkhurst went on to open a series of photography studios around Santa Fe. In the late 1940s, he was gored by a bull, and never fully recovered from that injury. Parkhurst closed his photography business in 1951 and died the following year at the home of his daughter in California. (Courtesy Palace of the Governors [NMHM/DCA], No. 007763.)

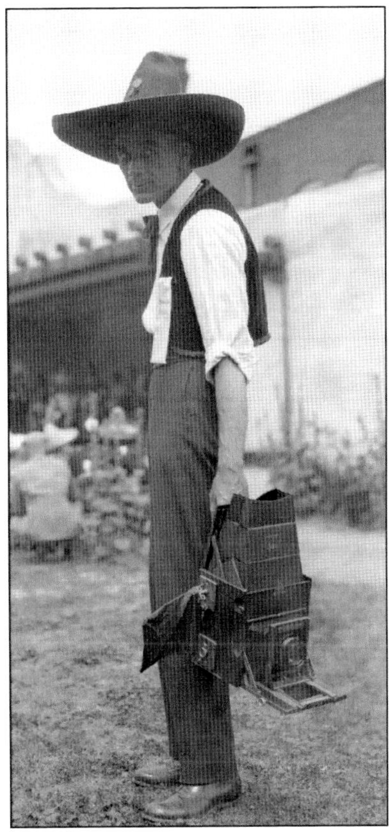

Wesley Bradfield was the son of a Methodist clergyman. While working for the US Forest Service in Michigan, he was sent to Santa Fe in 1909 to do field research. He later resigned, went into the curio business, and in 1912 was sent by Edgar L. Hewett, the director of the Museum of New Mexico, to take photographs of the great Mayan monuments in Quirigua, Guatemala. He went on to do field expeditions in and around New Mexico for the School of American Research. Bradfield later became the curator for the Museum of New Mexico and died in Santa Fe in 1929. (Courtesy Palace of the Governors [NMHM/DCA], No. 008802.)

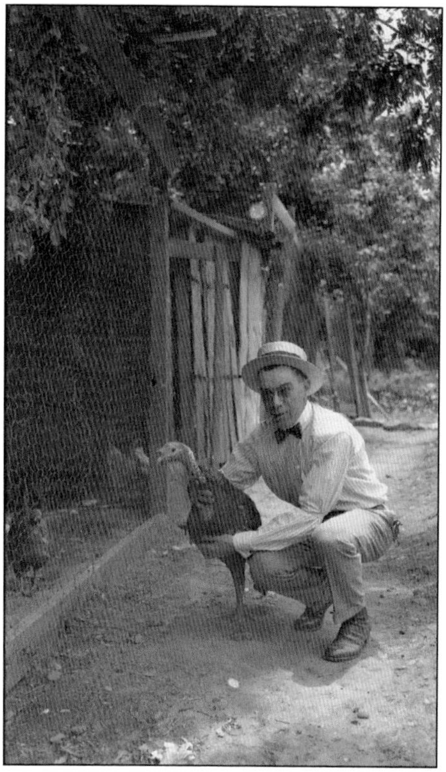

William H. Roberts was born in Colorado in 1887. He came to Santa Fe in 1916 and became a partner in the Rising-Roberts Undertaking Parlor. In addition to his funeral business, he fumigated for bedbugs, charging $7 per room, and was also a part-time photographer. He was a member of the Scottish Rite Masonic Temple, Shriners Club, Lions Club, and the volunteer fire department. His mother was Leah Harvey, for whom a school had been named in the 1940s. When Roberts died in 1968, he requested that his ashes be scattered at the top of La Bajada Hill along with those of his mother. (Courtesy Palace of the Governors [NMHM/DCA], No. 163321.)

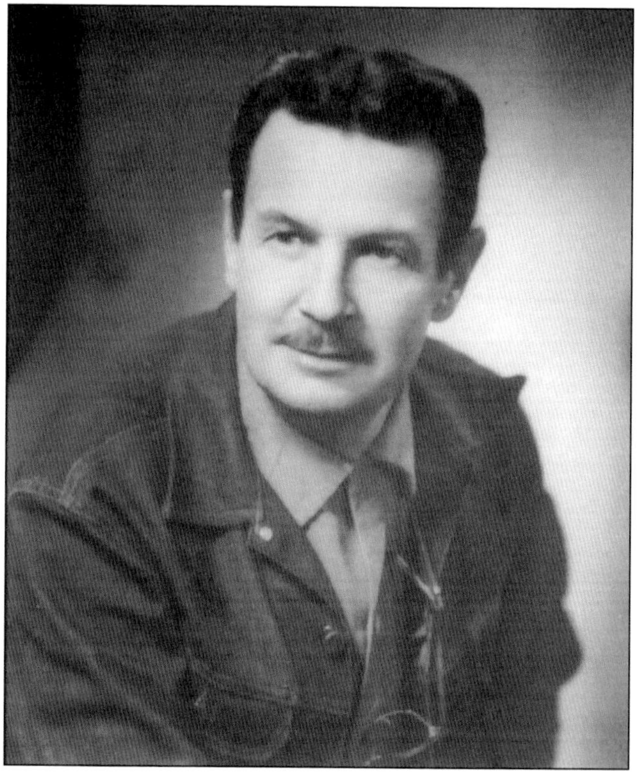

Tyler Dingee was a self-taught photographer who was born in 1906 in Brooklyn, New York. In 1945, he and his wife made a three-month trip to the Southwest and decided to settle in Santa Fe, where he opened a photography studio. Dingee partnered with local architects and photographed much of their early work. In 1960, his photograph of the Palace of the Governors was adopted by the US Postal Service as the official stamp to commemorate Santa Fe's founding 350 years earlier. Dingee was killed by lightning the following year while on a fishing trip with his brother-in-law, artist Will Shuster, in Estes Park, Colorado. Both Dingee's cocker spaniel and Shuster's poodle were also victims of the bolt. (Author's collection.)

Wyatt Davis was born in 1906 in East Orange, New Jersey. His father, Edward Davis, was the arts editor for the *Philadelphia Press*. Early on, Wyatt was introduced to some of the leading artists of the era, including John Sloan, who invited him to visit Santa Fe. That was the beginning of Wyatt's love affair with New Mexico. In 1936, he was hired by the New Mexico Tourism Department, for which he created thousands of images around the state. Today, his big-view camera that he used for decades resides at the Albuquerque Museum as a reminder of the heyday of early photography in New Mexico. (Courtesy Palace of the Governors [NMHM/DCA], No. 151129.)

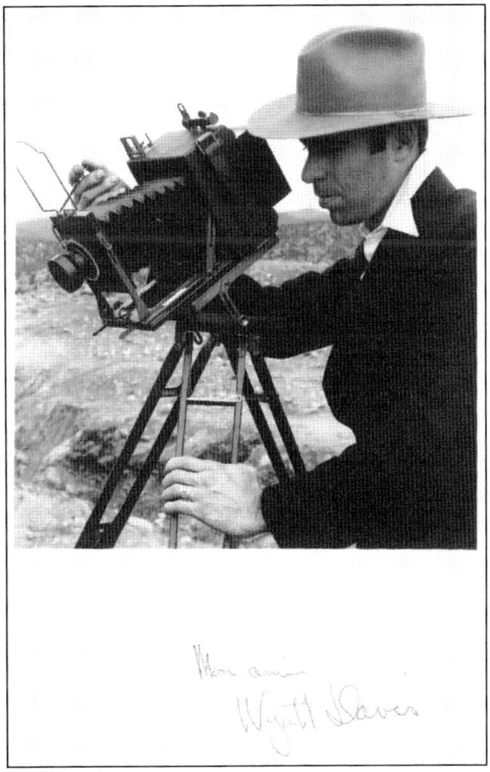

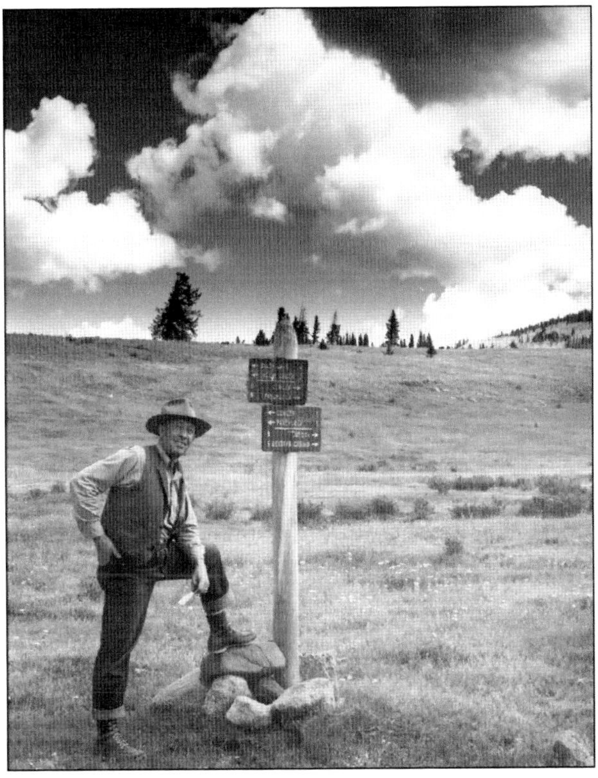

Harold D. Walter took the first photographs of Smokey the Bear in 1950. The five-pound black bear cub had just been rescued from a fire in the Capitán Mountains. The badly singed cub was found clinging to a charred tree. Smokey the Bear became a living symbol of the danger and devastation of forest fires, and for the next 25 years, he was an American icon. That campaign earned more than $1 million in promotion for the Forest Service. When Smokey died in 1975 at the National Zoo in Washington, DC, the Forest Service flew his body back to New Mexico for interment in the same forest where he had been found. (Courtesy Palace of the Governors [NMHM/DCA], No. 182956.)

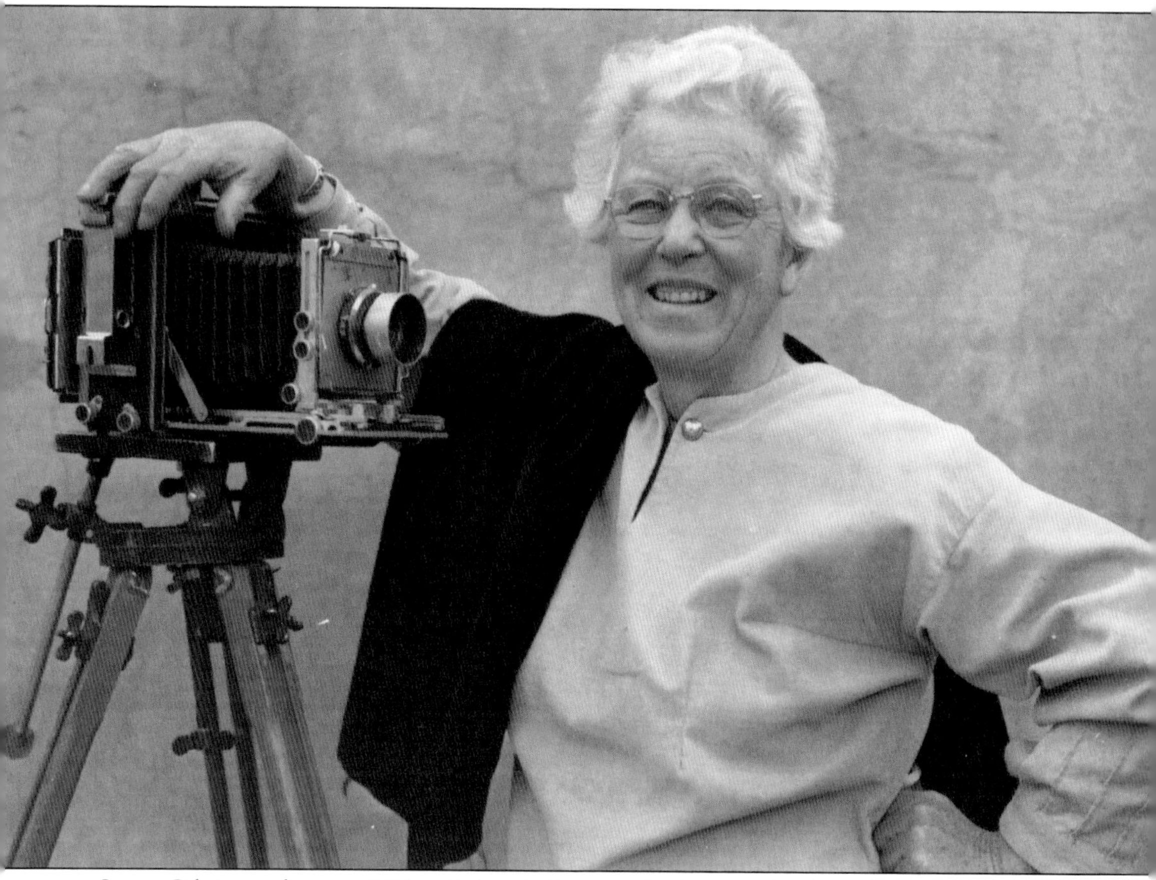

Laura Gilpin was born in 1891 in Colorado Springs. On her 12th birthday, her parents gave her a Kodak Brownie camera. From that moment on, she and her camera were inseparable. Her career spanned 60 years. She is best known for her documentation of Navajo people and of Southwestern landscapes. No other female photographer in the American Southwest did as much during the 20th century. She traveled to the Panama-California Exposition in San Diego in 1915, followed by the Panama-Pacific International Exposition in San Francisco the same year. These two events awakened her interest in the landscape and cultures of indigenous people. By the 1930s, she was concentrating on photographs of the Navajo and Pueblo Indians of New Mexico, to critical acclaim. Early on, Gilpin became quite adept at the process of developing platinum prints, which provided a broad tone of scale for her black-and-white photographs. She is considered one of the great photographers of this medium. From 1945 to 1975, her work was exhibited in more than a hundred shows in galleries and museums throughout the world. At the end of World War II, she moved to Santa Fe, where she died in 1979 at the age of 88. (Courtesy Palace of the Governors [NMHM/DCA], No. 050822.)

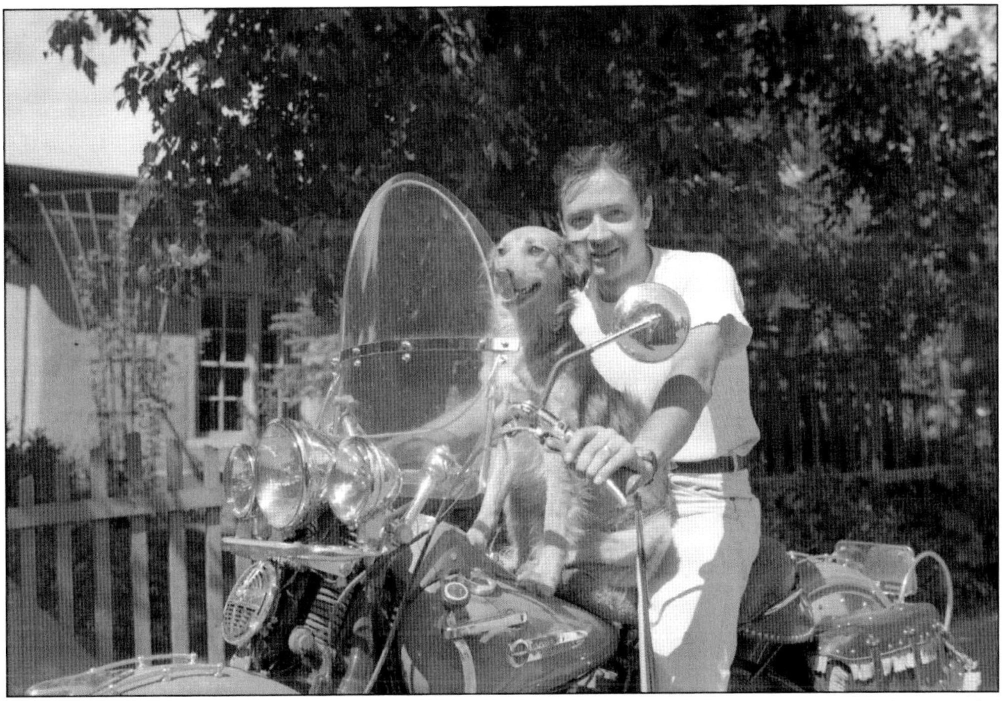

John Candelario was born in Santa Fe in 1916. He is seen in this photograph with his dog, Cindy, on his Harley-Davidson, named "Tarzan." A self-taught photographer, he was the grandson of Jesús Sito Candelario, who ran the curio shop on San Francisco Street during the latter part of the 19th century and the early 20th century. Later, the photographer managed the shop for his grandfather. Throughout his successful career, he remained a local Santa Fe boy, and he died in his hometown in 1993. (Courtesy Palace of the Governors [NMHM/DCA], No. 177025.)

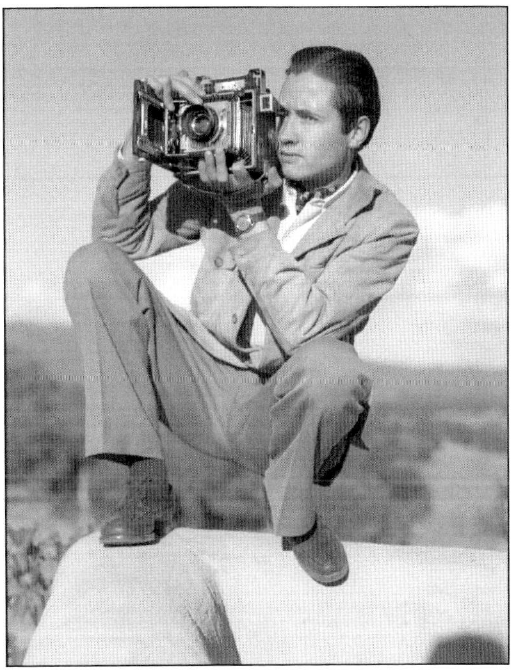

John Candelario was mentored in photographic techniques by many well-known photographers, including Ansel Adams and Laura Gilpin. In the early 1940s, his exhibit of northern New Mexico was held at the Museum of Modern Art in New York. In 1946, he was elected to fellowship in the Royal Photographic Society for his work in platinum-print photography. In 1954, he became a cinematographer, and received many awards, including an Emmy and Peabody. (Courtesy Palace of the Governors [NMHM/DCA], No. 177045.)

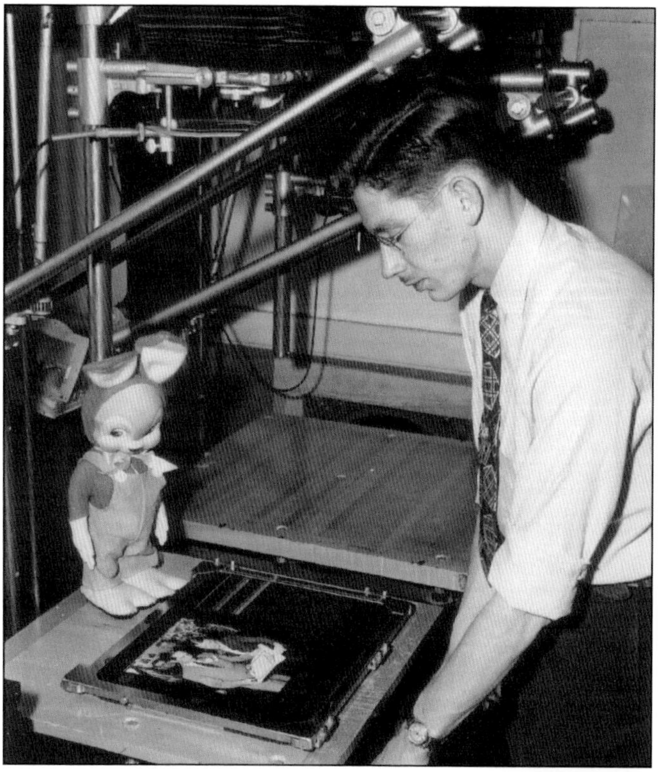

When World War II began, Robert H. Martin joined the Army and became the photographer for the Zenith Radio Corporation, one of the major defense contractors for the government. By 1946, he was hired by Los Alamos National Laboratory as the official photographer of the top-secret nuclear project. The Chicago native married Manuelita Ortiz y Pino, a member of one of New Mexico's most prominent Hispanic families. In addition to his work at the lab, he spent decades documenting Santa Fe culture and history. (Author's collection.)

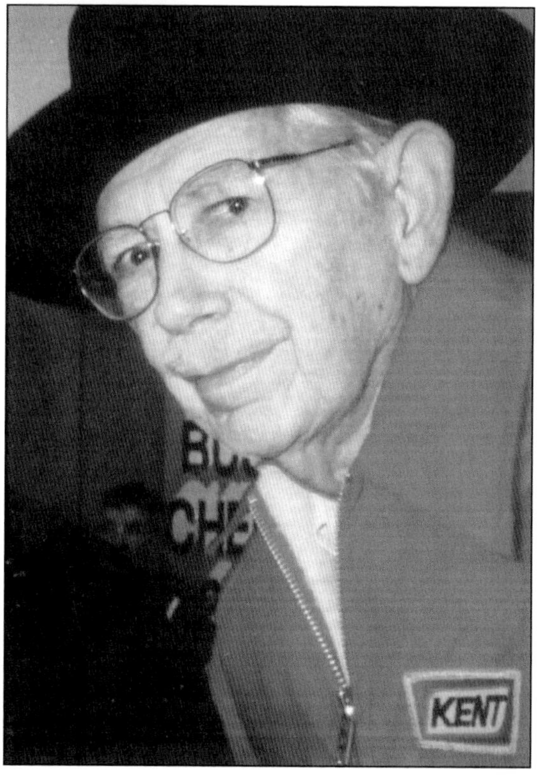

Robert H. Martin retired from Los Alamos National Laboratory in the 1970s when he came down with cancer from the radiation that he had been exposed to during his work there. Martin is believed to be one of the longest survivors of radiation-induced cancer. He died in Santa Fe in 2004 at the age of 83. Martin took this self-portrait shortly before his death. (Author's collection.)

About the Archive

The Palace of the Governors Photograph Archives in Santa Fe contains more than a million photographs dating back to 1850. This treasure trove of imagery encapsulates the history of New Mexico and the region. From anthropology to archaeology to people, each image provides a piece of the puzzle that tells the story of a time long gone, ensuring that it will not be forgotten. The earliest collections at the photograph archives came from the Historical Society of New Mexico. Founded in 1859, the society's photograph collection was housed in the Palace of the Governors. Fifty years later, in 1909, the Museum of New Mexico opened its doors, and the historical society continued to house its collection at the palace. In 1977, the society's photograph assemblage was donated to the State of New Mexico, which oversees the museum system. In addition to this vast collection of photographs, the archives contain thousands of images that were created by major professional photographers of the Southwest. Equally important are the private family photograph collections that have been donated to the museum for the sake of posterity.

The Palace of the Governors Photograph Archives is considered one of the most important historical collections in the American West. Adding to the significance of this collection depicting the ethnology of this region are photographs from Latin America, the Far East, Oceania, and the Middle East.

The Palace of the Governors Photograph Archives collection is as diverse in content and subject matter as the early process of photography, which began in Europe in 1839 with pioneers such as Louis Jacques Mande Daguerre, for whom the daguerreotype is named. Through trial and error, the commingling of light, copper, iodine, mercury, and salt captured the world's first images. Today, the adage "A picture is worth a thousand words" is even more relevant with the explosive growth in digital media that has become a ubiquitous part of our daily lives.